PHILIP WILSON STEER

DEDICATED
TO
THE MEMORY
OF
GEOFFREY BLACKWELL
FRIEND AND PATRON
OF PAINTERS

1 STEER *by Sickert*

LIFE
WORK AND SETTING OF
PHILIP WILSON STEER

by

D. S. MacColl

with
a full catalogue of paintings
and list of watercolours in public collections
by
ALFRED YOCKNEY

FABER AND FABER LIMITED
LONDON

First published in Mcmxlv
by Faber and Faber Limited
24 Russell Square London W.C.1
Second impression February Mcmxlvi
Printed in Great Britain by
R. MacLehose and Company Limited
The University Press Glasgow

CONTENTS

The places from 'Walberswick, 1884' to 'Walmer, 1934'
are from a list made out by Steer, with some marginal titles
of pictures added by Mr. Geoffrey Blackwell. 'Churt', a
slip, has been corrected to 'Chirk' and 'Walberswick', in
1888, is from a note of the four years to 1891 by Fred Brown
furnished by his sister. 'Boulogne?' also 1888, is not in that
note.

ILLUSTRATIONS

The reproductions in this volume do not attempt to furnish a corpus of its subject's work; they consist in portraits, chiefly photographic, of Steer and others in his family circle, one or two of places, and small-scale reminders of paintings or drawings to illustrate the text. Thanks are due to the galleries, publications and private owners who have given their consent to reproduction; copyright charges have been met in all cases where they have been claimed and it has been possible to trace ownership. Captions have been shortened so as not to encumber the plates: further particulars will be found in the following List.

Titles of pictures and drawings are in italics. Those without artist's name attached are of works by Steer. Owner's name of works reproduced or other source follows in small italics.

PRELIMINARY

Normal is null, since in the Art of God
The very Great are also very Odd

An artist unvexed by craving or gift for a double life might be lucky were he to leave no record but his work. Unfortunately the blank is never complete: some incident or legend survives to tempt and to inflate speculation. Shakespeare's second-best bed has swelled into one greater than that of Ware: the phrase in an early letter of Turner about house property has been mis-read into the disclosure of an unhappy love-affair, and his visits to collect rent at Wapping have become a tale of debauchery in the loose mythology that has grown about his name. In the last resort there may be legal matter to disinter, leases, contracts or law-pleas, and if, like Frans Hals, a painter has ever come into court for over-festivity he may be branded as an habitual sot, against clear pictorial evidence of his steady hand.

On the other side are visual artists blest or tormented by an itch for words as well: poets like Michelangelo or Rossetti, fascinating memoir-writers like Cellini or Haydon, copious note-book jotters like Leonardo, lecturers like Reynolds, first-rate critics like Fromentin, correspondents and diarists like Delacroix, who wrote better than at all times he painted. Constable, unburdening to Leslie or Fisher, pictures his intentions vividly in words; Van Gogh's wrestle with themes and technique pours in a huge fascinating stream over against the mental and verbal poverty of Cézanne; Turner himself was a suppressed poet, publishing, in Academy catalogues, scraps from an Epic, the 'Fallacies of Hope', with such occasional flashes of inspiration as:—

> While the fierce archer of the downward year
> Stains Italy's blanch'd barrier with storms.

Steer was of the dumb variety, measured against his close comrade and neighbour, Tonks, who loved intellectual intercourse so much that in his later days he put correspondence in the daily programme before painting.

For Steer the receipt of letters was more often an infliction than a pleasure, since he was punctilious in reply but hated the distraction and toil of writing. His letters, accordingly, are matter-of-fact, and even to frequent correspondents like Tonks, Ronald Gray and Geoffrey Blackwell have little overflow beyond reports of health, lodging, weather and suitability of his pitch for painting. His mind was ruminative rather than speculative; he had a definite and shrewd judgment of events and persons, private or public, but had never, like his colleague Fred Brown, worried his way into a reversal of orthodox religious beliefs. He was a Tory in faith, politics, national prejudice; distrusting foreigners, priests, and dealers in fundamentals. Adhering to old fashions in dress as well, he wore the white shirt and stand-up collars of his youth to the last. Travel out of England became taboo, because 'abroad I am a foreigner'; Scotland, even, was not native enough. He once grumbled over his friend Daniel's talk of 'first-class minds', saying, 'I know I have a third-class mind.' He had digested some of our classic writers, but, once embarked upon steady production, merely skimmed the daily paper and sale-catalogues, saving his eyes, so that he might be about the business his Maker had contrived him for, and that only: painting.

No one could be less like the novelist's and dramatist's idea of an artist, from Ouida to Henry James or Shaw; the inspired improvisor, the riotous spendthrift, plunger from ectasies to black depression, the figure in a scene of elaborate or exquisite decoration, the prophet and mystic. He was anything but a showman of his art or life; simple in his ways as those French contemporaries, Fantin and Degas, or the English Charles Keene, masters all. The second of them was so inveterately of a particular burgess tradition that if, when he dined out, he found flowers on the table, he threatened to leave were they not removed. To Steer, as to him, the playboy part of Whistler, the spectacular dress, quarrels, bailiffs, press campaigns and libel actions were distasteful, and their reflection in his early comrade, Sickert, did not make for comfortable relations as time went on. When that fascinating visitor, deep in debt or obligation, left a taxi ticking at the door for hours or chartered it for the correction of a proof in Essex, Steer was shocked, but he was moved by the letter from Venice in which Sickert spoke of the lessons in painting he owed to his old companion. In early 'New English' days Steer had been the guest of Sickert and his first wife at the Cobdens' home in Midhurst, and the two had painted one another exquisitely.

An odd scepticism about my attitude comes out in the following letter; but, more to the purpose, Sickert's feeling toward Steer. The portrait, abused by Henry Butcher at an Academy banquet as that of 'an intoxicated mummy', was on the painter's easel when I first visited him

2 SICKERT *by Steer, 1890*

(*a*) 'Madam, will you walk?' Steer deserts the outfield at cricket

(*b*) The Football Team
Tonks, Aitken, Steer, D.S.M., Blackwell, Mrs. MacColl

3 Sports at Great Haresfoot, Berkhamsted

in 1891. I prevented him from spoiling it, and had that personal reason, as well as its merit, for wishing to secure it for the Tate Gallery. Steer presented it through the Contemporary Art Society.

[1917]

My dear Steer,   6 Mornington Crescent, London, N.W.

Do you think

Firstly that when MacColl suggested your giving my head of the George Moore that he meant he would accept it? or do you think it was merely a polite boutade without any consequence?

Secondly, if he would, would you do this handsome thing and present it? It would be agreeable and useful to me and the more agreeable part would be the public association for ever of your name as donor of a picture of mine. A sort of crystallisative reminder of the to me agreeable fact that our names have from the beginning been very much linked together.

If the answer to my second question is affirmative sound him next time you see him as from yourself—not as from me. If he were disinclined, I may be supposed to have no cognizance of the scheme. 'Sly' 'devilish sly' is for Bagstock.

Yours W. S.

Don't bother to answer till we meet.

Unlike Degas, whose witty and malicious tongue spared few of his contemporaries, Steer preferred to be silent about fellow-painters if he could not praise. Once, when reputations were being canvassed at the Chelsea Arts Club, he sat mute, and when appealed to said that one should remember it was difficult to paint even a bad picture. When he was brought to speak at all about his own painting he exaggerated a prosaic, work-a-day attitude. 'Did you find', inquired an interviewer, 'as much thrill from painting in your later days as when you were a younger man?'[1] 'Thrill? Painting is a job like any other, something one has to do between meals.' 'No', he added, 'it is not always good to feel a thrill.' Sometimes he had been rather pleased when things went well, but often that was a sign they were going ill; and the critical faculty gone to sleep.[2] 'When you look at your past pictures do they give you pleasure?' 'Not exactly pleasure. Some one likes more than others, but wishes they were very much better. Painting a picture is like getting into water. You do not know what you are in for till you have taken the plunge, and then you either come out, having swum successfully to the shore, or else you sink.'

It is a man in his eightieth year who is speaking, annoyed, probably, at being interviewed, bent on lowering the eulogistic temperature by cutting out thrills and frills, but the truth remains that Steer was, to outward

---

[1] *The World of Art Illustrated*, May 3, 1939. My acknowledgments are due to the writer and editor, whom I have vainly endeavoured to trace.

[2] Tonks drew this moral from his own watercolours at Tivoli, when he came to review them. 'So, my dear Steer', he wrote, 'keep depressed'.

view, a plain man, one intermittently possessed and almost bored by the burden of his genius. Only his deep eyes and something of greatness in his presence, indefinable but unmistakable, spoke of the sleeping powers. Once engaged on 'the job' he was another person, intensely absorbed and applied, and determined to win through. His father, as we shall see, had displayed a will-power like Jacob's in serving seven years for a bride: the son was also like that patriarch in wrestling with the visiting tyrant of his working hours till he had won a blessing. The single faculty for which he would claim credit in his talks with Ronald Gray was 'sticking to a job and seeing it through'. He either did a thing thoroughly or let it be. When he ceased smoking fifty cigarettes a day he dropped the habit entirely.

His obstinate minimising of any pride or conviction of achievement had another illustration in what a Midland dealer told Henry Rushbury. About the time of the O.M. ceremony this hopeful buyer had rung the bell in Cheyne Walk. Steer himself opened, still in court-dress, and the visitor explained that he had come to buy 'masterpieces' at what price the painter chose to ask. 'I don't paint masterpieces', said Steer, and shut the door.

He was again unlike the artist, whether of fiction or reality, who has to struggle with poverty. In the early years he was allowed £150 a year by his mother, a sum equal to £300 and more as things are now, so that with occasional sales he could get along, afford a studio in those cheaper days, and engage models. At her death in 1898 he inherited something like £500 a year. Added to this was his salary at the Slade and a steadily increasing income from painting. He could instal himself comfortably in the Chelsea house, free from drudgeries of constant teaching or uncongenial portrait-painting which lie in wait for the needy beginner.

He had a distaste, which grew with the years, for social pomps and entertainments along with a preference for one visitor at a time. No ascetic, he was amorous of women as of sunshine and curios, yet romance or passion never entangled or distracted his life and work, nor did he marry. Like his Chelsea friends Tonks, Ronald Gray, George Moore, Sargent, Henry James, he remained a bachelor of art.

His life, then, was of a very untroubled and private sort outside of his painting, and he would probably have chosen, were it possible, that no biography should be written. He discouraged any such proposal in his life-time, dreaded the pretensions of a conventional 'Life and Letters', and had the older-fashioned Englishman's reserve about any invasion of his privacy. 'Nobody', he said moreover, 'knows me intimately enough. It would be like the book on Sickert: all the real things would be left out, and all the things that did not matter would be shoved in.' He recognised, however, that some account of his life was inevitable after his death, and

4 PHILIP, FATHER OF PHILIP WILSON STEER

5 MARY PAIGE *by Philip Steer*

left discretion on that head to his niece, Miss Hamilton, along with the correspondence and the documents he had regularly stacked, with so much else, at No. 109.

I therefore, on her appeal, agreed to expand the sketch I had already published, with Steer's approval, in the Spring number of 'Artwork' for 1929, and supplement it with the facts she could furnish about her uncle's family, upbringing and other circumstance. These are largely based on the clear memories of her mother, Mrs. Hamilton, Steer's elder sister Catherine, who continues to paint flowers at the ripe age of ninety. Without their devoted help and that from other members of the family the record of early years, and much else, would have been impossible. I have further been able to draw upon letters preserved by Tonks and two other intimates, Ronald Gray, a yet older comrade, and Geoffrey Blackwell, a patron and friend of thirty-four years. My debt to other friends or acquaintances of Steer are duly acknowledged in the text, but my thanks are due on the threshold to Mr. Lockett Thomson, of Barbizon House, for ready help with photographs, catalogues and other material. His father, David Croal Thomson, gave Steer a first exhibition at the old Goupil Gallery, and with him and with his associates, Mr. and Mrs. Marchant, Steer characteristically maintained an almost exclusive business alliance. Gray has also allowed me to make use of a notebook for the final years; G. L. Behrend, a painting companion of eleven summers, has made me free of copious notes and letters, and Blackwell put on paper his recollections and impressions of what was an ideal association for painter and patron. To him Steer reported on each summer's settlement, and he was given the lead among those eager to have first sight and choice of the season's production.

Blackwell's too early death on the eve of the 1943 exhibition at the National Gallery, to which he had largely contributed, carried away a man of many-sided interests and of sensitive, cultivated mind, as well as a genial host, whether at Berkhamsted or in London. A dinner given to Steer, Tonks and the writer during the last War at the Conservative Club, which Steer loved for its old-fashioned solidity, not to speak of cuisine and cellar, became an annual event. Others were charily admitted; Augustus Daniel, Charles Aitken, Alec Martin, Gerald Kelly and a few casuals; immense talk accompanied and followed the good things provided. Steer said little, but beamed at the chatterers over the one glass of port that defied doctor's orders. Once a new-comer was distasteful to Tonks and thunder hung over that evening. At not too late an hour the great man was packed into a 'growler' for safe passage home with Tonks for convoy. Hansoms he rigorously proscribed, as perilous machines.

Blackwell was eager in urging that a Life should be published 'while the iron was hot', and when, owing to a serious collapse, I had to renounce the task I had taken up with dubitation because of the scant material then in sight, he strove to stay me with flagons of choice vintages. Alas! I was condemned to a milk diet. That experienced biographer, my friend Joseph Hone, was willing to step into the breach, spite of enforced distance in Dublin and the slightest of personal acquaintance with Steer. On my recovery he generously waived his claim and transferred such correspondence as had already reached him.

The earliest worker in the field remains to be warmly thanked. Mr. Collins-Baker had for many years collected information about Steer's work, and in conjunction with his wife, a Slade pupil of Steer, had begun a card-index of paintings, including those in the Chelsea house. Mr. Baker renounced his project of a book when he left the National Gallery for a post in Pasadena, U.S.A., and a notice in 'The Art Chronicle' for 25 December 1909 and references in his 'British Painting' (1933) are all that found a way into print. The card-index was transferred to Mr. Isherwood Kay, a colleague at Trafalgar Square, and at his death to the British Museum. With Mr. Collins Baker's ready consent it has served as foundation in the full catalogue of paintings prepared by Mr. Alfred Yockney for this book.

Originally, aware of the reserve, whether in speech or letters, of my subject, and his uneventful career, save in paint, I had spoken of an 'expanded sketch' only: but on casting a net of correspondence in likely waters I was able to fish up memories that in a few years more might have been *spurlos versenkt*. The 'sketch' was 'expanded' accordingly, with a growing interest for myself, not naturally an historian, since I see habitually by detached picture rather than in continuous narrative.

Acknowledgements, beside those made above or in the text, are due to others who have helped me: to my friends Boris Anrep and Ralph Wilson, who saved my eyes by reading and marking letters or copying passages; to Sir Eric Maclagan and Professor Hind for easy access to books and answers to inquiries; to my wife, finally, for some emergency typing, least service in the constant and valiant care by dint of which I have survived at all.

* * *

It is a fond illusion of the critic-kind that biography gives a precious key to interpretation of an artist's work. All that matters of temper and taste is written in the work itself, to be deciphered there: the rest of the story is superfluous or irrelevant. Yet from the days of that proto-gossip, Giorgio Vasari, there has been a constant appetite for anecdote and traits of character, down to the most trivial, in the lives of painters and other artists. The hunger for such glimpses, endearing or disconcerting, arises less from any revelation of genius they may furnish than from the contrast between a fallible mortal's course in the violent or humdrum outer world and the imagination which could invent or distil from it something of beauty incorruptible. The historian's part is to authenticate, date and locate the work; the critic's to discriminate and praise; the biographer's to write one more chapter of the Human Comedy.

In one of Henry James's sketches there is a character whose form is present only when others are there to look at him. Steer, the still centre, the magnet of a devoted and actively gyrating circle, was something like that. I have judged it illuminating therefore, to include some account, not only of his family circle and domestic setting, but of the 'sodality', to borrow Tonks's word, that reflected his inspiration, cherished his foibles and was more vocal than himself. By its consent the stranger, under whose gaze Steer's unassertive features might tend, at times, to fade out, may be convinced of a massive presence in absence.

The great are apt to be odd as mortals see them. Steer's brand of oddity was a protective screen of ordinariness to disguise acutely sensitive feeling and to hoard against busybodies and tedious gossips the inner travail of what from on high had visited and disturbed him.

I
ORIGINS
AND CHILDHOOD

Philip Wilson Steer was born at Birkenhead on 28 December 1860, a day of heavily falling snow: he was third child and second son of his parents, who had been married seven years. His father, Philip Steer, born in 1810, was the eldest son of yet another Philip Steer, of High House, Kingsbridge, Devon, and grandson of Henry Sture of Hendham, Woodleigh, owner also of the estate of Bickley in the parish of Halwell, both in the same county.

Tonks used to declare that Steer was of the yeoman kind, and it is certainly more natural to think of him as rooted in the English countryside, solid, taciturn, weather-wary, than as a wild marauding Viking. Yet it was to such invaders from Denmark or Sweden that his brother Harry traced, to his satisfaction, all the Steers, Sturs, Stures or Styrs to be found in the annals of the island since the days of Ethelred the Unready.[1] The descendants, if his conclusions are sound, of Danish and Swedish freebooters had become peaceful squires and yeoman farmers in Devonshire; but a more adventurous branch emigrated. Henry Sture's second son, Henry, born 1780, crossed the Atlantic in 1824 after serving his apprenticeship at the Royal Dockyards, Plymouth, and eventually founded a great New York firm of Steers, ship and floating-dock builders. From their yards was launched the first American man-of-war, 'The Great Harry', and the celebrated yacht 'America'.[2]

From this line, remotely perhaps of alien freebooters, immediately of yeoman-farmers and shipbuilders, Philip, father of Philip Wilson Steer, breaks out as something of a 'sport'; an artist, namely, and romantic lover. He is described as remarkably handsome and a fine horseman. He showed early promise as a painter, had drawing lessons from a neighbour in Devonshire, an old man of remarkable character who was a student of both sciences and art. The young 'Philip Steer, Portrait Painter', at High

---

[1] 'Notes on the Sture Family of England', by the Rev. W. H. Hornby Steer, B.A. A summary of his conclusions, along with an account of what is certain in the record of the painter's family, will be found in an Appendix, p. 170, furnished by his son, Lt. Col. W. R. Hornby Steer.

[2] See 'The Yacht "America",' by Thompson, Stephens and Swan, Charles E. Laurent and Co. 1925.

House, Kingsbridge, attracted the attention of a benevolent baronet, Sir William Elford, of The Priory, near Totnes, a collector of pictures and amateur artist, who became an attentive, if somewhat fussy, coach and patron to the beginner. Under his guidance Philip Steer copied portraits, among them Sir Joshua Reynolds's of himself at Plympton,[1] and in April 1836 obtained a commission from a Mr. Cornish 'who wants to have one of his hands appearing with a scrowl of musick in it, signifying that it is a manuscript of Heber's Hymns which he has set to musick'. Next he was set to do the head of a model 'from Nature, like Opie', for practice and as a bait. Finally came a portrait of the baronet's wife under the reasonable conditions laid down in the following letter.

26.6.1837

My dear Sir,   The Priory
   Lady Elford has been desired by her family and friends at Manadon to sit to you for her portrait and I have told her that I have no doubt of your painting one which will neither disgrace you the artist or the house in which it will be placed, but that the only mode by which such an effect can be produced will be by her sitting to you in a plain unaffected garb without any pretensions to finery—That you shall not be encumber'd with any advice or suggestions by herself or any friends who may see the progress of it, by which you will be likely to make the best of your own observation and skill.
   I am quite sure that this mode of proceeding will lead to the attainment of the best effects and that a picture made out under such circumstances is most likely to hold an equal rank in public opinion with the other original pictures you have already executed.
I am dear Sir,
Yours very truly,

Mr. Steer   Will Elford

   From portraiture Philip Steer turned to landscape, and a letter, signed W. R. Courtenay, speaks of commissions for views of Salcombe and The Moult, and of a third. Others are in possession of the painter's family. From those years must date the professional card thus set forth

MR. P. STEER,
Portrait, Animal and Landscape Painter

Prices of Portraits
Miniature Size:

Bust . . . . . . £2 2s. size, 10 inches.
Small size . . . 4 4   ,, 2 feet.

[1] That portrait recalls an earlier tie between the Elford house and a Devonshire painter. When Reynolds, in 1773, was elected Mayor of his native town he wrote to the Sir William Elford of that date, asking him to see to the hanging of the self-portrait Sir Joshua was presenting. Elford carefully set it 'between two old pictures', and the donor was tickled to find that they were early works of his own. Elford and his partner in a Plymouth bank bought a picture by another Devon artist, Haydon.

Life Size:

Bust . . . . . . £5 5s. „ 2 ft. 6 in.

Kit Cat . . . . 6 6 „ 3 feet.

Half the price, as is usual, to be paid at the First Sitting.

Terms for Drawing, Painting, &c.

Per Month, Two Lessons a week, one hour each £0 14 0

Ditto, Two Lessons a week, two hours each 1 1 0

Six Persons wishing to form a Class, can attend at 7s. 6d. per hour.

For his landscapes the painter made close study of trees and clouds. Of the latter Luke Howard had, in 'The Modification of Clouds' (1803), given the accepted nomenclature, a basis from which Ruskin was to develop his unexampled mingling of scientific analysis with impassioned observation in 'Modern Painters'. The existence of those landscapes by Philip the father calls for stressing because confusion, accidental or intentional, may arise between his works and those of Philip Wilson, the son; but the example of his portraiture reproduced is sufficient witness to his merits as an artist in his own right.

After working in London for some years Philip Steer settled in Bideford and began to teach painting. To his classes came Emma and Susan, daughters of the Rev. William Harrison, who was then taking duty as *locum tenens* at Instow Church. Harrison was a native of Chester, born in 1780. He held a Cure at Holy Trinity there, and afterwards was perpetual Curate of Woore in Shropshire.

In 1815 this clergyman married Miss Mary Hornby, an heiress of considerable fortune. She had artistic leanings, and left behind her pleasant water colours, drawn and tinted after the fashion of her time. Of their two daughters Emma, born 1816, was educated by her father, who gave her a first lesson in Latin grammar on her third birthday! Later she was a boarder in Miss Bireley's school at Stratford-on-Avon, then one of the most fashionable and exclusive in England. Afterwards she lived quietly with her parents at Woore. She was a voracious reader and fortunate in having the run of a large library, whose eighteenth century and contemporary English books moulded her to a width and tolerance in advance of her time. Her intimate friend and confidant was her uncle, George Harrison, Mayor of Chester in 1824, ironmaster, owner of paper mills and a shot-tower, also connoisseur of wine, grower of pineapples and collector of pictures and objects of art. Through his friendship with Josiah Wedgwood Steer's sister has inherited some unusually fine black basalts, made to special order. Emma's arts were embroidery and pencil drawings.

Between the tall young master and his pupil Emma, who was no more than five feet high, a friendship sprang up which turned to deep attachment; but they were parted for seven years when the Harrisons moved to Hanwood, Salop, in 1846. Philip Steer felt he was not well enough off to seek consent to an engagement. The young people, thinking correspondence without her parents' knowledge would be dishonourable, decided to wait in silence, broken by no letter or other signal than some occasional newspaper, a poem from Emma's pen on her beloved's birthday and two copies of 'Ossian', which they marked and posted backward and forward.

In 1853 the marriage at last took place after a short engagement. Emma was apt to stammer if upset, and broke the news to her father in a letter, going out for a long walk while he digested it.

Their first child, born the following year, was Catherine, and the birth of the elder son, Henry, followed after the Steers had settled in Birkenhead. There and in Liverpool was little public care for art. Philip Steer strove to kindle a flame, arranging lectures by a certain Frank Howard, of high repute in his day (c. 1805–1866), and not to be confused with the Luke Howard already mentioned. This intimate friend and mentor of Philip Steer deserves to have his reputation taken out of near-oblivion's cupboard, set up and dusted. The photograph reproduced, with its rich amplitude of mane and whisker, preserves the striking figure he must have cut as practitioner and prophet of the arts. His father was Henry Howard, R.A., once famous, now not a little mouldy, as an 'historical' painter. Frank became assistant to Sir Thomas Lawrence; on his own account exhibited at the Royal Academy and elsewhere subjects drawn from Shakespeare, other poets and the Bible; on Lawrence's death took to producing small portraits, and in 1845 settled in Liverpool. He further practised what were later to be called 'Arts and Crafts' in grievous designs for church windows, racing-cups and the like for the silversmiths' firm of Storr & Mortimer (later Hunt & Roskell); twenty years of this as their 'Principal Designer', while working for Messrs. Elkington as well.

On the top of all this he was a voluminous author, with 'The Sketcher's Manual', 'Colour as Means of Art', 'The Science of Drawing', etc., to his name. From his 'Spirit of the Plays of Shakespeare in Outline' P. W. Steer, at the age of sixteen, took 'Antony and Cleopatra' for a wall-painting in the Music Room of his father's 'Apsley House' at Whitchurch.

The four volumes of Shakespeare illustrations are a remarkable feat in modulated outline, inspired by Flaxman and Retzsch, but dispensing with their occasional use of shadow. A very different line of work is revealed by *Epsom in 1833, after the victory of 'Dangerous', from a contemporary print after Frank Howard.*[1] Here is a scene, whose background might be photographic, pictured six years before Daguerre's invention, of which Frith took full advantage twenty-five years later.

The hand-books cited above are the work of a keenly analytic mind brought to bear on the principles of composition followed by various masters, and on the 'strong' and 'weak' points underlying them in every picture-field.

Those activities were not anything like enough for the volcanic man. He excelled as a lecturer, whether at the 'London Institution' or in those honourable if dingy resorts of anxious culture, the 'Mechanics' Institutes', that we of a less eager age were to know in their decline, along with their middle and upper-class cousins, the 'Literary and Philosophical Institutes'. In these he popularised, as after his death, Matthew Arnold was to urge, the Best that had been Thought and Said about his subject, and boldly illustrated doctrine by carrying a picture, whose subject had been dictated on the spot, through five-lecture stages of 'Invention' and 'Execution'. This he did in Liverpool and performed also at Grange Mount, Birkenhead, Philip Steer's 'School of Fine Art for Ladies, with a class for Gentlemen on two evenings of the week'. His friend thought him a brilliant artist, 'but too outspoken to please the people of Liverpool', not at any time very susceptible to such cultivation, and relapsing from bouts of mental improvement into comfortable contentment with the less than second-rate.

Only, I think, Benjamin Robert Haydon had carried lecturing to so bold a pitch of demonstration, exhibiting, as he did, on his platforms nude models in the poses of Parthenon figures and analysing their anatomies.

Neither Frank Howard nor Philip Steer found a place in the 'Liverpool Academy' (1810–1867) and their names are absent from Mr. H. C. Marillier's 'Liverpool School of Painters' (Murray, 1904). Mrs. Hamilton notes that 'Howard's tongue was a little too long, but that he hit the nail on the head. He offended the Liverpool public, as he said they had only one thought, Palm Oil and Cotton. He was a keen musician and wrote criticism for the Liverpool Press on Music and Opera'.

Such was the sea of Culture on whose waves Steer's father swam dutifully and happily, while that portent, Frank Howard, walloped up from the deeps. The mother, a hungry reader, was doubtless called or considered a 'blue stocking'. There is a touching relic of the couple's affection and ambition in some lines written by Emma for a sketch-book she gave her husband as a birthday gift. Their prim, eighteenth century-like wording

[1] 'The Derby in Art', by A. E. Johnson, in the Strand Magazine, June, 1938.

6 (a) FRANK HOWARD

6 (b) CATHARINE STEER
(afterwards Mrs. Hamilton)

(*a*) Photo used by Frith for his picture, 1858

(*b*) By Frank Howard, 1833, after the victory of 'Dangerous'

7 DERBY DAY

is inscribed on 'superfine satin' paper, with a pretty stamp of rose, thistle and shamrock:—

> Accept, my love, this trifling gift,
>   And on its sev'ral pages trace,
> Whate'er may be thy fancy's drift;
>   Fresh forms of beauty, lines of grace.
>
> No touches from a limner's hand,
>   Should fall unheeded to the ground;
> So whether simple, frail, or grand,
>   Let thine, within these leaves, be found.

To the fond partners, after a seven years' wait as for their betrothal, was born a son who was to fulfil, and more, their artistic longings, but to be strangely resistant to the Howard medium. Like a sea-urchin, at a hint of dangerous contacts withdrawing his tentacles from the noise of argument and scriptures of the ink-beast, he shut-in his gift against dilution or infection, opening only at a hint of 'food convenient'. 'Turner': yes, as we shall see, but not all even of him; the English discoverer, not the Italianising tourist.

On the other hand the child of so long an idyll was to have the advantage of growing up in a house where paints and brushes were common objects and an eager father at hand for eleven years to demonstrate their use. No wonder then that at fifteen a precocious son had reached the virtuosity of *A Dead Bullfinch*. He stood in need of no further 'education', though schools of art may have had their uses in providing models and the spur of companionship.

Owing to the serious illness of his mother the infant Philip became wholly the care of the children's nurse, Margaret Jones ('Jane') afterwards Mrs. Raynes, a passionate and energetic young Welshwoman of whom the other children stood in great awe; to the new-born baby she gave her whole love and devotion. This rugged, loyal and zealous Celt served with the Steers until her marriage. She and the cook had torn one another's hair out in rivalry about a lover, Raynes by name. 'Jane' lost the battle and consoled herself with his brother, who had a job at Paddington. Till his death she slaved, doing the entire washing for a neighbouring hotel, day in, day out, and tending his children. When she had buried Raynes she returned as cook to Steer's mother, on whose death in 1898 she became housekeeper to Steer himself at the house he took in Cheyne Walk, and was there till her death in 1929 at the age of ninety-one.

The child's baptism was delayed until October 1861 when he was ten months old, owing to a severe attack of bronchitis, a complaint that was to be his enemy through life. He was named Philip after his father and

Wilson after Bishop Wilson of Sodor and Man, a connection of his mother's. One of his christening presents, a Carolean porringer, came from the Bishop, but was stolen from the Avenue Studio. Philip the younger was a fine infant and much to Jane's gratification strangers would stop her to ask who was the lovely boy in her perambulator. His father was exceedingly proud of the child's forehead, and in a letter to his grandmother wrote: 'He shows the germ of a reflective mind, which I trust and pray may open and expand in great splendour at some future day.'

When the boy was two years old Jane presented him with a paint-box for his birthday, which he always took to bed and slept with under his pillow. He could be safely left alone in the nursery if she gave him a cup of ink and water, a paint brush and piece of paper, and would sit on the floor absorbed and happy till her return. His favourite picture book then and Bible of art afterwards was John Cassell's 'Art Treasures Exhibition'[1] with its numerous illustrations after the masters. Among other portraits was one of Turner by John Gilbert. Every evening on his way to bed the child went to see his father with this book. He was asked 'Who is the greatest painter?' With solemn slowness he would find the page, lay his hand on it and declare 'Tur-ner'. That worship was strong to the end as at the beginning. In Steer's bedroom hung a watercolour by Turner, where the morning light fell, and he said he never came to an end of it. His mother, writing to the child's great-uncle, George Harrison of Chester in 1864, told him 'Little Philly is busy doing a sketch in water colours under his Papa's direction. He says blue is his favourite colour'.

In 1864 the Steers moved from Birkenhead, having bought the Grange, Whitchurch, near Ross-on-Wye. Philip Steer renamed it 'Apsley House' in admiration for the Duke of Wellington. A red-brick Tudor building with Georgian additions and panelled rooms, it had belonged to the Vaughan family and a condition of sale was that a boy's portrait of the Lely school must go with the house to prevent ghostly visitations. An old and pleasant garden with well-timbered policies completed a fortunate home for the painter-to-be.

Mrs. Hamilton notes:—

In the photograph [reproduced p. 16] the little room on the left was our Museum, where we spent so many happy hours. It was built on to the house by a previous owner who was a J.P. and he used it as a Magistrate's Office.

[1] 'John Cassell's Art Treasures Exhibition, Containing Engravings of the Principal Masterpieces of the English, Dutch, Flemish, French and German Schools, with Biographic Sketches of the Painters and Critical Notices of their productions: Cassel, Petter and Galpin.' On the title-page is a group by Watteau. The Exhibition illustrated was the famous one held at Manchester in 1857, the most remarkable assembly of masterpieces from private collections ever held.

This view was taken by my Father when first we went there, before the garden was altered. Later there was a lawn and fountain in front of the window, and there is a wing on the right side where the dining room now is which does not show in this view. The house covers two sides of a square.

The children had grey ponies, but 'Phil' was not fond of riding. Once, when the Great Powers were safely out of the way, his brother and sister decided he ought to have a lesson, but when they whipped the pony into a canter the child fell off upon the much-admired forehead and to the youngsters' panic a large bump rose; this they tried to cure by putting his head under a pump. The loyal little boy did not give them away when final reckoning came.

He endured teasing with calm, but once, when he was five years old, he considered his brother and sister had gone too far and things could be borne no longer. He picked up a hoe and threw it at them with one word only—'Damn'. This was characteristic of his attitude through life, a patient tolerance of annoying things and people until they crossed the fair limit. He was a dignified child and would brook no liberties taken with his toys by other children: he was deeply attached to a little waggon which Jane had made for him by the village carpenter. He lived in an imagined world very intensely during his early years, but after his seventh birthday constructive powers began to develop rapidly and he made his own toys, especially little boats.

Steer's father arranged a museum for the children and trained them to become ardent collectors of shells, plants and minerals. Phil's interest was centred in minerals and fossils. His love for these and especially for crystals continued through life and he possessed some very fine specimens. At 109 Cheyne Walk the back part of the Entrance Hall was crammed with shells and minerals; others were mingled in the rooms with Chinese bronzes. He often wondered at people's indifference to the beauty of such things. He was one of the few customers of Mr. Botley in Church Street who collected minerals solely for their beauty. Specimens of these were warmly welcomed gifts from his family at Christmas-time, and it was his habit to speed a specially favoured guest by slipping into her hand at parting a rarely-coloured fragment.

The Steer children took long walks over the Herefordshire Hills with their father, distinguishing the song of birds, and trained to watch clouds. 'They learned that the Heavens declared the glory of God and the Firmament shewed His Handiwork, but also how to make squirts out of cow-mumble stalks.'

In 1871 the father died after a short illness. Up to that time the children had been taught at home by a governess, but in 1875 Steer joined his brother at Hereford Cathedral School after attending a preparatory school in Whitchurch run by a lady who had been on the staff at Eton. He left the former in 1877.

To this account of the family circle, from notes by Miss Hamilton, her mother adds the following:—

At Cheyne Walk, Phil and I would amuse ourselves, recalling our childish adventures, our parents and kin, our friends, most of them now dead. We often spoke of our father's only surviving brother, Uncle Tom, who was crippled when a baby by infantile paralysis. He farmed the lands of Borough, Devon, for some years, riding over the estate on his pony with special stirrups for his knees, and on Sundays was carried into Church by his man. He had a reverence for the land; loved wild things, wild flowers and children: we held him in high affection for his noble and amiable character, and whimsical sense of fun. He lived with his mother, who died at the age of 95.

She speaks also of Steer's reaction as a painter to the Devonshire scenery of his family's holdings.

My brother used to go on visits to Borough, near Kingsbridge, when he was quite young. This was the estate our Grandmother bought, which later came to him and his brother, and is now owned by his nephew.

Later in life he had an invitation from his cousin, Mrs. Ewen Stabb, to pay her a visit at Ashburton and paint on Dartmoor; but the scenery of Devon never appealed to him; and as far as I know he did no painting there, as he thought it too enclosed, and preferred a long vista and open country with cloud effects.

To G. L. Behrend Steer said, 'Cream is the only attraction Devonshire has for me, being by nature greedy.'

8 APSLEY HOUSE, WHITCHURCH, ROSS-ON-WYE

9 The Infant Steer with his Nurse

II

BOYHOOD

Numismatics

In 1875 Steer's sister Catherine married 'a dynamic and magnificent-looking explorer', Charles Edward Hamilton, just back from his travels in South Eastern Africa and the land of Moab. The boy took wholeheartedly to this bearded giant and would sit for hours listening to his adventures as anthropologist and naturalist. Hamilton came of a long line of sailors and soldiers, one of whom was the Elizabethan adventurer, Sir Antony Shirley; his father and two uncles had fought at Waterloo and another uncle had been killed at Trafalgar. This was, perhaps, what fired Steer to an unlikely desire in one who had fought shy of riding, namely to enlist in a Cavalry regiment; but the phase passed, and his next ambition was to take up what was then for him the most entrancing study on earth, Numismatics. He had been an ardent buyer of coins from his early teens, and continued so till his eyes failed, forming an important collection of Greek, Roman and English examples; but he rarely spoke of them save to the elect. He would carry a new acquisition in his waistcoat pocket for days, to handle and ponder.

In the 'Art Journal' for March 1893 appeared Steer's solitary contribution to the Press, an article on 'The New Coinage' with reproductions of Poynter's and Brock's designs; a testimony to his interest in the subject, and probably instigated by Croal Thomson, the editor. It is reprinted on p. 173.

A friend of Hamilton's, F. G. Hilton Price, F.S.A., senior partner in the banking house of Child, was at the time a frequent visitor to Apsley House. During one visit he wrote a small monograph on the Druidical Stones at Trellech near Monmouth, and commissioned Steer to illustrate it with a lithograph.[1] Interested in the lad's knowledge of coins, he procured a nomination for him to enter the Coins and Medals Department at the British Museum.

Here are passages from two letters to the boy:—

---

[1] This was an innocent bit of careful drawing; a 'gent' in pot-hat and overcoat stands against one of the stones to give scale.

13.10.1875.

My dear Philip,   Temple Bar
    I am very glad to hear from you—I have written to my friend Mr Franks, asking
him what forms have to be gone through with—I believe a nomination is necessary—
However that may not be difficult to obtain.
    I will do all I can to help you into the Museum.
    How glad you must be to have a cabinet for your coins—
    I will let you hear from me again shortly . . .

25.11.1875.

    At last—I have seen one of the Chiefs of the British Museum.
    I find upon enquiry that first of all, a nomination is required—wch can only be
obtained from the Official Trustees, of w^m there are 50. The best to apply to, are the
Lord Chancellor—Bishop of London—Lord Chamberlain, Chanc^r of the Exchq^r
and other officials of the Government.
    The next stage is to make up y^r mind to wch depart^t you w^{ld} join—then to have y^r
name placed upon the list for appointments—w^{ch}, I am assured by my friend, are very
numerous.
    Après cela—the usual Competitive Examination for the Civil Service.
    A University Education is of great importance, as most of the heads of departments
are M.A.s of their Universities.
    Languages should be got up—a fair knowledge of Greek & Latin, French & Ger-
man are requisite to enable you to keep up with the times & dive into the past.
    Mr Franks told me that any one knowing Sanscrit or Chinese c^{ld} be certain of
ultimate success—scholars in those tongues are well paid for translating documents.
    No one can get into it *after* he has attained 24 years of age.
    One of the Private Trustees will tell me something further about it shortly—I spoke
to him last week ab^t getting a nomination.
    You should spend a month or two in the Brit: Museum—studying the objects. . . .

    The prospect of learning Sanscrit or Chinese on the top of the rest must
have been somewhat daunting; but the budding official in numismatics
was put under a tutor for elementary preparation. This was Dr. Purcell
at Whitchurch, a brilliant and somewhat eccentric scholar. Steer said he
learned more from him in a few weeks than from anyone else who ever
taught him. Then followed, from January 1878, a London course of in-
tensive study under a tutor for the Civil Service examination, but he
found the routine of précis writing intolerable: spelling and punctuation,
even, he never really mastered:[1] his heart went back to its first love, and
he dashed to his rooms after work to paint as long as light lasted. It was
at this time, not two years earlier as has been stated, that he painted the self-
portrait which is reproduced. Its romantic swagger may be profitably
compared with the simplicity of the Uffizi portrait, painted in middle

---

[1] For clearness' sake I have added a comma or full-stop occasionally to the breathless text of
his letters.

life, but it has remarkable precision of drawing undistracted by preoccupations of colour.

The Black Forest

At sixteen, before he went up to study for the British Museum, he had visited Germany for the first and only time, under the care of a family friend, Miss Sharp. He stayed in Paris on his way out and in a letter to his mother wrote ' . . . in the afternoon I went to the Louvre, the pictures were most exquisite. I like the pictures by Murillo best. . . .' Perhaps the delightful *Angel Kitchen* had attracted him. From Paris he went on by Strasbourg to Bad Rippoldsau in the Black Forest. In a letter home he wrote, 'I have just been to take a sketch, but the place is so enclosed in hills that one cannot see very far'. In another he says:—

There are about 250 Germans here they are about the most ugly people I ever set eyes on. We have made the aquaintence of some French ladies and one Englishman they are about the best people here. I can pick up a good deal of French from hearing them talk as they cannot speak English. The scenery here is not very pretty as there is nothing but fir trees. . . . I dont much care for the Germans they are so dirty in eating. There is splendid cool air here it is 2000 feet above sea level. . . .

John Kemp's School

After the idea of work at the British Museum had been dropped it was decided he should enter the School of Art at Gloucester under John Kemp. He attended, at first, three times a week, but owing to distance from the station, a drive of six miles, Kemp advised that he should live nearer and attend every day. His mother accordingly sold the house at Whitchurch and took one at Gloucester so that he could attend all day and every day and have a comfortable home. He carried away from Kemp's teaching at least one useful maxim, viz. 'shaddas (shadows) have edges.'

In April, 1881, he qualified for a certificate of second grade in perspective at South Kensington, with the note, 'Excellent'.

III

PARIS

1882–1884

Julian's: École des Beaux Arts

Steer lived in Gloucester with his mother till he had finished with the School of Art. Disappointed at being turned down as a pupil by the Academy he decided, like so many of his time, to study in Paris and entered Julian's Atelier in October, 1882. He enjoyed life in Paris, and worked industriously, going little outside the daily round of hotel and atelier; was strictly careful about money, and still much of a mother's boy, with mind turned homewards.

Passages from his letters follow:—

5.11.82.

My dear Mother   Hôtel du Beau Séjour

To morrow we leave this hotel and go to the Hotel Britannique in the Avenue Victoria which seems very nice. We have been all day looking about for a studio some of them are very queer places. I think we shall go first of all to Julian's where Bouguereau and Fleury are professors. It seems to be about the nicest. I did not see Floyd there I suppose he has not come back yet. Last night we went to call on Browning and found him at home he was very pleasant and asked about J. Kemp, he recommended Julian's to begin with and meanwhile to look about and see if we fancied the work of any particular man and then to leave. I shall be very glad to get settled down into permanent rooms and unpack my things. . . . We have got on so far with our French pretty well but it is very difficult to remonstrate with a garçon for charging too much. One of the English students at Julian's was very kind in showing us over and giving us all the necessary information. There are plenty of English and Americans there. Yesterday we did not get up till ten o'clock we felt so tired after our voyage the night before and then we went to the Palais de l'Industrie a sort of Exposition where a military band played not at all Sunday music. In the afternoon we saw there some beautiful pictures. Tell J. K[emp] I will write to him when I get settled down to work. The charges at Julian's are for the whole day per month 50 F or 200 F for six months which is at a cheaper rate, or one can go for half the day at about half the cost. I think we shall go for a month to begin with. It is getting dark so I will say goodbye. Tell Harry to keep his peccer up.

6.11.82   Hotel Britannique
                                                                       20 Avenue Victoria

The last letter you got from me was only an apology for one. I was just starting off

10 (*a*) STEER AT 10

10 (*b*) A DEAD BULLFINCH (*painted at 15*)

11 (a) John Kemp, 188-   11 (b) Theophilus Morgan

to see 'La Mascotte' which I did not enjoy much not being able to see the jokes and the house was so frightfully hot I dont think I shall go to another theatre in a hurry. I am very happy here this hotel is kept by two ladies one is English and called Scott and the other is Swiss and called Perret they are very kind. There is a nice room to sit in, in the evenings Scott and I generally play Besique, an English lady and gentleman that have been staying here gave us their box, everyone meets together in the sitting room and at six o'clock table d'hote, so I think the arrangement is much better than moping in lodgings. I am getting to feel more at home now in the atelier, last week I got rather a bad place so my work was not very satisfactory but I hope to do better this week as I have a good place, one has to get to the studio very sharp on eight on Monday if you want to get a good place as it is a question of first come first serve. I managed to get there this morning in good time. Most of the fellows wear blowses so I invested in one they say it saves one's clothes. There have been several nouveaus since us, we had a 'punch' this morning to celebrate someone's arrival. Paris is a dreadful place for fleas, I have caught two already the streets are so full of dirty people. You must not expect me to write oftener than once a week as it comes rather expensive. I will try and keep a letter on hand and write a little when I think of anything. . . . We do plenty of walking every day the studio is just a mile off and we do it twice each way because we come back for lunch. . . . I suppose Harry is getting on with his work tell him if he wants to think Gloucester streets sweet to come here and smell these and if anyone wants another snif they must be a 'glutton' as old Aston said but that is chiefly in the small streets.

21.11.82

Dear Harry

Many thanks for your long letter I am glad to hear any gossip which you can scrape together. It is a month tomorrow since I commenced work at the atelier, for the next month I shall only go there in the morning and go to the Louvre in the afternoon to copy because these dark days we have to leave off work at four instead of five so it is absurd paying for what one does not get. There are a couple of students who have taken medals in the Academy schools very decent sort of fellows they say it was a good thing for me that I did not succeed in getting in so that is encouraging. The weather here at present is very wet rain every day, the Seine has risen so high that the boats cannot run and hear it has overflowed the opposite side. I think after your exam it would do you and Ma good to come over here for a bit there would be no difficulty you could stay here and it would cost very little the living here seems to agree wonderfully well with me I have not been at all bilious we have cafe au lait and roll and butter for breakfast then at half past 12 we have lunch or dejeuner proper at which we drink claret and at six we have a capital dinner which consists of soup two courses of meat sweets cheese desert and cafe noir, drink claret and water. I quote all this for your benefit as you are in search after the philosopher's stone, it seems to suit me extreemly well. . . . How is Mr. Pop? I suppose his little wants are attended to as usual there is a cat here but I dont care much for it. . . . Last Saturday night we went to a kind of music hall where there was a variety entertainment there was a strong man who hung by his legs and held a cannon weighing 700 lbs in his teeth and a girl who sang English comic songs. We are keeping up our French as well as we can there are two Americans here who are learning and they are glad to speak I think I am learning some of the phrases. I have no news as we do nothing except our regular duties.

29.11.82

Last Sunday we went to Versailles and spent a very pleasant time there. . . . We go now nearly every afternoon to the Louvre I am copying a head out of a Vandyck picture it is the Madónna being worshipped by a Dutchman and his wife and I am just painting the head of the Dutchman. I am trying this week to do the 'esquisse' the subject is Clytemnestra after the murder of Agamemnon I dont know how it will turn out. . . . The clergyman here has evenings once a week when he invites anybody who likes to go so we think of going some day.

7.12.82

. . . The days are so dark now that one cannot see after four o'clock and hardly till then to work, in the afternoons now I go to the Louvre I am copying a head out of one of Van-dyck's pictures. I dont much care for copying it is rather dry work I dont think I shall do any more after this one. . . . I'm afraid you must think my letters very dull stupid pieces of composition but I live quite a life of routine so there is nothing startling to tell you.

I think I am gradually improving in my drawing although I dont seem to see it much myself but I suppose if one keeps pegging away one is bound to improve—it makes one feel very down in the mouth sometimes, if all is well next week I shall try and paint the model, hitherto I have only drawn in charcoal and shaded with the same. Last week I did the esquisse Clytemnestra showing the bodies of Agamemnon and Cassandra to the crowd. I think it was not bad for me the professor said it was 'tres gentil' but not horrible enough, I am trying the subject for this week Priam beg-ging the body of Hector from Achilles, they seem very fond of giving subjects from Homer, if Harry has a translation of Homer I should like it, is'nt there one by Pope in the house? Paris is beginning to look gay now for the new year this is the season for Paris they say all the French families come for the new year.

22.12.82

I shall spend Xmas in a rather novel way this year by rushing off as usual to the atelier and working all day this no doubt sounds very heathen but the reason is that they are going to do the studies for the 'concours' which means for a prize of 100 francs for the first and then the others simply get marked. These 'concours' take place once a month during the winter, both the studios do the same model and the same pose and without the professors seeing them while in hand, and then one professor from each studio decides the prize, in the last one an Englishman in our studio was first for the painting but only marked 3d as two drawings came first, of course I dont go in with any expectation of even a place but still one likes to do as the others do. Last night I was at a dinner given in honour of some of the English students who are leaving Paris we dined at a small restaurant in the quartier Latin it was quite a typical students dinner there was present [James] Charles and [J. E.] Christie two academy students the latter a gold medalist and very jolly fellow he recited Burns' Tam O'Shanter exceedingly well and sang lots of Scotch songs. Then there was Taylor the son of Tom Taylor he is a little priggish, a Norwegian merchant who has taken to art and many others too numerous to mention 14 altogether. After the cloth was taken away a bowl of punch came on flaming and we turned the gas down and sang the Rhine wine, and then every one either had to sing a song or tell a story some of the stories were very good there is a man called Laidley[1] who has been a barrister who has stories for all occasions.

[1] W. J. Laidley, afterwards guarantor of the first New English Art Club exhibition and author of 'The Origin and First Two Years of the New English Art Club (Lane, 1907).

Then to finish we all sang Auld Lang Syne and joined hands round and after that the landlord came in so we had to drink his health and sing the Marseillaise altogether it was great fun, and now after this disjointed rigmarole I have only room to add love to yourself and Harry who I hope is all right now.

7.1.83

Dear Harry

Many thanks for your long newsy letter . . . . I dare say you remember me saying some time ago in a letter that I should try and get into the Beaux Arts well you will be glad to hear that I have succeeded—there is a doctor Wells staying here studying who is a very nice man of I should think 40 years of age one evening we were talking and he happened to mention that he knew a lady living in Italy who was intimate with Cabanel so I told him what an advantage it would be for me to get into the Beaux Arts whereupon he offered to write and ask her for a letter to Cabanel which she duly sent and which I took myself this morning accompanied by a drawing to Cabanel who was very courteous and asked me my age and some other questions and looked at my drawing which appeared to give him satisfaction then he wrote out a form requesting the director of the Ecole National des Beaux Arts to enrole my name among the list of his pupils the whole thing has come about so quickly that I can hardly realise it yet,—of course it is an envied position among students I shall have to pay 60 francs on entering and then never anything more I am just as free there as anywhere else to come and go where I like, it has required a little of what professor Moore calls 'push' it is rekoned the strongest studio in Paris in point of work. By the same post I send an illustrated paper with the news about Gambetta I went and saw him lying in state which was not anything much. The funeral was tremendously grand they say the procession consisted of 300,000 persons troops it took 3 hours passing one spot I saw the start which was the best part because all the troops were drawn up and then they were manoeuvring about which was interesting. I daresay you will read a much better description of it in the English papers than I could give you. . . .

Thursday

. . . I have not been to the Beaux Arts yet but intend going on Monday I expect to have a rough time of it at first but I know a few fellows there so they will put me up to a few wrinckles as to how to act.

13.1.83

Dear Harry

. . . On Tuesday I made my first appearance at the new atelier which was rather a serious undertaking according to all accounts but the reality was not so bad all I had to do was to get on the platform where the model poses and sing a song which was not heard because as soon as I commenced they all began screaming and yelling, if they see you are good tempered over it they dont carry it very far I shall only be able to work there every other week as it is so crowded so I am thinking of joining some other place as well.

I had a letter from Kitty the other day which I have answered I also wrote to J. Kemp and now with best love to the mater your affte bro.

P. Wilson Steer

Further letters were unfortunately destroyed. He was at home for the vacation of 1883 and visited the Hamiltons at Headcorn in Kent. His mother gave up her Gloucester house in that year.

*   *   *

Fellow-Students

So far I have followed, in the main, a chronicle from family sources. About the Paris period Steer gave me some additional facts for the sketch I wrote on the eve of his National Gallery exhibition.[1]

James Charles, who was his senior, and chief student friend in Paris, told him of what he had escaped through his rejection by the Academy School. From Bouguereau's teaching he gained little, partly through ignorance of French, but also because of that master's piecemeal methods of correction; Cabanel, at the Beaux Arts, which he entered after the summer vacation, taught effectively by himself drawing.

Unreadiness in the language not only insulated the youth from the general life of Paris, but had other effects; it prevented intercourse with French students, of whom the leading figures were René Menard and Etienne Dinet, known afterwards, one for his love of Greece, the other for his Eastern scenes. Of the British a genial companion at the Hôtel Britannique, near the Châtelet, was G. R. Halkett, the talented caricaturist, journalist and editor of later years. At Julian's were T. B. Kennington, a brilliant student, and James Christie, the huge ruddy Scot, whose performances of 'Johnson on Boswell' and 'The Curate on the Prodigal Son' were a rite afterwards at dinners of the New English Art Club as much as Walter Sickert's scene from 'Hamlet'. At Cabanel's were Edward Stott, Arthur Rendall and one of the Dalziels. Yet another fellow student was William Patrick Whyte, who sent congratulations on the 1909 exhibition of Steer at the Tate Gallery, 'as delightful an experience as I ever had in my life.'

Ignorance of French had a third and final result. An examination in that tongue was introduced at the Beaux Arts, comprising history and other subjects, to cut down an excessive number of foreigners. Steer was obliged to pack up and go home. His stay had been less a *beau séjour* than a camp in the characteristically chosen 'Hôtel Britannique'.

[1] 'Artwork', Spring number, 1929, pp. 7–22.

IV

RETURN TO ENGLAND

London: Royal Academy and other Exhibitions

Since Mrs. Steer had no fixed home at the time of her son's return he probably went very shortly after it to Walberswick. One of his comrades there was Arthur Hoeber, who wrote reminding him of those days, from New York in 1909, where he was doing work for the 'International Studio' and 'Globe' as art-critic. He mentions as others in 'the old crowd' 'Bill Allen' and 'Rowe'. These were probably R. W. Allen and T. Trythall Rowe, foundation members of the 'New English' in 1886. In 1885 he set up in London at Trafalgar Studios, Manresa Road, Chelsea. Mrs. Steer had joined her elder son Henry at Tunbridge Wells, but when he came as senior curate to St. Jude's, South Kensington, they took a house in Stratford Road and Philip went every Sunday to lunch there, making friends with his nephew and niece and bringing his own comrades to the house. There was always a bed ready for him when 'flu or bronchitis struck him: he arrived in a cab and stayed till he was well.

To these details of the family background Mrs. Hamilton adds:—

Philip had a great dislike to artists and students who put on what he called 'fancy dress'; yet, though anything but a dandy himself, always had his suits made by a good Savile Row tailor, plain and comfortable.[1]

Before his Paris schooling Steer, as he told me, had been fired, like the rest of us, with admiration for Burne-Jones at Sir Coutts Lindsay's Grosvenor Gallery exhibitions in the late seventies; particularly his *Pygmalion* series; for Watts and Millais as well. Whistler attracted but puzzled him, as he did Ruskin, by his extreme mistiness. In Paris he remembers being struck by the picture of a parrot by Signac, but the most striking confrontation was that of Manet, who died in 1883, not in 1884, as has been stated; in the latter year a posthumous exhibition of his work was held, and seen by Steer, who was partly puzzled, as before by Whistler; but this lesson also sank in.

[1] Not 'always'. At the beginning of the 'Great War' he employed an obscure but workmanlike tailor who built him a suit in whipcord, calculated as if for eternity.

In his picture *A Girl with a Goat on Sandhills*[1] bought by Mr. Galloway of Altrincham from a Manchester exhibition in 1883, for £33, Steer is said to have acknowledged a strong influence of Cazin. In 1883 and the two following years he was hung by the Royal Academy. In the first, from 23 Brunswick Road, Gloucester, No. 206, *What of the War?*, painted while he was at Kemp's school, was a portrait of Mr. Bick, brother-in-law of the master, reading a newspaper. Mrs. Hamilton recalls that John Kemp tried to dissuade Steer from sending 'so immature a work' to the R.A., but his cousin, Louis Trant, a lad of his own age and a painter, overbore the objection. The portrait, lately acquired by the Tate Gallery, is well up to R.A. standards and thorough in its realism, but does not suggest the painter's hand. (See p. 29.) In 1884, from 'Magdala', Denby Road, Bournemouth, No. 472, *Fantaisie,* the head of an Italian girl, was bought by Mr. Charles Deschamps of Old Bond Street for £42. In 1885, from Trafalgar Studios, Manresa Road, No. 643, *Discovery*, was a woman with a mask, which its author afterwards destroyed. The R.A. chapter ended some years later with an advertisement in the Press that Steer and Sickert had had the honour to be rejected; a 'gesture' that must have been due to Sickert's impish taste in publicity rather than to his friend.

In the years 1883–1888 Graves's 'Dictionary of Artists' credits Steer with four pictures at Suffolk Street, four at the Grosvenor Gallery under its changed direction, and one elsewhere. The pictures shown at the Grosvenor Gallery provoked a remarkable storm of abuse in the papers, *On the Pier Head* and *Chatterboxes* in 1887, but particularly *The Bridge*, a scene at Etaples now in the Tate Gallery collection; a rather commonplace but harmless enough scene of a man and woman against railings in the twilight. 'Either a deliberate daub or so much mere midsummer madness' is a phrase from the 'Daily Telegraph's' wordy scolding. Steer's period, in succession to Whistler's, as the most contested painter of his time, had begun.

It is the custom of critics to search for recondite or revolutionary qualities in a painter whose work the general public mislikes. Time reduces the novelty to an exacter measure. It is not the newness so much as the goodness of a genuine artist's work that renders the public uncomfortable and hostile. It has settled down to the tameness which the last leader's impulse has suffered from the diluters, and resents any bracing of its vision.

For once, it appears, Steer's stubborn heart had a misgiving under this pelting. 'About 1887', writes Ronald Gray, 'I was catching a train at

[1] Lately in possession of Mr. Owen Hugh Smith. The subject is Cazinesque, the paint of a pleasant crumbly texture. See p. 32.

Victoria and Steer walked with me to the station. He was depressed and said that he really felt like chucking painting because he never sold a picture and each time he exhibited he was abused. Even at the New English Art Club, founded in 1886, his first entry was not auspicious; his picture was skied. This was *Andante,* a girl with a violin and two other figures. He was dissatisfied himself, for afterwards he cut it up. The moderate esteem he enjoyed from fellow-painters themselves in those days is witnessed by the following voting-list for the Committee of the Club in 1888. His name is fourteenth out of twenty-five.

1.	Clausen, G.	44 votes	13.	Parsons, A.	24 votes
2.	Sargent, J. S.	44	14.	Steer, P. W.	23
3.	Brown, F.	42	15.	Shannon, J. J.	21
4.	Tuke, H. S.	33	16.	Gotch, T. C.	19
5.	Bate, Francis	32	17.	Thomas, J. H.	19
6.	Christie, J. E.	29	18.	Hacker, A.	16
7.	Kennington, T. B.	29	19.	Charles, J.	15
8.	Lee, T. S.	28	20.	Mann, A.	14

Only a few divined what was in him. Here are the impressions of George Clausen, his older contemporary; a survivor of the earliest 'New English' group, as he recalled them for me in his ninety-second year:—

12.10.43   Cold Ash, Newbury, Berks.
I shall be pleased to tell you the little I know—not much, as I was never one of his intimates—I don't think he had many; I always found him a reticent man, though we were friends for many years.

My first acquaintance with him was in the early days of the 'New English'. I remember some one condoling with him on having a picture rejected at the R.A. and he said quietly, 'It doesn't matter'. My impression at that time was of a man with a lazy mind, but gifted with a wonderful sense of colour; he never made a mistake about that. Since those days I have come to the conclusion that it was not a 'lazy mind' but a concentration on the problems of colour, almost to the exclusion of everything else. Whether consciously or not, he tried to express the fresh vision of a child, and was indifferent to other things until, in his later landscape work, he seemed to realize and aimed to interpret, the great forces of nature. He never spoke—to me—about his own views. He came under many influences, but it was always the colour problem which attracted him; and also a certain elegance. He was an intense admirer of Watteau, and he liked Gainsborough also.

It was through A. G. Webster, painter and brother-in-law of Clausen, that an older friend of Steer, Fred Brown, came to appreciate his work on a visit to the R.B.A. galleries in Suffolk Street. This, Brown wrote to me in 1930, was before he knew Steer personally. He goes on:—

I was introduced to him by Jacomb Hood after my return from Paris (in the winter of 1883–4) but how long after I cannot say. I took the two Bartletts [first promoters of the exhibition which led to the New English Art Club's foundation] round to Steer's studio in the winter of 1885 or early spring of 1886.

Thus began a notable alliance for the furthering of young art in that and following decades.

12 STEER AT 18, 1878

13 (a) What of the War?   13 (b) Steer in the 1880's

V

THE NEW ENGLISH
ART CLUB

Foundation and Early Years: 'Natural'
Light-and-Shadow Colour

Glory to Thee in field and vineyard, Source Divine!
   Requicken woods and sward, in duskiest house prevail,
From darting eye of newt to swan's wing slip and shine,
From magnitude of line
   To minim of detail.

Thou, calling to joy the sister, twin-born, sombre,
   Who lies and lengthens out beside her brother bright,
Hast known of all that charms to find a doubled number;
No mourning, muted umber,
   Shade, richer than the light.

Sun! giving to air its silvers and its roses;
   In fount or mud or shrub obscure an avatar!
Stripped of thy sorcerer's call that wakes them and transposes
To strange apotheosis,
   Things were but what they are.

After the Hymn of Chanticleer to the Sun by Edmond Rostand

Writers about what it is their pleasure to call 'the Naughty Nineties' have been too exclusively engrossed in the 'decadents' of that period, fascinated by a cult of 'strange sins' and general perversity. The sins or vices in question are no more than two: both unhappily familiar, and the limits of perversity are quickly reached, since only virtue is infinite. The other chase ends in dead boredom, such as the tedious monstrosities on which the well-named painter Bosch lavished so high a painter's virtuosity. Wilde exploited wittily a trick of inversion borrowed from De Quincey; Ernest Dowson, with his one memorable and cynical line, was not the leading poet of the time; that place is shared by Housman and Yeats. The brilliant devilries of Beardsley's spider-line took the fancy of all Europe, but his was only one in that bright focus of the talents whose name and record have been so strangely omitted from the 'End of the Century' legend.

The New English Art Club was founded in 1886. Then, as before and since, a mob of disgruntled outsiders was impatient for the Academy sluices to unlock or meditated schemes of 'reform', mutiny and reconstruction. The crowd this time was largely of Paris-trained students. Paris, to the old-fashioned, was still a name of dread, associated in the matter of pictures with lubricity, bloodshed and bad colour. A dealer offered to the suspects his rooms for an exhibition, and when that scheme aborted, one of the band, W. J. Laidley, came forward with a two-year guarantee of rent. For the second year the Dudley Gallery, blessedly small, was secured.

The original members were a mixed crew. Prominent were the followers of Bastien-Lepage's large-scale 'open air', of whom James Charles, George Clausen, La Thangue and Stanhope Forbes were the most able; there was also a Scottish contingent, to be named later the 'Glasgow School'. The earlier exhibitions were not unpopular. From the first of the groups Clausen and what came to be known as the 'Newlyn School' were drafted off to the Academy and most of the Scots seceded when a picture by one of them had been rejected, leaving, however, W. Y. Macgregor. Control passed to what were popularly dubbed 'impressionists', a 'clique', as Brown[1] frankly describes it, led by Sickert and including Steer, Sidney Starr, Théodore Roussel and Francis Bate.

> *'When three men stand together*
> *The Kingdoms are less by three'*

It is small States like Athens, the Italian Renaissance Cities, Elizabethan England, little Holland, Belgium, that are fruitful for the spirit rather than imperial conglomerations, and so, in its degree, was what may be called the second state or foundation of the 'New English'. What Sickert's intrigue had provoked became in the hands of Brown, its organiser, Bate, its honorary secretary, Steer, its immovable and massive constant, a rallying ground for the budding talent of more than one generation; a welcome cockshy for the critics, a titillating scandal for the public.

The 'London Impressionists'

The scandal obtained a name when the painters I have enumerated, with the addition of Francis James, Bernhard Sickert and George Thomson, held an exhibition in 1889 at the Goupil Gallery under the title 'London Impressionists'. Senior to the others as a painter, and with authority as a friend of Whistler and Degas, Walter Sickert took the criti-

---

[1] See his 'Recollections' in 'Artwork', Winter, 1930, and for a fuller history, 'Fifty years of the New English Art Club', edited for the Club by Alfred Thornton in 1935.

cal lead among them and wrote the unsigned preface to the catalogue. This protested against William Morris's condemnation of modern painting and against the kind of 'decorative' painting that accompanied the doctrine. The full text of the document will be found on pp. 175–6.

'Impressionism', at the time of the manifesto, was the nickname for any new painting that surprised or annoyed critic or public. Sickert was interviewed before the exhibition by Herbert Vivian and asked 'What is an Impressionist?' 'I don't know', he replied, 'it is a name they will give us in the papers,' and it was probably applied by the dealer concerned as a rough and ready means of attracting popular interest. It has, however, remained as a prized label for the use of categorists.[1] Clearly the argument of Sickert's declaration has nothing to do with the strict usage of the word 'impressionism', which arose from the title, *Une Impression*, attached to a landscape by Claude Monet in an 1874 exhibition, and it properly belonged to two features in that painter's practice. The first was a keying-up of lights as near as might be to their natural pitch, with a reading of shadows in terms of their colour rather than of their tone.[2] The brown chiaroscuro with scanty glazings of blue, which had been the sufficient whole of painting to a Van Goyen, was renounced for parti-coloured webs more akin to Oriental painting in effect, but allowing for the naturalism of complementary tints which appear in shadows. That was one feature: the other was what may be called a 'snatch technique', timed to the intervals during which the incidence and quality of light remained fairly constant, so that a given subject, haystack, line of poplars, cathedral front, could be noted with speed approaching the pace of a shorthand reporter keeping up with a fluent speaker. As Sickert has pointed out it was the attempt to 'finish' such sketches in the open that was fatal for Cézanne.[3]

Sickert has no more to do in his introduction with the painting of Steer than with that of Monet. His exposition is Whistlerism of the 'Ten O'clock', and represents a stage on the course that ran away from the Camelot of William Morris through the Chelsea of the Nocturnes to the Camden Town of later days. London is not yet the squalid East End, but the riverside, whether under work-a-day illumination or transmuted by gas-lamps

[1] My old friend Alfred Hunt spoke habitually of the landscape painters who, in the eighty-nineties, dominated the Academy, Peter Graham, McWhirter, Colin Hunter and the rest, as the 'Scotch Impressionists': David Murray, the latest to be admitted, had done his best to bar the door behind him. William McTaggart, who had developed a fresh-air-and-sea painting parallel to, but independent of the French, remained isolated in Scotland.

[2] Ruskin, diviner-in-art, had given the text for this: 'It is an absolute fact that shades are as much colours as lights are.'

[3] Anglo-French Review, April, 1920.

to a blue envelope for 'palaces in the night'. Before dealing with Steer's part in the show it may not be out-of-place to say a word about his associates in the exhibiting group.

WALTER SICKERT himself, shiningly blond and handsome, fashionably tailored, a brilliant wit and man-of-the-world, had acted in Irving's company, studied for a short time under Legros at the Slade, learned etching and become a disciple of Whistler and from 1883 onwards of Degas. Discipleship to Whistler was a mixture of bliss and servitude. Thus in the evening the Master would whistle up a cab and Walter was charged with a weighty lithographic stone in case inspiration should come during or after dinner. At the Café Royal or elsewhere the waiter was enjoined to place an extra table for the stone, and Walter, bearing it again, untouched, went forth when the evening ended. In Monet's dazzle of outdoor sunlight Sickert, no more than Whistler, was a fellow-snatcher: his shadows depended on a conventional india-red foundation. He was at home rather in a shadowy glimmer of the music-hall scenes Degas had introduced to painting, reconstructing them from notes and memory. He was a native of paint, giving a pleasant quality to every touch. He had a struggle throughout for drawing, but a fine instinct, and his surrender to the camera and his latest work, the refuge of a tired old age in reproduction of other men's designs with bright arbitrary colours, are not to be remembered against him. With 'loyalty' to institutions or persons he had no patience. 'Loyalty to whom? to Winter?' he asked, when the 'New English', of which he was an in-and-out member, was discussed. Winter was the delightful Cockney sales-secretary, who kept a furtive little figure of his own sculpturing on his desk in the hope of 'chatting' a collector into buying it. Sickert joined any new exhibiting body that promised to revive an illusion of youth, but was in theory an anarchist about juries, thinking pictures should be hung together in the alphabetical order of their authors' names. He regarded sales as a dealer's business: he made no attempt at nursing his prices, but rolled up a number of canvases when in need of cash and despatched them to his agent for what they would fetch. Lavish in acquiring studios and stores for his pictures, in London or abroad, he centred much of what heart he had on Dieppe and its fisher-quarter of Le Pollet, dear to him since childhood. There, once and again, I found him the best of companions, and the most frequent and fallacious discoverer of new techniques. He would turn up before breakfast outside the window with a yesterday's canvas and when asked 'Was it a Moonlight?' would declare, 'No, a broad sunlight in the right scale of tones'. Everything in Dieppe was the best of its sort. He believed a very poor kind of canvas on sale there was one hallowed by the practice of Velazquez; he used, from

14 (a) GIRL WITH A GOAT ON SANDHILLS, *exhibited 1883*

14 (b) KNUCKLEBONES, WALBERSWICK, 1888
Sickert after Steer

15 (*a*) EMMA, STEER'S MOTHER

15 (*b*) ASLEEP, 1893

old affection, watercolours that turned black, and recommended a kind of fish-glue for a ground that came away with the paint. His most specious discovery was of a varnish for watercolour drawings, which, if the over-painting went wrong, could be dissolved away, leaving the under-design intact. Unluckily it embrowned the colour. But through these and other diversions he pursued a huge canvas of the Grand Hotel with all its heart-breaking exactitude of windows, or caught between sun and dusk a be-witching glimpse of the great church from the Café des Tribunaux.

Two others in the band, THÉODORE ROUSSEL and PAUL MAITLAND, were also Whistlerians; the former an ardent Frenchman, theorist and practiser with a 'tone detector-r-r'. He invented a method of colour-etching applied to flowers, and painted the picture of a nude model resting, now in the Tate Gallery, remarkable for a quality of flesh-painting marred by the 'Canterbury' chair and other properties. Maitland was his mildly 'damned soul' in low-toned riverside views, but once broke into a bid for stronger realism in a *Hollywood Arms* with an enormous 'Sugg' gas lamp. FRANCIS JAMES became limited in movement by physical disability, and worked in watercolour, mainly from flowers. A pen-drawing of him, by Starr, appeared in 'The Whirlwind', Herbert Vivian's weekly, whose lively blasts help to illustrate the later eighties. SIDNEY STARR (a too tran-sitory meteor), nearest in the group to Steer, was a promising artist who went off to the United States and did not return. BERNHARD SICKERT, over-shadowed by his brother's brilliance, painted gently in the vein of Camille Pissarro and won praise from George Moore. GEORGE THOM-SON, a Scot with a strong burr and rather gruffly gloomy address, painted a remarkable view of St. Paul's, rescued by Steer from the floor of his studio and now at Millbank. He became teacher in a ladies' college and afterwards retired to France, occupying himself with a study of 'glazing' and 'scumbling' in oil technique. He, like Sickert, wrote on exhibitions in the evening papers, which did not, in those spacious times, limit them-selves to personal paragraphs.

When I was writing on FRED BROWN for the 'Magazine of Art'[1] Sickert wittily but wickedly and unjustly said, 'Brown was caught up by our movement as by a cow-catcher on a train'. Actually, by a rare honesty and tenacity of character, he was the linch-pin or even a driving wheel in successive moments of a fight for the young of his time. It was he who drew up the constitution of the New English Art Club, was a pillar of integrity on its committee and juries, educated generations of artists in two schools, and meanwhile took his own scrupulous course in painting; neat the end of his long life producing the remarkable garden scene bought by

[1] 'Professor Brown, Teacher and Painter', October 1894.

the Chantrey Fund and more than one deeply studied portrait of himself. As the form of his name suggests, he came into painting by way of 'Fred' Walker trans-lighted; 'subject pictures', also, such as *Hard Times,* bought for Liverpool, and solid portrait studies, but was deflected to landscape in the track of Steer. His daily task, in term, was teaching. In the early days he had a house in Edith Grove, Chelsea, with a studio built by an architect brother. Later he moved to Ormond House, near Richmond Bridge, where he lived with his sister and others of his family till his death. The rooms were hung with choice examples of work by his friends and pupils, to whose purchase he devoted anything he gained by painting.

FRANCIS BATE had been the author, two years previously, of a book[1] which ran through two editions, a whole-hog plea for 'Nature' in paint, stripped of all Old Master conventions or 'decorative' admixture. 'Nature', in 1887, meant especially an effort to rival the scale of natural lighting out of doors. Since this is confessedly impracticable with canvas and pigments, whose scale, under an indoors light, is comparatively one of greys only, the argument lands the author in a paradox, but the impossible thus attempted is what spurred contemporary painters, abandoning the 'chiaroscuro' to which Constable had clung, to push their tones into an upper register. Here was one 'convention' more, but a compromise that captured fresh elements of natural beauty. Bate's own painting in the early 'New English' years was defiantly near to earth, a *Mangold Wurzels under Rain,* for example, but he boxed the compass later with a *Rock of Ages*, to which a nude woman clung amid the billows. He was for thirty-one years a perfect honorary secretary of the New English Art Club, with a firm hand, a ready and humorous tongue; he was, by another paradox, the teacher of Roger Fry, the first change in whose chameleon course was from bald realism to revolt against modern French painting and pastiche of Gaspard Poussin. Bate's retirement from his post in 1933 left the New English at a climax in its career. A dinner was given in his honour at the R.B.A. Galleries, where the Club held a fiftieth exhibition, and an album of drawings by fellow-members was given as a memento of his services.

I return from his companions to Steer, but before dealing with his part in the show a general caution seems to be called for in the matter of 'influences'. It is tempting for the categorist to make much of an English influence on French landscape dating from the exhibition of Constable's *Haywain* and a corresponding influx of French influence here from Monet and his followers. I do not myself believe that the course of French land-

---

[1] 'The Naturalistic School of Painting': Offices of 'The Artist', 1887. I had not seen this till now, when I unearthed, from a reference in 'Who's Who,' a copy in the Art Library at South Kensington. Bate himself had none.

scape would have been very different if Constable had never existed or never been medalled in Paris: his chief impact was on Delacroix. Nor do I think that the influence of Monet was very strong with any of our painters who count. It must be remembered that his characteristic 'snatch' serials began subsequently to the exhibition I am dealing with, and the pictures previously shewn in London were of the less congenial Varangeville and Belle Isle harvests. Some 'influence' of course there was, and a hint is enough for the sensitive, but what affected both countries was a general influenza of direction and exclusion which might be called, borrowing from Bate's title, 'Naturalism'. The word 'Naturalist' has been annexed by science, but that, rather than 'Impressionist' is what we want. Artists are apt to have room in their head for no more than one idea at a time, and the prevailing idea of the eighty-nineties was to exclude mythology, legend, history and contemporary dramatic incident from painting under the silly byword 'literature' in favour of 'The Thing There'. Whistler was strong upon that, though he had one adorable lapse, the project for a *Venus Anadyomene*. When I praised once the aptness for his scheme of a bit of wall-skirting in a portrait I had watched him painting, he took me up quite severely, 'But it's *there!*' So with Sickert: he however, reasoned out the principle. 'Supposing', he said, 'that you paint a woman carrying a pail of water through that door, and drops are spilt upon the planks. There is a natural, necessary rhythm about the pattern they make much better than anything you could invent.' Belief in a logic of beauty coherent with natural effect was the sustaining conviction, whether recognized in words or not, for the painters of our period.

There is something of an inverse superstition in a supposed strong influence of Turner on the French, when Monet, Pissarro and Sisley were refugees in London during the 1870 War. Monet joined with other French painters in a polite letter to Sir Coutts Lindsay in which Turner is referred to, and certainly all three painters were interested in Turner and other English painters. Pissarro's letters to his son Lucien testify to this, but also to a dissatisfaction with Turner's treatment of shadows. Pissarro was forty, the other two thirty years old, by no means callow students. Mr. Clive Bell's supposition that Monet's painting was affected by Turner's *Interior at Petworth* is negatived by the fact that the canvas in question had remained rolled up from the time of its painter's death and was not seen till 1911.

Steer, my readers will be surprised to learn, delivered himself on the subject of 'Impressionism', like so many of us. A paper by him was unearthed by Miss Hamilton, clearly in his writing but undated and puzzlingly headed in pencil by another hand:—

The following paper was read by this gifted artist at a Conversazione of the Society of Arts last week.

The Society of Arts had no record of such a 'conversazione', but the puzzle was afterwards cleared up by press-cuttings preserved among the papers of Steer's Mother. The 'Society of Arts' was that of Tunbridge Wells in October 1891, and the paper had been originally read at a meeting of the Art Workers' Guild in London. Steer was probably drawn in by Charles Furse, who wrote an article on the subject in the 'Albemarle' for September 1892, which I controverted under the title 'The Logic of Painting' in the following number.

I recognise some of the bricks in Steer's composition. One passage recalls Sickert's impersonation of Cobden-Sanderson, announcing from the hearthrug, 'Imprhessionism, then, is the exprhession of my imprhession.' The reference in the matter of focus to Reynolds's 'dilated eye' I must have supplied. But Steer's concern is, like Sickert's, to repudiate the nickname 'Impressionist' except as a description of good artists, ancient or modern.

During his very insular stay in Paris Steer seems hardly to have so much as known that there an 'Impressionist' School existed. It was an exhibition at Dowdeswells in the early eighties that brought him up against Monet, Pissarro and Renoir; there was another, with twenty Monets, including the Belleisle period, at the old Goupil Gallery in 1889, and Monet, like Degas and Ruskin, was exhibited, by loan, at the 'New English'.

Whistler

Of Whistler Steer never saw very much, fearing that intimacy might mean 'a whole-time job', and Whistler, who liked courtiers better than possible rivals, and disliked also the more than republican constitution of the New English Art Club, since it had no President, was rather suspiciously aware of Steer from the first, and ceased to exhibit with the Club after 1889.

He became definitely inimical when the Club continued, after his quarrel and litigation with Sir William Eden, to hang watercolours by a declared enemy, and those who refused to be bullied and remained on friendly terms with 'The Baronet' were reckoned outside the pale. Steer was one of those and during this trouble there was an uncomfortable incident at the Chelsea Arts Club, where I had been dining with him and others. It was announced that Whistler had arrived, and presently he marched in to the upper end of the long room and with his sharp eye must have marked my companions filing out. I was sorry indeed that he could not have talked to Steer, who never ceased to admire the pictures that were

16 (a) EDWARD STOTT (*pencil drawing*)

16 (b) SION HOUSE, 1894

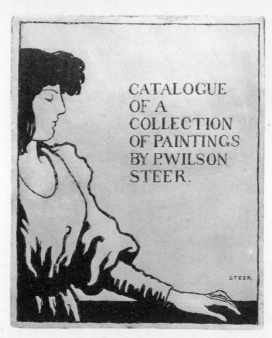

17 (a) CATALOGUE COVER FOR EXHIBITION OF 1894

17 (b) ROSE PETTIGREW, 1891

a strong influence in his early London years. Fashion has recently belittled Whistler, or ignored, but he will return from the purgatory of the too-famous-in-their-time, and remain. One pledge of that, the *Mother,* hangs or hung on a screen at the Louvre among the famous French of the late nineteenth century. Square-set, a classic in disposition, spacing and thrift of accessory, subtle in tone, colour and surface, that tender expression of New England age whispered down its noisier neighbours, the exuberance of Courbet's *Studio,* the riot of Delacroix' *Sardanapale.* Whistler was a puritan of paint, a Preraphaelite of the third generation, supplying a tonality, learned from Courbet, to the rawer naturalism of a Madox Brown. His fastidious taste could not abide much of daylight London, and it was a tragedy of misunderstanding that led Ruskin, champion of Preraphaelites, to denounce the transformation of noontide squalor into nocturnal changelings, inspired by Hiroshige. Rossetti himself, poet of the P.R.B.'s, had lent something of his early magic to the *Little White Girl,* as Swinburne divined.

Steer and Seurat

Steer's contribution to the 'London Impressionists' exhibition was eight pictures, namely

32	*The Citadel*	36	*The Outer Wall*
33	*The Beach, Walberswick*	38	*The Mill Stream*
34	*Knucklebones*	39	*A Tidal Pool*
35	*Pretty Rosie Pettigrew*	40	*A Tannery*

The *Citadel* was probably that of Boulogne. With the exception of *Knucklebones* and perhaps Nos. 35 and 39, the pieces are difficult to identify. *Knucklebones* has been mistaken, because of the broken texture of the shingle, for an exercise in Seurat's 'pointillisme'; it is actually a pre-raphaelite-like rendering of pebbles, a fact brought out by Sickert's translation of it for the 'Whirlwind' into black and white (see p. 32).

In one later picture by Steer there is direct evidence of Seurat's influence by way of Pissarro, who in 1886 had broken out in spots, through a passing infection from the 'Neo-Impressionists.' This is the *Procession of Yachts* of 1893, now at Millbank. In George Moore's 'Modern Art', pages 88–89, is described an exhibition where those two painters showed yachts in profile, almost identical in style and displaying the new technique. Steer borrowed from their design for his areas of sail punctuated into phrases by masts, but he left the dots to their owner, using only broken touches.[1]

---

[1] Part of Steer's picture appears in the portrait by Augustus John, painted for Newnham College, of Miss Jane Harrison, its first owner.

The design and distantly allied technique of this picture were all that Steer took in from Seurat.

Divisionism

Seurat's heresy, which should have remained decently dead, was revived when Fenéon's collection of his work came upon the market, and has won popularity of late years with the 'gobemouches' of criticism. George Moore's protest, therefore, calls for renewal, and the craze for a brief excursus.

In the early eighties the treatise on 'Colour' by the American, Ogden Rood, first published in 1879 and translated into French, German and Italian, stirred anew the curiosity about 'complementaries' and 'primary' colours in relation to the spectrum which had already teased painters like Turner and Delacroix in the days of Field's 'Chromatology' and Chevreuil's treatise. Goethe himself had taken a hand in theory and the devoted Eckermann, neutralised for any literary purposes of his own by the Olympian tyrant, had tactfully to put the master right on some points of colour vision.

I remember a conversation at Brighton early in the eighties with a lady, an ardent student of painting, and in particular of Watts's iridescent effects. She insisted that every area of colour should be furnished at its edge with a rainbow aura. It was vain to urge that the colour would do anything in that way of retinal reaction without the effect being doubled by painting it. That itch for bringing complementaries into the open must have been widespread, but a match was set to the smoulder of theory at an early exhibition of the 'Independent Artists' of Paris, a body founded concurrently with the 'New English' in 1886. In that year was shewn Seurat's *Isle de la Grande Jatte* with fully developed 'pointillage', or 'divisionism', dots of supposed 'primary' paint, as minute as the brush-tip could produce, with the intention of recombination at picture distance.[1]

Seurat, son of a small-bourgeois official, the crank of one idea, reproduced his father's type as a crank in painting; ruined a fine original sense of colour by substituting the ridiculous showers of dots, which produced, actually, not more vivid colour, but a foggy whitish grey, and being a hopelessly inept designer he either clamped upon his meagre drawing a tyrannical geometry, or chose out of all possible material in harbour scenes of the richly paintable Honfleur the most wretched assembly of forms.

Signac, his fellow-champion of the process, declared later that the dotting was a 'mediocre proceeding' and at the same time guyed it in his

[1] See the final section in my 'Nineteenth Century Art' for an examination of the fallacious theories and ineffective practices involved.

practice by enlarging the dots to brick-like dimensions, incapable of optical mixture at any distance. The force of false theory against glaring evidence was exhibited when Seurat's picture, *La Poudreuse,* vulgar in every respect beyond parallel, was exalted to the height of a masterpiece.

Science and Art

A chapter might be inserted here on the influence, fruitful or fatal, of Science upon Art, but a few instances must suffice.

A perfect conspiracy of the two is in the architecture and sculpture of the Parthenon, where science is completely digested, but informs the whole, down to barely traceable optical subtleties; so, in a modern instance, the drawings of Ingres are enriched by a science that does not stick out of them.

The 'Goths' of France made heavier demands upon science for their building than the Greeks and advertised its stone engineering of arcade and buttress, with glass encroaching towards 'Crystal Palace' proportions. Here was high tension between the partners, flowering in outrageous beauty.

The budding of book-sciences excited Renaissance Italy. Perspective kept Paolo 'Uccello' as happy as the birds, outwitting sleep upon his feet all night to bend over diagrams of the exciting new lore, telling his protesting spouse, 'O what a delightful thing is this Perspective!' but it had doubtful virtues for his practice. The prone warrior in the *Rout of San Romano* is a miniature out of scale. With Mantegna, contrariwise, perspective was an engine for breath-taking charges on the vision out of space in the Eremitani frescoes, *Dead Christ* and other master works.

Leonardo is the outstanding genius whom Science destroyed. Wide, hungry, but incoherent of mind, he smothered his early inspiration under a confusion of research and invasion by incompatibles. Horses were, I was going to say the most 'stable' element in a bewildered world, but 'stable' was not their place; upstairs, downstairs, in Our Lady's Chamber they prance about the divine beginning of a Nativity. Shaky in perspective, distorting heads by ill-placed ears, or fish-like eyes, ridiculous in his notion of wave-action, the master of line reduced his vision of a Monna Lisa into a 'jocund' hussy, the cutves of whose eyes and other shapes are not even axial, against a landscape that does not join. His colour was blackened by false theory, a photograph-like tone pursued towards infinity that kept pace with the declension of his moral taste in humanity to such sickening depths. The painting of Ingres has the like double degradation.

By that distant son of the High Renaissance, the English Christopher Wren, Art was wed again with Science. For the Astronomer who was lawfully at home in the high vault of the Universe, it was byplay to build its microcosm in a terrestrial cathedral.

The part of science, implicit or explicit, in the modern work of art came into hot discussion at the end of the nineteenth and beginning of the twentieth century and I must confess to having taken a hand in attempting to rationalise the slang word 'impressionism', embodying the French-English bid for high-pitched natural colour and complementary shadow in a doctrine which should include also the effects of intense or distributed attention exercised through our eye's variations of clear vision and focus. Bate, I find, had also touched on this, as did R. A. M. Stevenson in his 'Velazquez'. These conclusions were printed as a series of papers in 'The Artist' and compressed for the fourteenth edition of the 'Encyclopaedia Britannica'. I lectured also, in that centre of missionary propaganda, Exeter Hall, for the 'Ethical Society' under chairmanship of the philosopher, Professor Bosanquet. Among what, at 'Revival' meetings, were called 'anxious inquirers', on the close of proceedings, was my young friend, Roger Fry, in whose essays the doctrine persists, somewhat smothered by 'overtones'. It was an ardent and amusing time. My witty friend, Pringle Nichol, was asked by a French visitor what, exactly, the 'Ethical Society' might be, and replied, 'Madame, c'est le "Moulin Rouge" de Londres.'

To sum up after this excursus. A healthy artist finds food convenient for his talent in congenial contemporaries and fore-runners; but the talk of French 'influences' on English painters of the eighty-nineties and Steer in particular has been much overdone. The new 'naturalists' in the two countries were cousins who ran a parallel course, and there was a lineage here through Buxton Knight and others, back to Constable. The outburst of sunset colour in early Steers, might be more reasonably traced, if a special source is called for, in the astonishing effects of the Krakatoa eruptions in 1883, whose dust continued to blaze in the evening skies of 1884. But neither was that a necessary stimulus. Every now and then there come sundowns of heart-shattering splendour, the despair but the temptation of any painter with eyes in his head. Such an hour I remember in a Cornish port when, looking inwards to the harbour, one incredulously followed a changing web of intense hues striking on the wavelets of a cross-rip against colder reflections of the eastern sky, and then, turning about, was awestruck by figures of common men, women and children, high on the harbour wall, translated into sublime statuary against the conflagration of the West. A youthful and vigorous painter can make dashes at noting such effects, or recollecting them; a marvellous constitution like Turner's can be on the watch for them early and late. Steer made his fascinating shots, but must have been dissatisfied with weakness of composition in such snatching, almost burglary, of nature's more recondite treasure. In later days he was neither an early riser nor one who neglected the dinner-hour for a raid on sudden illuminations, but as the autumn evenings closed in he could extend his range from shining whites of cloud and light-drenched or darkened greens in noonday hours to more flagrant effects. Some of those, caught over Battersea from his windows, are especially lovely.

VI

A CAMPAIGN

1890–1909

Exhibitions of 1894 and 1909

I now reach the time when I came to know Steer's work and afterwards himself. The first meetings, about 1890, remain vague. These
were no doubt at the New English Art Club. We were friends
quickly. My mother made him welcome at Longridge Road; he liked
to talk with her and my sister, who remembers his admiration for a
pretty schoolgirl niece. My sharper memories are two. One is of a walk
from Richmond to Twickenham by the river-side track that passes
Marble Hill. It was haymaking time; his fancy had been fired by two very
attractive fellow-passengers in the train, and he lamented that they or others
known to us were not among the haycocks for gallant conversation. We
found that little-spoiled survival of eighteenth-century planning, Mont-
pelier Row, giving on Marble-Hill Park. By the bowling-green of the
little old inn, the 'Rose and Crown', at its highway end we took tea and
talked the sun down. I rediscovered the spot in 1897, when hunting for
married quarters, but it was not till I was settled in No. 13 that the earlier
visit came back to me, and explained a dream-like recognition. Steer was
in 1890 a tall slim youth, with noticeably deep eyes and a dancer's feet,
exercised not at 'balls' but at shilling 'hops' where models might be met.
Another meeting, to which I will refer later, was at my Longridge Road
studio; George Moore, with a French painter or writer, and Furse were
other guests. Then I remember giving a sitting to Steer in his studio at
Maclise Mansions, overlooking Addison Road Station from the high
side-window which appears in the background of *Jonquils*. If the portrait
at all exists it may some day dimly come through a landscape, for I was
unluckily over-busy just then to return. Steer made only two changes of
address after that time; to The Avenue, Fulham Road, in 1894, and to
his house, 109 Cheyne Walk, in 1898.

During the first two years of the New English Art Club I was lecturing
about the country or travelling abroad, and little in London, so that I did
not see its exhibitions till 1888; but I remember the 'London Impres-

sionists' of the following year as marking a new watershed. The Grosvenor Gallery Exhibitions, followed by those of Rossetti after his death, had published for us youngsters what had been going on secretly of a purely English movement in the second of its pre-Raphaelite periods; here was a successor, in step with contemporary French painting: Whistler had been a midway precursor.

In 1889, still distracted by lectures, I began some spasmodic attendance at the Westminster School, whose master was Fred Brown. Charles Furse had recently left; Tonks was on the point of leaving. The first crossed over to Tufton Street from his father's Westminster canonry now and then: Tonks brusquely claimed the seat I had taken on my entrance: it was his way of beginning a life-long friendship. With these and Brown I entered the circle of the 'New English'. In January of 1890 I was invited to write for the 'Spectator' and given full freedom by its editors, Hutton and Townsend, the latter swallowing some dubitations. The opportunity of addressing its very large public was a remarkable one, as if a heretic had been offered the pulpit of St. Paul's. The April exhibition of the 'New English' included *Jonquils*. I discoursed upon the Club and gave first place to Steer.

I had not been a reader of art criticism and did not realise how sharp a tack the paper was required to take. My predecessor, Harry Quilter, had declared of one of Steer's early pictures that:—

if it be executed in all seriousness, it is one of the most extraordinary examples of artistic perversity which it is possible to conceive . . .
> Life and thought have gone away
> Side by side,
and taken hand in hand both Art and Commonsense.

He 'turned to pleasanter things'. The first of these was Hacker.

Not all were so violent, though the 'Impressionist' manifesto had drawn fire. A huge amount of space was given to art criticism in those days, and there was good stuff in minor papers; but veterans will remember how strict a hierarchy was maintained in 'solid' journals, and how any preferences were effectively submerged in tepid lists of the mentioned. The young can imagine the state of affairs by inverting the present manner of criticism, in which what are thought to be 'advanced' artists meet with the indiscriminate deference once awarded to Academicians. Of the newer order the chief writers were Charles Whibley of the 'National Observer' and George Moore in 'The Speaker'. The former, strong, like the rest of us, for Whistler and also for his Scottish followers, was cold about Steer, as was Stevenson, when he returned from Liverpool, still tied to his Barbizonians. Moore was a doubtful convert. In his 'Conversations in Ebury Street', where he paints Steer after his inimitable fashion, he says of him: 'Steer, whom I had the wit to pick out as the only painter in London who could fill the blank that Manet's death had made in my life.' That was to anticipate and telescope a little, for Moore was not strong on chronology or, indeed, on facts—witness some mythology about myself in the same volume. Coming from Paris and intimacy with Manet, Degas and the Impressionists, he was naturally more cool and critical than an eager beginner in London. I first became aware of him as critic in his brother's paper, 'The Hawk.' He was severe about the 'half-baked boys' of the 'New English', but of course spotted the *Jonquils* of Steer and wrote warmly of it. Then he was put off for a time, and until publication of his 'Modern Painting' in 1893, when he quitted the field, was still rebuking me, not without some reason, for my completer enthusiasm.

It may be permitted to a contemporary critic to recall, by quotation, some of the argument in a hotly contested campaign during the decade 1891–1901. The exhibition in the first of those years brought the portrait of *Mrs. Cyprian Williams and her Children,* now in the Millbank Gallery. I wrote of its 'beauty of an original kind, rather promising a new master than referring to an old'.

Next year, 1892, in November, appeared the article that George Moore grumbled over. Here are the passages that provoked him:—

The exhibition is a triumph for Mr. Steer. The word masterpiece is not to be lightly used, but when one stands before his portrait of a girl in blue,[1] it is difficult to think of any collection of good pictures in which it would look amiss, or fail to hold its own. If we talk of English masters, Romney is the name that most naturally suggests itself, because in the bright, clear face, brown hair, and large simplicity of presentment, there is a good deal to recall that painter. But Romney's colour would look cheap beside this, and his drawing conventional in observation, however big in style. This excellence of drawing deserves to be insisted upon, because while everyone with an eye feels the charm of Mr. Steer's colour, it is usual to balance that recognition with a sneer at his peculiarities as a draughtsman; but the grace and nature of this portrait are surely as obvious as the loveliness of its colour; there is a look of scarcely arrested life, of movement caught in passage, in the drawing of the shoulders and the action of the whole figure. The chair alone is an example of what good drawing and good painting are: the bit of furniture has given up all the beauty in the play of its form and colour with the air; there is no inch of it that is a bored statement of fact, or a slurred substitute for observation. From corner to corner of the canvas the colour-play goes on; subtle touches of other tints building up the broad impression of blue in the dress, and hints of reflected colour in the face and hands relating them to the objects round. The face itself, fresh and clear beyond most painting, is a joy to the eyes. A picture like this unites so many qualities, that it must catch almost all onlookers by one or another

[1] This was catalogued as :—

Molle meum levibus cor est violabile telis
Et semper causa est cur ego semper amem.

18 (*a*) BOULOGNE SANDS, 1892

18 (*b*) YACHTS, 1892

19 (*a*) PUSSYCAT IN STEER'S HANDS

19 (*b*) CHILDREN PADDLING, 1894

charm. The other two pictures depend more entirely on the pure painter sense. But *Boulogne Sands* is the very music of colour in its gayest and most singing moments, and every character and association of the scene helps by suggestion in the merry *fête* of light. The children playing, the holiday encampment of the bathers' tents, the glints of people flaunting themselves like flags, the dazzle of sand and sea, and over and through it all the chattering lights of noon—it is like the sharp notes of pipes and strings sounding to an invitation by Ariel. It is all this, yet nine out of ten people will get no further with it than to notice that one of the little girls has awkward legs . . .

The third of Mr. Steer's pictures is another holiday piece of colour—a procession of yachts under a press of white canvas, framed by the masts of a schooner at anchor nearer shore. As in the other scene, the handling is of the kind that suggests by a sort of metaphor the rain and beat of light upon things. One painter, a Whistler say, feels when he looks at a sail the fluid sweep of its form, how it comes and goes like a smooth gradual gesture against the sea; and this impression he renders by a technique that fits his feeling. But if you are more struck with the way the charges of light patter and break upon those reflecting surfaces, the more flowing and melting technique must give place to something like the handling here. It becomes a subtle problem in the dialectic of painting how far the more obvious characteristics should give way to the more subtle, how far the expression of truth in colour should be allowed to invade the facts of form and texture. The sky of the beach scene, for example, if it be taken as representing form and texture, is ridiculous; it is like something rough and chippy, and if that suggestion gets too much in the way, the method has overshot its mark. Its mark is to express by a symbol the vivid life in the sky-colour, the sea-colour, and the sand-colour, and it is doubtful if the richness and subtlety of their colour can be conveyed in any other way. This matter of handling, then, is a moot point, a question of temperament and balance of interest; but the beauty of Mr. Steer's colour is not a moot point, and the sooner the colour-blind cease to pride themselves publicly on disliking it, the better for their own reputation. The simple fact is, that for range and delicacy of colour-combination, there is no living English painter to be put beside him.

To Moore's criticism, reprinted in his book, I replied at length in an article on 'Handling', which it would be disproportionate to reproduce here, though it would have its relevance to a more recent discussion, for 'The Times' art critic, Mr. Charles Marriott, has asked me what, if not 'divisionism', is the 'word to describe the broad stippling, or hatching or something between the two—a division of substance rather than colour or tone—which distinguishes the more characteristic works of Monet, Pissarro and Sisley'. The answer, of course, is 'broken handling', to be distinguished from 'broken colour', which is not 'divisionism' either.[1] Moore was right about the dangers of the dotting touch and Steer settled the discussion by modification from harsher to more fluent or fatter pastes, but that controversy on disputable ground lost him, for a space, a powerful advocate, who cast back, in revulsion, to the near monochrome of what Sargent called 'those old Dutch things'.

[1] Pissarro did become 'pointillist' for a short spell, as we have seen, but revolted and thereafter merely stippled.

What I had called the 'Girl in Blue' (one of the famous Pettigrew sisters, who sat to Millais for his *Ornithologist* and to other painters) was bought by a master at Haileybury. The *Boulogne Sands* was bought by Brown. My friend Jane Harrison bought the *Yachts* for £25. When I see the *Sands* again I can understand the bewilderment of my readers at so high an exaltation, and my conviction on the main issue, that a master was in the making, makes me tolerant of the enthusiasms of young critics now, however ill-directed or unmeasured they may appear to me. It was interesting to find that at the National Gallery Exhibition of 1943 the earliest pictures of Steer roused the keenest admiration among those critics of fifty years later.

Sales were events in the early New English days, and it was uphill work to persuade an amused but incredulous public. The *Cyprian Williams* portrait was a commission from Francis James. Another fellow-painter, John Lavery, brought Mr. William Burrell to Steer's studio, and the £45 he gave for the *Jonquils* was the first substantial price; a brother George acquired a study of Miss Pettigrew at the same time. Mr. Croal Thomson, the dealer, was an early purchaser and remained a staunch backer. Augustus Daniel showed the taste which carried him to directorship at Trafalgar Square by being the first of the leading collectors in the field. Herbert Trench took my word for it that Steer would prove a safe investment even for a civil servant's purse, and began an accumulation which finally filled a large drawing-room on Richmond Hill. Sargent took over one of them; Sargent who said, 'I wish I could paint faces as Steer paints landscape.' Others passed to Mr. Blackwell's collection. Cyril Butler was another early and steady supporter. That collector, member of a family which is formidably engaged in the government and education of this country, deserves a niche among the courageous patrons of the nineties and early nineteen hundreds. Shrewd, genial and hospitable, he made his country-house at Shrivenham a resort for youthful artists and devoted a kind of small dower-house on the estate to the use of some of them, Havard Thomas, the sculptor, for one. Steer decorated a drawing-room for him with panels of Girls at Play. Portraits by him and pictures, including the *Music Room,* now at the Tate, adorned other rooms. Their possessor became Honorary Secretary to the Contemporary Art Society on its formation, but had joined by then what Steer described as the 'exstinct volcanos' among buyers, except for small ventures with the on-coming juniors.

The campaign carried on till 1896 in the 'Spectator' was renewed, from 1897, in 'The Saturday Review', and an article headed 'When the Wicked Man . . .' of November, 1900, marks the situation then:—

Steer is the greatest colourist and most absolutely born-painter the English school now possesses. . . . He has three landscapes in the present exhibition, the first of white noon, the second of the last orange hour of sunlight, the third after sunset, when the beams travel up the green-gold dome and flush the wreckage of clouds with rose; in each you see the strong eye that will not clap an all-applicable preparation on the difficult scene, but admits every beauty which a different radiance offers, and snatches harmony close up to nature. Let me use definite measures to put Steer's qualities in relief. The noon-day picture is the kind of effect Constable battled for, white clouds reflecting silver on green countryside and trees. Constable is in the National Gallery and Steer in the Dudley Gallery, and it is thought irreverent to make these comparisons; but I affirm that I have never seen a Constable in which this radiant chord was so certainly expressed; in the shadow of Constable's clouds there remains a disappointing rustiness, in his blue a blackness, in the foundation of his trees a brownness, which it was his special aim, mind, to get rid of.[1] I do not know, and it has been my tedious business to seek for ten years, the painter in Europe who could have painted the shadow in the foreground of this picture, so luminous, so fresh-coloured, yet dark, so elusive, with no forced brown, violet or other recipé in it . . .

And now consider: here is a painter about whose position there is no serious question among those who know; ask, not the critics, but the one or two men among his colleagues who have a right to speak, and you will find that their really anxious and interested consciousness is of Steer's existence. The dealers, alive to such implicit judgments, know that his day will come, but nervously stand back in case it should be not to-morrow, but the day after. The Chantrey Fund, which lavishes thousands on a Dicksee, has never found a hundred for a Steer; the committee appointed to select English pictures for the Paris Exhibition, and perfectly aware of his claims, never invited him to send; the critics of leading papers mention him not at all or with strange disproportion. No painter of this rank, surely, has been so scurvily treated by his country since Manet, Manet who during the greater part of his career sold nothing, was excluded again and again from entrance to the Salon and from its rewards, till a new generation of his successful borrowers for very shame took him in; Manet who was expressly excluded from two Universal Exhibitions, and only triumphed there after his death. One can understand the hesitation of the sheep-like public, of the buyer who is not certain of a speedy return; one understands too well how the wheels of reward are worked; but surely if critics, who have no money to lose, and the best reason for whose existence is a generous readiness to champion unrecognised talent, fall in with this neglect, they are either ill-equipped for their office, distracted by considerations that ought to have nothing to do with their judgement, or superfluously timid.

In February, 1894, there was a first collected exhibition of Steer's work at the Goupil Gallery in Lower Regent Street; forty-three pieces, thirty-eight of them oils, five watercolours done at Boulogne, of which more in Chapter X. Among the pictures was work of the previous summer at Richmond, Surrey; the 'Star and Garter' and Sion House the chief, with one or two from subjects at the 'Hare and Hounds' Hotel, where he put up; others from excursions to Twickenham, Kew and Hammersmith.

[1] The great sketch canvases, the Haywain and Leaping Horse should be excepted, and other, smaller works in which freshness has been preserved. Constable feared 'cutting his throat' with the palette-knife, and the sketch was apt to be overlaid with gallery 'finish'.

The English line was thus taken up again from its beginnings at Walberswick in 1884–6, Swanage, 1890, Hayling Island and Cowes, 1891–92, and was not again to be interrupted, save at Montreuil and briefly, Paris, in 1907. Other pictures, already mentioned as sold, were lent by their owners; some of the early French scenes were included, and a couple of flower-pieces, work, no doubt, of rainy days.

Here is my notice of the exhibition in the 'Spectator' of 17 March:—

Anything like a strong painter appears so rarely above the horizon, that a certain warmth of greeting would seem justified by the event. But nothing is more irritating to those surprising people whose conception of modesty in a critic it is that he should treat evident genius with the lukewarm appreciation due to mediocrity, and of justice, that he should discourage promise till the last possible moment by every device of facetious misunderstanding. I observe with satisfaction that the moment seems to have passed when Mr. Steer could be comfortably treated as a jester, and that even the most belated reverberators of opinion hesitate between their two manners of facetious and fulsome reporting. And the second stage of a good painter's reputation declares itself, when his weaker work is exalted, and his characteristic work lamented, as being unworthy of his powers.

I have used the word strong of Mr. Steer, because I wish to convey not that he is a perfect or complete painter, but that he possesses the essential qualities of a painter in a marked degree. He has the instinct for composition, and the instinct for colour. We are accustomed, in these days of universal study, to a vast number of painters who have built a considerable amount of culture on a narrow basis of instinct. Mr. Steer works by instinct much more than by culture. Hence he fails at times completely in a way the cultured painter does not fail, because with the latter it is an affair of ropes and leading-strings; the cultured painter does not allow his instinct to lead him astray, because he can hardly be sure that he hears its voice, and would distrust it if he did. Therefore, he holds by the ropes, never comes a bad cropper, but also never gets anywhere. He remains tastefully clutching; the tug of the leading-strings directs the ponderous tripping of his feet, jerks him back from all natural excursions, and betrays itself at every step in his timid explorations of the main road. The instinctive painter also will strike the main road for parts of his journey, but because it is his natural way, not because there is a handrail to hold by; and sometimes he will charge the fences with disastrous results. It is better to start with instinct than with culture, because instinct arrives at the results that culture approves but never can create, any more than an assiduously fed pond can turn itself into a fountain. This is a commonplace, but the ponds are so common too, and seem to pass for fountains because of the number and elegance of their ducts, the far-fetched quality of their stagnancy. The moral is to be grateful for the rare case of a fountain. Now, I think a picture like *The Sofa*[1] is enough to prove the presence of this original living source of painter's vision, an energy that relates the picture, in its degree, to all great work. It has not the appearance of being modelled on any previous picture; it does not remind one directly of this master or that, but it is akin to them all in virtue of an inventive act of seeing that confers dignity and simplicity on the things seen, and this act, a determination of the disposition and reliefs of the things seen, has persisted through the execution. A good many people can

---

[1] This picture was bought by my friend C. R. Ashbee.

see a picture in the actual, vaguely; to hold a picture till it is painted, across all the minor problems of emphasis and subordination, is a harder task, and it is this grasp that gives largeness and immediacy of address to things like *The Sofa*. The painter has not stopped to flirt with a pretty intruding motive in a corner, nor allowed an interesting detail to come forward and make a speech; he has held his picture. These same gifts of a composing and a tenacious eye come out in two other pictures, the *Procession of Yachts* and *The Girl in Blue*. In the first, the passage of the tall phantoms is punctuated by the masts of the nearer vessel in a way that could only be expressed by a musical analogy. It is like a fine piece of phrasing upon the metrical intervals of bars. In the other picture, how freshly the inspiration has been held, and how directly presented! By neither of these, again, are we directly reminded of pictures seen before, but we are reminded of the same qualities in good pictures. What has been said of their composition is true of their colour. Who remembers exactly that brown and golden white and purple blue, and so on, of *The Sofa* anywhere else? Yet there is nothing extravagant in the scheme. An eye that can afford to be hospitable, because it knows a colour when it sees it, has gathered the harmony from very simple materials fused in a glow of lamplight. It is Mr. Steer's discovery, but it is as old and orthodox in nature as any other harmony.

I have insisted on the original and natural turn that Mr. Steer has given to the essential and ancient gifts of a painter, composition and colour, because it has been made a reproach to him that he imitates the styles of several incompatible masters. Now this charge of imitation and eclecticism really comes home not in the fundamentals just dealt with, but in the field of texture and handling. In that matter Mr. Steer does not seem to feel a certain inspiration, and is tentative. One canvas recalls the thin painting of Degas; others are broken in handling, and are a little like Monet; yet others have the full, fluid Whistlerian brush. Of the three manners, the second is the more experimental and doubtful. I attempted, in a former article, to explain why a painter should be tempted by such a device, how expressive it is of certain qualities at the obvious sacrifice of others. I need not return on that; it gives a few speculators pleasure to understand the reason of a technique; it has given a great many people pleasure to affect not to understand the explanation. Mr. Steer's later work is less heretical and depends for play of colour more frequently on semi-transparent painting over a coloured ground. The little panels and the ships at Cowes are painted in this way, and the reddish-brown of the ground unites the superposed colours in a very curious and charming series of greys. It has the danger, however, of a unity that comes of process, and the patches of uncovered ground in one or two look a little tricky.

I have praised Mr. Steer as a painter strong in essentials, but not complete. The pleasure to which he is least sensitive is that of delineation. Delineation is only one part of drawing, which includes the putting of bodies in their places and making them look like bodies—qualities which are always present in Mr. Steer's work. Drawing, as commonly practised, means putting a very precisely wrong line round something which is not a body, in a place where it ought not to be. But this common defect of over-definition does not make against the artistic charm of beautiful line. It is the pursuit of effect that seems to render Mr. Steer sometimes oblivious of everything else that makes a picture. In the *Girls on a Pier*, he forgets composition; in the *Girls Running*, composition and colour; and even in the *Paddlers*, a picture in many ways beautiful, there is a desperate shot at an effect in those white blobs in the water, which no doubt stand for sparkles of reflection. It is an effect outside the scale of paint.

E

There are more general questions raised by the exhibition that it would be tempting to discuss. It is clear that the modern picture in a light-blue key is more difficult to hang than its predecessor in the key of mahogany-brown. But pictures so fine as the *Classic Landscape* and the *Sion House* would deserve pains in the arrangement of their setting.

Moore was right to accept the *Paddlers* without boggling, as I did, at the blobs of white pigment, to represent sun-dazzle, like Constable's famous 'snow', which was a corresponding snatch at the unattainable sparkle of light on leaves, and has equally been appeased by time.

Steer's former teacher, John Kemp, unable to visit the exhibition, wrote enthusiastically about the cover of the catalogue, reproduced on p. 37.

3.3.94   Rockleigh, Clevedon, Somerset

I am writing to thank you for your kindness in sending me a copy of your catalogue.

It was very good of you to think of me, but you know how great an interest I take in your work and progress. I shall keep this catalogue among my treasures, for the striking beauty of its *cover*.

I do not know when I saw anything that delighted me so much. It is so original, so beautifully drawn and so very decorative. The way in which you have disposed the masses of black, from the straight line below, to the mass of hair above the drawing of the arm and hand, taking off the square edge of the sheet, and the combination of simplicity and refinement throughout, make it one of the most delightful compositions and it is so peculiarly your *own*, not Walter Crane-ish or Morris-ish, though there is a strong Japanese feeling. But I know you have looked a great deal at Japanese work. I hope the exhibition will prove a success in every way.

Steer had written, before the opening of the show:—

I am up to the neck in work for my exhibition, for one thing I am in the agonies of designing a poster.

My eulogy of Steer, it will be observed, was not untempered by critical reserves, and since I have been admonished that my admiration was due to friendship I reprint in the Appendix, p. 180, two further excerpts from articles maintaining that balance. Admiration came first; friendship followed, and my friends were uncomfortably aware that they must look for more severe, rather than more lax, treatment because of that relation.

Journalist dulness or excited fuss came to a head during the exhibition of Degas' admirable picture, now in the Louvre, called in a Grafton Gallery exhibition *L'Absinthe,* but properly *Au Café.* Morals were thought to be outraged by the scene of two people taking what in England would be afternoon tea. J. A. Spender, eminent journalist and apostle of the middling in art as in politics, wrote as 'The Philistine' in the 'Westminster Gazette' a series of articles reprinted as 'The New Art Criticism', and roused in correspondence the whole battalion of British shockables against the deplorable taste of George Moore and myself. We had given a point to the enemy by accepting the exhibition title as a clue to the slack figure of the woman. Sickert set us right: she was a model of the engraver Desboutins, who figures so magnificently in the picture. The Scottish owner, under the outcry, sold it to Count Camondo, by whose bequest it became a national treasure.

In 1906 I left current criticism for office at the Tate Gallery, and the fight was transferred to other ground. In that year Herbert Horne and Robert Ross, who had been consulted about an addition of three English painters' self-portraits to the historic collection at the Uffizi, nominated Steer along with Holman Hunt and Sargent. A vigorous study for Steer's portrait belongs to Sir Augustus Daniel's collection: a variant was obtained later by Mr. Sydney Cockerell for the Fitzwilliam Museum. Of other portraits our frontispiece by Sickert renders the youth of Maclise Mansion days; Steer returned the ball with a head of Sickert at a bristling-moustache moment as well as a lovely Whistler-like full length now in the National Portrait Gallery. Steer is one of the group in Orpen's *Homage to Manet*. There is another portrait, from one of the later summer tours, by Ronald Gray, and a back-view of Steer sketching, by Connard. He figures also in an 1893 or 4 group by Rothenstein, and in an unfinished picture with Tonks and Sargent; in two drawings also, a closely studied head and the Steer his friends knew in conversation, a thoroughly characteristic *sic sedebat*.

By 1909 the top of the hill was reached; Steer entered the National collection with *Chepstow Castle,* the gift of Miss Mary Hoadley Dodge. Miss Dodge was in a difficulty. She loved the picture, but was about to travel, and the small quarters she retained in London had been panelled in a way that did not favour picture hanging. She consulted Sargent who reported to me, and at our instigation offered a masterpiece to the Tate Gallery. My trustees gulped, but swallowed, soothed by explanations from Lord Plymouth. In the same year, at the Goupil Gallery Exhibition of Steer's work under Mr. William Marchant, Hugh Lane acquired *The Balcony* and *Corfe Castle* for Johannesburg, and Mr. Geoffrey Blackwell came into the field. He had not till then taken much interest in painting, but was induced by an article in 'The Times' to visit the show, and became the largest collector of Steer's work. The article was by Charles Holmes, taking the place of Humphry Ward, the drab of whose cautious reporting made the best of preparation for the other's vivid conviction. 'The Times' critic had bought a Whistlerian Steer, the *Casino, Boulogne,* but did not greatly like that the purchase should be known.

The battle was won and a celebration of victory followed in 1929, when Charles Aitken, my memorable successor at the Tate Gallery, put all his tireless devotion into assembling a full retrospective exhibition, the first given there to a living master. Banquets followed, to Steer's discomfiture; one of them at the Chelsea Arts Club; but none was pleasanter than the quiet dinner given by Aitken near his Gallery, to a small band of the faithful.

John Kemp had again added his word about the Goupil show:—

8.5.09   Clevedon

I am writing to congratulate you on the great success you have had in the Exhibition of your works at the Goupil gallery, of which I have just heard from Thorne Waite. He writes: 'they are remarkably good pictures, remarkable for vivacity of colour and freshness,' and he goes on to say that on the opening day you were successful in selling about £2,000 worth! 'a record show and much the talk of the town'!

I felt I could not do otherwise than congratulate you on such a success, not only on your artistic work but on the solid recognition of their value. . . .

From other letters of cordial recognition, one from William Rothenstein may be singled, a renewal of unfailing homage:—

23.4.09   11 Oak Hill Park, Frognal

Just a line to tell you how greatly moved I was by the beauty of your pictures at Goupil's yesterday. I never saw them looking more noble, and I cannot now tell you how much I admire the beauty of your work; you always seem to me a sort of magician —I only wish I could learn more from you. The vitality of your pictures is magnificent, and I think everyone is bound to feel this; there is a splendid sense of bloom and health and bursting life about everything you do that fills one with joy. You deserve all the success you will get. No one has worked more steadfastly and more humbly than yourself, no one has ever had so little vanity and been more appreciative of others. I owe you more than I can well express; I wish I could have shown more result from your example; at least I glory in what you do, and what you have become, and the work you are showing now will establish you once and for all as easily first among us all as a painter.

In 1894 the mixed French-English outings had come to an end with visits to Boulogne and Rye. I may as well here correct a lapse of my friend Alfred Thornton's memory in his 'Diary of an Art Student in the Nineties', since it annoyed Steer. I had given Conder a rendezvous at Dieppe for July 1893 and invited Thornton to join us. He says (p. 37) 'Steer arranged to come, but on hearing that MacColl was to be of the party, despite his friendship for him, cried off, for he feared the nearness of so critical a mind, saying gloomily, "If MacColl met God Almighty he would criticise Him to His face." ' Steer, who had a very precise memory, indignantly denied the story to Gray, and I should have heard of his intention had it existed. The phrase quoted belongs to Tonks, for whom a breath of criticism was a blight.

On the eve of the 1929 exhibition I took over for a short spell editorship of the awkwardly named 'Artwork', a monthly issued by Messrs. Dent, and now extinct. I used it to start an 'English Vasari', inviting artists, or

20 (*a*) No. 109 Cheyne Walk, Chelsea

20 (*b*) Battersea Reach

21 MRS. RAYNES (*Steer's Nurse and Housekeeper*)

in case of their shyness, admirers to write notices of their career: there has been a spate of such publication since. For my first number I wrote the sketch of Steer's life and work already referred to and ended by printing one more tribute from the 'Saturday Review', which may round off those I have already quoted, since it expresses a profound feeling which has not varied in near half a century.

PRIVATE AMBARVALIA[1]

20 April 1901

Luce sacra requiescat humus, requiescat arator,
  Et grave suspenso vomere cesset opus.
Solvite vincla jugis; nunc ad præsepia debent
  Plena coronato stare boves capite.
Omnia sint operata deo . . .

The 'New English' opens at the very time of the Going About of the Fields, when even the critic, if he may not be altogether 'operatus deo', holiday-making in the country, ought to be turned loose in his stall like the other beasts with a flower or two about his head. I had to include the visit, then, in my private Ambarvalia, and in the modern dearth of ceremonies it became almost a rite. We have lost all of that solemn celebration except the impulse to go about, but the least religious of moderns is caught with some nostalgia of the feast, when he walks forth on the first Spring Sunday of the year. 'In sacred light rest the fields, the labourer rests, the plough is idle and heavy work at a stand.' The modern has forgotten how to be 'busy for the god', has forgotten the song and the way the garlands were woven; unchaste, un-dressed, unsprinkled, un-crowned he goes; yet the god returns, and at a bend of the way surprises him, filling his heart with tender compunction and awe, and ministering to a truant the great sacrament of his light.

I had gone out on Easter morning, crossed a 'swelling flood' to where fields stood 'dressed in living green', and paid those maimed rites in a chance-found sanctuary. It was a slope of grass curiously stencilled with the shadows of bare branches, and in the middle space thick-springing crocuses broke through the turf. On their purple and white and gold the light played, swelling and falling in slow, heart-thrilling cadences, like music in a solemn antique mode out of the winter-wounded earth.

And when, among the jumbled observances of my Spring Festival, I paid my visit to the New English Art Club, I found as always, in the painting of Mr. Steer, something congruous with that experience of light undefiled and colour born again; a painting that was not mocked by the first daffodil basket in the street. *Hydrangeas*, with its high singing carmine and pearly greys of the blood, the flower-lights and shining shadows of its tissues will remain in my memory with the blossoms of the season. To this painter it is given to make living colour out of pigment, and the more the fitful sunshine lightens upon it, the more its radiance quickens. I shall see a great deal of pigment in the coming month, tamed into official systems, pensioned off into decent retirement, lashed in tormented moribundity, cooked into various careful glues, jams and poisons, but I hardly dare expect to find anything in English painting so in tune with the Ambarvalia, its sacred light and flowers.

[1] For a description of the feast, see Walter Pater's 'Marius the Epicurean.'

VII

CHELSEA

1898–1942

The House

George Moore accuses the Maclise Mansions studio of being 'at the top of five flights of black stone stairs', which may or may not be exact, but the place could not be called engaging, and the studio that followed had the rather dismal character of a toplit room.

The Chelsea house was very different; one where Steer could set up his rest. Fronting all there was of sun from morning till night, it commanded a view of the river with its barges and old Battersea beyond. When darkness fell a Whistlerian nocturn succeeded. Dated approximately 1790, the house had lost, to nineteenth-century bad taste, its original window-panes, and there must have been rehandling of the entrance also in the interval. A former tenant, it appears, kept a pony-trap in the space behind the house and this was reached by an inclined plane in front and passage beneath the building.

The recessed entrance opened on a roomy hall running to the back; on the right, in front, was a pleasant morning room which figures in the tea-party picture and the *Sodales* by Tonks; at the back was a dining-room hung with French eighteenth-century engravings.

On the first floor the whole front with its three tall windows was sitting and painting-room combined. At the back, across a passage, was a room stacked with studies and pictures in all stages of completion. Above were bedrooms. Over these Steer had been persuaded, when he was painting the lady to whom Hugh Lane was engaged, to construct a sun-trap of a studio, top- as well as side-lit. The engagement was short-lived, the portrait unfinished, and the studio lapsed into a lumber-room.

Behind the house was a rather grubby backyard, but in one corner of it a few spring flowers contrived to show themselves. Steer had got hold of a disused Park seat and in sunny spells sat out and watched them.

When he took the house he had bought for it flowered chintz curtains, Aubusson carpets, Regency and Louis XVI furniture but added to these comfortable English armchairs. In forty-four years the collecting habit of its tenant crammed the house with pictures, bronzes, china, pottery, coins and medals. Cupboards were full and ledges piled with bric-à-brac, shells, mineral specimens, and many parcels had never been opened. It was the painter's hobby to hunt in obscure junk-shops for unsuspected treasure, and the Chinese painting, now in a national museum, was bought near Stamford Bridge for half-a-crown. Once he backed his taste at Christie's by bidding for a still-life, catalogued as a Manet, but doubted in the sale-room and by most of us afterwards; a puzzle, but a fine work; Steer wrote to Blackwell on 12 July 1918:

I am pleased to have got the alleged Manet as it is a good picture whoever it is by, and it was a bit of luck that the dealers doubted it, otherwise the price would have been prohibitive. For my part I cannot see who else could have done it. Moore says it is too thickly painted for Manet, but I seem to remember seeing early Manets quite as thick. However, it will be an interesting problem until it is solved, which no doubt it will be some day.

Moore who had written, 'the Manet is not a Manet, but one of Martin's little jokes', recanted; he wrote[1] from Paris:

I spoke to Duret yesterday about your picture, describing the composition to him. He says that Manet did paint oysters, but it is so long since he saw the picture that he cannot identify the composition from a verbal description, but if you will send a photograph he will tell you at once. I am beginning to think that you are right and that the others, myself included, are not unnaturally wrong, as you alone have put your whole life into canvases. You should and do know more about a picture than anybody else.

Moore must have seen and forgotten a well-known oyster-piece by Manet that hung in Madame Eugène Manet's house.

Steer lent the picture to the Tate Gallery for many years; and Louis Dimier, the French connoisseur, seeing it there, pronounced it to be by Ribot.

In the studio-sitting-room were Sickert's portrait of Steer as a youth, a good bit of painting by Couture, a Whistlerian Nocturne by Greaves, Oriental screen and paintings. On the mantelpiece were two fine pieces of Vauxhall glass. A bureau faced the fireplace, with a chair on the door side, a cabinet on the other. Other rounded cabinets flanked the chimney-piece; yet others stood between the windows. Facing these was a sofa, usually encumbered with papers and portfolios. Close above this hung a row of watercolours by friends, namely Gray, Tonks, Sargent, D. S. M., Harrison. A superb drawing by Augustus John of an old woman, nude,

---

[1] I have the kind permission of Moore's literary executor, Mr. C. D. Medley, to use this and other letters.

had held the place of a second Sargent, and John tells how Steer, solemnly handing over a fiver, said, 'This ought to remain in the Family.'

Steer's pictures, *The Balcony, Music Room, End of the Chapter* and so forth, some portraits also, preserve aspects of his studio in their backgrounds.

In the early years at Chelsea he entertained his friends, but perhaps the tax on 'Old Jane's' powers became too heavy, or, as is the way with such domestic tyrants, she grudged to others the toil she lavished on her master. I remember more particularly one pleasant dinner at which my wife and I were guests along with the Rothensteins, Tonks, Moore, Collins Baker, recently married, with his wife Muriel, ex-Slade student, wearing very becomingly a kind of bridal wreath. Our host knocked with a knife-handle on the floor for the change of courses, and excellent of their solid kind they were. Moore was irrepressibly determined to talk of 'horn-calls' which Elgar had written for a play of his, and only a burst of helpless laughter at last smothered the subject. Steer disliked dinner-parties of the fashionable sort and the risky process of changing for them, but there were houses in Chelsea Village where he was happy, such as Miss Sargent's, 'Peter' Harrison's, the De Glehns', George Moore's, Hugh Lane's, and he could be lured as far as Hampstead to the Rothensteins, the Wethereds, our house, the Hugh Hammersleys'.

Hammersley was a partner in Cox's Bank, known to all service men in the 'Great' War, but afterwards absorbed in Lloyds. His first wife was a Scotswoman, alert in mind and an admirable hostess, whose looks are preserved in portraits by Sargent and Tonks. 'Admiral's House', at the top of Hampstead, with look-out tower and secluded garden, was theirs, and the dining-room walls were hung with Sickerts. Steer figures in Tonks's caricature group of a tea-party there; Sargent, Will Rothenstein, Max Beerbohm and others.

Another house for which Steer made an exception was that of Judge Evans and his wife in Bayswater. The Judge had crammed the walls of his house from skirting to ceiling with pictures but still pursued his pet avocation[1] of 'getting a little bit of' some fresh painter, and savoured and shared it as he did a fine Stilton or bottle of vintage port. His wife was his partner in taste and discrimination for pictures and drawings and has added another collector's hobby, namely country houses which call for redress. She it was who gave a first impulse to the formation of a Con-

---

[1] Is it impossible to persuade our statesmen and public speakers, and those writers called 'publicists' that 'avocation' means not the same as 'vocation' but its reverse: not a man's ordinary job, but his pastime? So again eminent novelists commonly use the word 'prone' for a figure thrown down or recumbent on his back when they mean 'supine'.

temporary Art Collections Fund when I wanted to secure Augustus John's *Smiling Woman* and other things outside the horizon of the Tate Gallery Trustees. Of Steer she writes:

Not long before he died I found myself telling him something about my father that I had never dreamt of mentioning to anyone before. I never heard him say a thing that was not rooted in sense and sensibility. One of my proudest boasts is that in a letter he told me I was a valued friend!

There were the draughts of course.

About 1933 he made an exception to his rule of not dining out, but on arrival said a man had sneezed in No. 31 bus, and he had bought a box of his favourite lozenges, a sort unknown to me. Tonks was tickled to find us both sucking. Another time he came worried because Henry James had kept him talking, dragging his words out as was his wont, at a street corner, and Steer was *inclined* to think the wind was East.

As time went on his range was restricted and his most frequent outing was to Tonks's studio after dinner. A screen behind the door formed a recess which held the fire-place. To the right was Tonks's round writing-table, bearing drinks, and behind it the shelves on which his Littré's French Dictionary and other engines of literature were disposed. To the left a little old-fashioned sofa was Steer's seat, whereon, if talk became too abstract, he could abstract himself in a light slumber. This is the scene of one of those little pictures in which Tonks, uniting the two sides of his talent, gave a new turn to the eighteenth-century 'conversation piece', making it fondly humorous instead of primly civil, and quickening thus the more static poses of his painting with biographic life and fun. *An Evening in The Vale* portrayed George Moore, reading the manuscript of his latest novel to the host and his friends, St. John and Mary Hutchinson; Steer too, but relaxed in his seat, hands crossed above his dinner, eyes closed and mind evidently lulled and gently rapt away, though not beyond the alert of a good story or personal discussion. A second scene was the morning-room in Steer's house and presented a back view of its master, giving tea to his old nurse and her gossips in all the wide-spreading bagginess of the clothes that shielded him from insidious airs.[1] Nothing could be less like the conventional interior and company of an artist. The room spoke of no 'aesthetic' mode, looking, but for a good mantelpiece, like the cosy parlour of an old-fashioned lodging-house; one, however, in whose cupboards and on whose walls a treasure of prints and china had survived. Our house, to Steer and Tonks, with their accumulation of collector's lumber, was a byword of 'chastity'. In yet another of those pieces, *Sodales,* the room was Steer's again, with two figures about the fire, one of them a fourth in this rare sodality, a super-Sickert, sprawled horizontally in a

[1] See p. 60.

suit such as the French stage would give an Englishman, slipperless feet and a prophetic Moses-from-the-Mount display of spreading beard. Prophesying he obviously was, or had been, developing his latest decalogue, half-profound, half-cynical, for circumventing the shoals of painting; but his host had foundered under instruction and was bowed over a tom-cat in his lap, which for once had not ousted the guest from his prescriptive seat. Clinically sharp, the conjunction, and along with its humanity and fun the room had yielded a little masterpiece of colour, Chinese in its discrimination of yellow and muted rose among the greys.

Steer, in any case, was frankly puzzled by Sickert's taste for the ugly-beautiful, sworn as he was himself to a gracious world like Watteau's. Once, Philip Connard recalls, Sickert, as they passed a rag-and-bone shop together, said, 'That's how I should like my pictures to look.' 'They do', said Steer.

The Housekeeper

MY SERVANT

Great-hearted, how begrudged by you she'd plod
Who slumbers now beneath a humble sod;
And yet we ought to take her a few flowers:
The dead, poor dead, have pangs as keen as ours,
And when October, stripper of old boughs,
Soughs lamentably round their marble house,
Sure, they must think us a most thankless crew,
To sleep snug under blankets, as we do,
While they, gnawed to the bone by dreamings drear,
Without a bed-mate or a gossip's cheer,
Skeletons old, wrought on by frost and worm,
Feel drip on them snows of the winter storm,
Time slip away, and friend nor kin restore
Rags of the wreaths hung on their iron door.
When, of an evening, the logs hiss and spit,
Calm in her chair were I to see her sit;
If, on a blue and cold night of December,
She showed, crouched in a corner of my chamber,
Grave-eyed, come from a deep-dug bed eternal,
To brood on her big child with eye maternal,
What could I answer to that pious soul
While from her hollow lids the tear-drops stole?

'Les Fleurs du Mal,' CXXIV

The devoted tyrant who filled so large and close a part in Steer's daily life deserves her niche in the gallery that holds the 'gouvernantes' of many famous Frenchmen, and of the Chelsea bachelors Moore and Tonks.

When she took up again the care of 'Master Phibby' she had a jealous eye to all his interests, from dry feet to picture sales, thinking the world unjust if any returned unbought from exhibition.

Steer used to say that she could give a very shrewd criticism on pictures and if he got stuck would appeal to her judgment, which he counted unerring: in a letter to his sister he quoted Jane as having said, when congratulated by a guest on an excellent pudding, 'There's art in everythink, even in painting pictures.' She had her likes and dislikes among the visitors. George Moore she detested: 'Who's that?' she demanded when he called, and, her suspicion confirmed, grunted 'Oh! *im*!' Hugh Lane was favoured but always announced as 'Mr. Huge Lane'. She was a very early riser and her greatest happiness was in cleaning and scrubbing. 'Hard work', she was fond of saying, 'never hurt anyone.' An eye specialist was amused at her answer to his question if she could see clearly: 'I can see dirt.' Miss Hamilton recalls:

Her delight was to turn Cheyne Walk topside turvey while Steer was away on his painting excursions. When 'Pom, pom, pom', sung to a hymn-tune, ascended from below stairs it foreboded her displeasure. She allowed no one else to wash his collection of Chelsea china, but so great was her energy that Steer kept finding yet another piece damaged. It was suggested that he might employ the expert washer from a Museum to save her and his treasures, but though he turned this over for some time he decided that it would hurt her feelings too much and sadly abandoned the idea. Yet there were times when he rebelled; he was incensed, on discovering a large fragment missing from the base of a massive Chinese porcelain pagoda, to be told that his 'Mr. Thomas' had broken it. That great, gentle tabby with paws as soft as clouds!

Steer fully returned his old nurse's affection. His letters often refer to her or quote her views: thus she authorises the Blackwells to consider seven pounds two ounces 'quite a nice-sized baby', but snorts over an operation for tonsils: 'Children did not use to have those kind of things.' When her strength failed at last and bronchitis beset her, the long care she had given was amply made good. Nurses were engaged and she was tenderly looked after, installed in the front morning room where she could still keep some control and see chosen guests. She nerved herself to attend the service for Hugh Lane at Chelsea Old Church, and stamped in my memory is the sight of the old woman being supported home on Steer's arm. He wheeled her about on the Embankment when she could no longer walk. Anxious, in her latter days, when he had to leave town for the summer's work, he would not go far afield and was determined not, if he could help it, to fail her at the end.

During those absences she was watched over by Tonks and Gray, if either was at hand, and Steer's letters gratefully acknowledge their reports. Here is a specimen from Tonks:

18.9.1925

When I saw Jane yesterday she had recovered from her attack. Her voice was weak, but she took an interest in my conversation, particularly when I told her negotiations were going on for a Sargent portrait, the price being in the neighbourhood of £30,000. She took a grim pleasure in the fact that money cannot be carried beyond the grave.

Steer, to his satisfaction, was with her at the last, on July 4th 1929. He wrote to Gray on the 7th:

It has come at last and the dear old lady passed peacefully away on Thursday afternoon, in the presence of me, the nurse and Flo. The bronchitis had become more acute for some days, rendering her unconscious, and her breathing became very short, and while I sat, looking at her face, from the foot of the bed, her lower lip began to twitch, and this was the beginning of the end, which came in about a minute. Fortunately, there has been a good deal to occupy me since this happened, and to-morrow is the funeral and I am glad to say my brother can take the service, at the cemetery [Paddington] where her husband has lain for about 35 years. As I daresay you know, you were one of her special favourites, and her loss will react on all of us.

To Tonks he wrote on the same day:

I was very much touched by your letter and I had to pull myself together to prevent the writing at times becoming a little misty. You were one of the old lady's great favourites and latterly she spoke more of you than anyone else.

Sparing, as ever, of words, Steer had put his deep feeling into a portrait. It is characteristic of the man that having for once broken away from the lovely-beautiful he has lavished on the plain, even repellent features of his old nurse and housekeeper a wealth of elaboration such as he rarely gave to one of his pretty models. She sat with her customary thoroughness, and unable, from failing sight, to judge of what was done, she would ask afterwards 'What has my boy done today? Has he made me beautiful?' Yes: in this unlovely-beautiful of character intensely read into paint a debt was paid to your watching-wizened face and hands gnarled and thickly veined by labour without stint.

Steer's family had been concerned about the position when 'Old Jane' became helpless and the care of her a problem. They made gentle suggestions that she should be comfortably pensioned off and looked after by a niece in the country, but she would not hear of it. 'I promised his father that I would look after Master Phibby till his death,' she declared, and her master acquiesced. Miss Dorothy Barnard, one of the little girls in Sargent's *Carnation, Lily, Lily, Rose* and afterwards a close friend of Steer, was told by him that the old woman had never realised her baby had grown up. When he was in the sixties and herself near ninety she would pop her head in at the studio door and say, 'Well, well—daubing away, daubing away!'

22 Mrs. Rayne's Tea-Party, *by Henry Tonks*

23 (*a*) New English Art Club Jury, 1904

23 (*b*) Steer, in his 'New English' Circle, Admonished
A drawing by 'Max

On the death of Mrs. Raynes her place was taken by 'Flo' (Florence Hood) a girl of seventeen from Fulham whom the dragon had trained in the way that she should go. For thirty-five years she faithfully served her master, cheery and indefatigable, tending 'Father', as she called him, to the last.

Necessary Cats

The fervent lover and the sage austere
    In their ripe season equally admire
The great soft cats, who, like their masters dear,
    Are shivery folk and sit beside the fire.
Friends both of learning and of wantonness,
    They hunt where silence and dread shadows are;
    Erebus would have yoked them to his car
For funeral coursers had their pride been less.
They take, brooding, the noble attitudes
Of sphinxes stretched in deepest solitudes,
    Seeming to slumber in an endless dream;
Their loins are quick with kindlings magical,
    And glints of gold, as in a sandy stream,
Vaguely bestar their eye-balls mystical.
                    'Les Fleurs du Mal,' LXVIII

Clan Chattan, the Cat Clan, extends beyond the Scottish Highlands, and artists so unlike as Baudelaire and Steer were both sealed of that tribe. 'Old Pussy Steer', irreverently so-called in our household, had affinities with those pets, susceptible as he was no less to 'magic kindlings' of the senses than to chilly outer airs, and disposed to somnolence when at peace. The sleek, comfortable aloofness of the cats appealed to him, and their dignity, though he may not have imputed the condescension of the proud uncanny creatures to their Egyptian godhead. The reigning tom-cat, accordingly, was a third important member of the household, and Miss Hamilton has furnished a chronicle of the dynasty.

Steer enjoyed the quiet companionship of a cat and used to say that he liked them because they were not sycophants and provided their own boots. He made friends with strolling cats along the streets in Chelsea, talking to them in a special voice. As a child he had his special pussies, the 'Duchess', a tortoiseshell, and her daughter, the 'Countess'. His first attempt to handle oils at an early age was a portrait of the sleeping 'Duchess', and in letters while he was studying abroad were inquiries for his 'Mr. Pop'. It was not until he settled down at Cheyne Walk that he was able to keep a cat of his own in London. In *Hydrangeas* the girl on the sofa is playing with the first Mr. Thomas, a black-and-white kitten, much beloved. After its death in 1906 a magnificent tabby was brought up from the country by his niece. This beautiful and sagacious creature ruled Steer for eighteen years. There never was such a cat! He could do no wrong and on the only occasion when he made a hole in his manners by jumping up on a mantelpiece and breaking a Sèvres vase he was forgiven.

When Steer began preparations for his annual outing this cat would become restive and distressed and afterwards mourn his absence, but upon the master's return after three months he was treated with hauteur for days. 'So you left me, did you?—Well then you can get on with it!' A chair was kept for him opposite Steer's. The great creature would leap noiselessly upon the table and contemplate anyone who sat in it with an expression of revolted patience till Steer would say, 'I am afraid you are sitting in Mr. Thomas's chair.' I had become the excited possessor of a dubious Monticelli and had taken it round one sunny morning for my uncle's verdict. As he sat contemplating it, in walked the cat and sitting down before the picture, yawned at it. 'Well,' laughed Steer, 'that's all old Thomas thinks of it and I believe he is right!'

He was heartbroken when the great tabby died of influenza in 1924. His last cat died just before the 'blitz'; a powerful striped tabby who hunted seagulls on the mud banks opposite the house. Once when Steer was seriously ill, Tonks with his medically trained mind was horrified to find the cat asleep on the end of Steer's bed, so he shoo'd it out of the room and shut the door. It came in again through another door, and Steer would not have it put out a second time.

An anonymous band-box was once handed in at '109' containing a kitten. Steer guessed that some of the Slade students had sent it to console him for a pet that had died; this touched and pleased him immensely. He was indifferent to dogs, though there was always one of uncertain breed on guard at Cheyne Walk, but they lived downstairs under the care of Mrs. Raynes and later of 'Flo'. They were always procured from the milkman, as Mrs. Raynes's theory was that only a milkman could supply them.

There was a fresh grievance for the pussy when Steer added to his summer absences visits in the Isle of Wight along with Gray at Easter-time to Dorothy, second wife and widow of Hugh Hammersley. That lady had precisely the qualities of hospitable care without fuss and of easy understanding to make her guest happy, and by an exception in his correspondence they became familiarly 'Dot' or 'Dotto' and 'Phil' to one another. In the punctual 'Collins' which did justice to her kindness and her provision in particular for the return journey he writes:

16.4.31

The dog was demonstrative but the cat treated me somewhat coldly but condescended to sleep at the foot of my bed.

10.4.32

Ron [Ronald Gray] and I arrived home safely on Friday after a delightful visit and I very much enjoyed the peaceful time you provided, which is exactly my idea of a holiday and I think on the whole we were very lucky in the weather as to day here it is dull and raining. To insure a good crossing I retired to the cabin and lay down before the boat started, which much amused Ronny, but I was taking no risks and consequently enjoyed the delicious hard boiled eggs and brown bread and butter which you had so thoughtfully provided, when we got into the train.

On arriving home I found the household struggling with a floor cloth which they had divided down the middle with the economical idea of turning the sides to the centre. I also got a warm welcome from the dog and even, strange to say, from the cat, who I think must have missed the siesta he is sometimes accustomed to take on my knee in the afternoon.

20.4.33

I found my home still standing and all well but was sorry to hear that my dear old cat took my absence rather to heart and roamed about the house and would not take his food as usual. However all is well now I have returned, but it is depressing to think of the same thing happening when I go away for the summer!

Steer painted the great 'Mr. Thomas' as a kitten, playing with the girl's hat in *The Muslin Dress*. His dread of house-cleanings and paintings comes out in a letter to another correspondent:

13.3.25

... I am in the middle of my third cold this winter which I think is a record for me. I attribute this last one to draughts on account of the house being painted and pointed, the outside now looks like a dolls' house ...

The Cronies

Next to the housekeeper and the cats, in Steer's affection, liking or tolerance came a circle of habitual visitors. Vignettes of the more constant among them will complete the painter's setting.

Ronald Gray

Ronald Gray, whose name often recurs in these pages, was the earliest of Steer's friends in the group. They were made known to one another in 1886, on the ice in Battersea park. Gray was the son of a severe Calvinist father who started an engineering business in the Danvers Street of 'Chelsea Village' days. Carlyle he remembers making friends with his small sister, and there were recollections of Turner, as 'Puggy Booth', being hooted and pelted by street boys or going on the river with his housekeeper.[1] Gray contrived to quit engineering for painting, studying at night under Brown at Westminster, but was checked in his career by tuberculosis in the knee-joint and illness following, which sent him to Australia for recovery. This was at a time 1901 to 1903, when memories would have been particularly interesting, but unluckily Steer's letters to him, which might have filled some gaps, have during War-time been mislaid. After his return he kept a constant watch over his friend's health and peace and accompanied him at times to painting grounds. Here is one tribute to his

[1] Gray's 'Memoirs', unpublished as yet, carry his story to the end of the 'Great War'.

quality in a letter from Steer to Tonks of September 7, 1921, from Southampton:

> Gray has been a perfect brick and has done for me all that any human being could possibly do. All I regret is that I am afraid I have made him waste a great deal of his time.

His services did not end with Steer's life: as will appear later, he had the exacting task of artistic executor. Hale and active at seventy-seven he is still producing his deft watercolours, landscape or portrait, at a time when his retreat, as a Brother of Charterhouse, is shut up and a studio for oil-painting hard to come by. I have tested his sociable qualities in long painting spells, Welsh and Cornish, and watched with admiration his easy gift for getting into friendly relations with men and women of every rank and kind.

Henry Tonks

Tonks's moods fluctuated between ravishment at having escaped from medicine to the pleasures and pangs of drawing, and a bitter sense of lee-way to make up, with doubts of his own capacity. So long as he was in labour with or nursing a new picture in secret, hope ran high. 'With the rest of us', said Steer, 'a picture is an everyday incident, with Tonks it is an event.' It was anguish to display the new-born. To me he wrote about the Sunday morning caricatures he threw off without effort and squandered on his correspondents, as he did his delightful letters:

> 29.9.16
> Such pleasure as I have derived from doing those drawings has been chiefly due to the feeling that them at least I have not got to show to the public; that only one or two will see them, and that Konody and such people have not got to judge them, and then you ask me to throw them to the whole collected swine. No, not even if Ian Hamilton consents to write a preface. They were done for you. When I exhibit a picture I always feel it has lost its virginity; in my studio it seems to have a kind of innocence, rather touching, even sometimes a kind of beauty, and just as a poor girl parts with hers, so my poor picture goes out into Piccadilly and offers her innocence for what it is worth. I dont want to get any thing out of these Sunday diversions. I should have done you others, but the very feeble capacity I have in these matters suddenly left me, and I found I was becoming silly, so I hope I stopped in time. . . .

In the end he ceased to exhibit, but the invitation to show his collected work at the Tate Gallery overcame his doubts and dread, and he was, for once, almost content. When, however, I had urged him, in a congratu-latory letter, to press further in oils the dramatic and composing gift shown in his caricature-impromptus, and crossed him coming into my club with a friend, he shot at me, 'MacColl, you're too didactic', the last words to me of the super-severe schoolmaster, my admirable friend.

Outside his studio were social and intellectual relations in rich plenty, and a Paradise Regained now and then, as on Lord Northbourne's Eastry estate, in the Highlands with the Hammersleys and with the Owen Hugh Smiths at Ardtornish. (All hands were turned out once to rescue his sketching-stool from a torrent ravine—the Highlanders loved him), and at the Old Priest's House at Sopley, near Christchurch, with a stream running at the bottom of a garden that grew succulent asparagus, marrow-fats and other kindly fruits of the earth. But most paradisal of all were the grounds of the Villa d'Este, one summer, with an ancient gardener for their Adam. Thence, Tonks declared, a summons ought to go out, 'Ad Este, Fideles!' to join a company of the Blessed. One crumpled rose-leaf troubled his peace: he was puzzled and cast down because watercolour washes were obdurate, with nasty hard edges. Of course they were, in that broiling sun.

There was an unceasing fund of amusement for Steer in Tonks's swiftly succeeding enthusiasms for new devices medical or artistic. He waged a tireless campaign against Steer's sluggish habit of body, and at one time, instigated by Arbuthnot Lane, was hot on the cure of *stasis*: all his friends must drink paraffin and the thin among them wear surgical belts: I skinned my throat and tongue and risked my life by taking a swig, not of paraffin, as I thought, but of Scrubbs' Ammonia, in the dark. For watercolours we must use a photographer's camera-stand, with ball-bearings, and he gleefully announced that he had circumvented the need for much 'faithful labour', say in painting a row of palings, by drawing them with a candle-end, and slipping a wash over the grease that left them white. He had Hambidge to supper and flirted with 'Dynamic Symmetry'. Even Steer took up a little instrument for dividing a canvas in 'golden mean' proportions for a rough and ready approach to composition.

As with Gray, so with Tonks, Steer was well-nigh a religion and also an anxious care for the doctor who survived in him; bulletins about his colds came with every winter's letter from Chelsea. Colonel Armstrong, retired from the medical service of the Indian Army, who saw Steer frequently in his blinded period and advised him less dictatorially, asked him, after Tonks's death, 'Did he miss him much?' He replied, 'No, friendship is often so exacting.' When John Fothergill gave dinner to the two, he put Steer's helping of pudding on a big Sunderland plate with the inscription 'Prepare to meet thy God'! He looked rather dazed at first, then slowly turned to Tonks across the table and said in a hollow voice, 'There he is!' Letter-writing to him was so perverse a misuse of the faculties that he supposed it was Tonks's device for maintaining his divine authority after death. When he must himself reply he minimised names and personalities.

F   W.S.

To G. L. Behrend he said, 'If I ever get a coat-of-arms the chief thing in it will be a waste-paper basket. It is my best friend.'

George Moore

To Moore his friends were chiefly of use as sounding boards, testing grounds, reference-resorts for novels in the making, but in his self-absorbed way he was attracted to the man whose work he genuinely admired, and constituted him Painter-Referee in succession to Manet. Steer, on his side, had a distrust of what Moore might do or say next in the way of indiscretion, and like Tonks he had to suffer from his vanity over portraits. Of one by Steer he wrote:

I am sure that your portrait of me is not good—I am *sure* that it is not worthy of you. The features are mine but the face is without character of any kind. It is very flat prose and you will agree with me that that is unpardonable. I will sit again at your convenience—but this is not worthy of you.

The letter is undated, but the address is 92 Victoria Street, where he spent some years up to 1900. Of this or another portrait Vernon Wethered writes:

Steer painted a head of George Moore which he gave to him. After Moore's death he thought he would like to have it back. Moore had used it for a frontispiece to one of his books, and apparently had thought it would bring him more credit if taken for a portrait by Manet. It was painted in the style of Manet and reproduced with the signature omitted might easily be mistaken for a painting by him. On enquiring after it from Moore's housekeeper, she told him she had seen him one day on the floor of his room scrubbing out the signature. The portrait couldn't be found, so Steer supposed Moore had destroyed it. That is the story, so far as memory serves, as Steer told it to me.

Before the date of that incident, having beguiled Steer to walk with him to Dulwich, in search of a haystack for 'Esther Waters', he made inquiry of various policemen, found his treasure, and on the walk home was so pleased with the success of the expedition that he suggested they should share a house together and keep a pony cart, in which they would be able to drive to London.[1]

In another dateless letter from Ebury Street he tried to draw Steer into collaboration as an illustrator:

I am anxious to publish an improved version of 'The Lake'—my best book, or to speak more exactly, what will be my most perfect work, if I can republish the amended text. It occurred to me that two or three illustrations might help to persuade Heinemann and that it might amuse you to do three or four pen and ink drawings of a romantic Lake. Dreams!

[1] 'Life of George Moore', by Joseph Hone, p. 211.

I will bring you the book just to set you going, but you have been dreaming and painting 'The Lake' all your life. Three or four pen-and-ink compositions. Landscape looks well in pen and ink. The drawings need not be carried far; better that they should not if the medium be pen-and-ink. Three or four after-dinner dreams.

Nothing came of the project.

All other letters to Steer are a song of praise about his painting. After a dinner at Ebury Street he read to a number of us as well as to its subject the letter addressed to Steer and prefixed to his lecture on the Impressionist Painters.[1] This was altered and expanded for the 'Conversations in Ebury Street' of 1924, of which Steer wrote to Geoffrey Blackwell:

13.2.24
I think the anticipation was worse than the reality, Tonks read me a few extracts the other evening.

He had presentation copies of all Moore's books, but appears to have dipped into only one of them. 'He seems', he said to Gray, 'to write about very trivial subjects.' Tonks, in the matter of Moore, oscillated between a sense of flattery in the friendship of so renowned a writer and exasperation with his peculiarities, and came away with Steer from the cremation service helpless with laughter at the comic spirit which had inevitably invaded those proceedings, as it did more richly the Irish obsequies which followed. Hardly a fellow-writer was present, but Ramsay MacDonald had wafted an eminent painter from an *n*th sitting, clad in a bright sporting suit.

Two characteristic letters of Moore to Steer may be added here. The first was inspired by a visit to the very remarkable collection of English paintings shown at Bradford in 1904:

8.11.04   4 Upper Ely Place, Dublin
After five days music at Leeds I reached a point at which I could not hear what was being played. Five days music reminds me of the Liber Studiorum; half a dozen drawings delight one, the fifty five or the seventy five or the one hundred and five make a sort of palimpsest of one's mind. I remember hearing the whole of Hamlet, six hours, it was magnificent, I was not bored but at the end the actors might have read passages from 'The Daily Mail' and I should not have known. On the sixth day I went to Bradford and I made some discoveries. I discovered the use of the Black Country. I could not understand why the north of England had been converted into cinder heaps and the sky into smoke cloud; now I know. These things have been done in order to provide a sufficient background for pictures. Until you have seen pictures in the Black Country you do not know how beautiful pictures can be, or how they can delight you. My visit to Bradford was an enchantment. I walked about like one enchanted, and it was a great pleasure to me to find that my friends had much more talent than I thought they had. I have always admired your talent but I did not know

[1] Dublin, Maunsel & Co., 1906.

that you had ever painted a picture so beautiful as *The Card Dealer*. That is really a beautiful thing, and I can hardly imagine that the time will ever come when it will not seem beautiful.

I liked Tonks's *After the Ball*—his lumpy women, Rothenstein's green shutter, Holman Hunt's *Hireling Shepherd* or Wanton's Shepherd (he is hugging a lady, a gentleman with a shock of purply red hair) pleased me very much. It is a beautiful picture and one that will not go out of fashion. There is so much in it that time will not destroy. I suppose you know it—the swallow catching the gnat, and the gnat is catching something else, I am sure it is, if I had had a magnifying glass I should have discovered what. There was a Maddox Brown next to it, a thing in pale green, flat on the canvas, very good. Nor did the Rosettis weary me. There was a Jones somewhere, but I won't tell you about Jones; you know what I think about him, the worst artist that ever lived, whether you regard him as a colourist, a draughtsman, a painter or a designer.

I wish you would send me the landscape, and will you please send it in a frame so that I will be able to see it on the wall. It will be difficult to get a frame here, and I will send you back the pink girl. I am most anxious to have a look at that landscape. Do you remember that I asked you to send me any piece of Chelsea china that you saw that you didn't want to buy for yourself, you will not be able to improve your collection, but I should like to have some more pieces—figures especially.

18.5.09   4 Upper Ely Place, Dublin

I have heard of the great success of your exhibition through friends, not through the newspapers (you know I never read them).

There was an article in the 'Times' I believe, a column and a half long, in which you were declared to be the first among English painters, and no doubt the other papers have said the same thing.

It is quite needless for me to tell you of the pleasure this gives to one of your oldest friends.

Do you remember the evening I met you for the first time in the Cock eating-house? And my first visits to Addison Road Mansions? I think I always knew that you were a great painter, and I have in a prominent place in my house the picture I took away from Addison Road Mansions—a girl in a black hat. It always gives me pleasure to see, and you, too, are a pleasure to see. I don't know which I like better—the painter or the friend; both seem to me so admirable.

William and Alice Rothenstein

When, after what Max Beerbohm has described as '*gaucheries* on the *Rive Gauche*' of Paris, 'Will' burst upon the town simultaneously with 'Max's' own descent upon it from Oxford, London was dazzled indeed. Rothenstein at once made himself felt in the two clubs, New English and Chelsea Arts, in the world at large with the portrait sketch-book that was his passport to all the eminent, but also with his vivid interest in all the intelligent, so that he began what may now be called his omnipresence. Those early days were of uncovenanted brilliance, but in 1899 he settled down, married, and determined, like Queen Victoria, 'to be good.' He developed, indeed, into the preacher who figures in the two New English

24 (*a*) PROF. FRED BROWN, 1894

24 (*b*) DAVID MUIRHEAD, *by D. S. MacColl*

25 (a) DOROTHEA HAMILTON, 1893

25 (b) THE REV. W. H. HORNBY STEER

groups by 'Max', where a Steer, massive and unresponsive, is lectured by one whose accusing hand and diminutive form swell with missionary ardour. It was in face of such calls to a life of 'probity' that Steer grumbled, 'Rothenstein does the same things as the rest of us, but always from higher motives.' The balance of amusing levity against excess of gravity, however, was kept in the Rothenstein partnership not only by William's own irrepressible wit but by a happy spirit of mischievous fun in his wife. Alice Knewstub was a daughter of Rossetti's assistant and inherited the beauty of a mother who had posed for the head of that painter's *Venus Verticordia*. A short experience of the stage had widened the range of her observation, and marriage took her into yet another field. Her talk was an unfailing delight to Tonks and Steer, hardly checked, though punctuated, by a monitory 'Alice!' from the other end of the table. Health, however, required of 'Will' a break from his happy painting-ground among the Whitechapel Rabbis, and his long absence in the Cotswolds broke up any close association with Chelsea. Tonks, a man of moods, and restive under edification, failed to pick up the threads again on the Rothensteins' return to London, and Steer, rather lazily, followed suit. William never wavered in his admiration of Steer's work, though he rebuked me for what he thought a too exclusive advocacy, and the portraits I have referred to are a record of their friendship; Steer's portrait of Alice remained in his studio and is now in possession of her son. William Rothenstein will count in the future not only in virtue of remarkable paintings in several branches of the art, but as an historian of high quality in two kinds: portrait-drawings that are a 'Who's Who' of his time, and pages that are eloquent of intercourse with his sitters, and of an intelligence matching theirs in description and reflection. His enthusiastic epistles to painters and writers Steer gently mocked as 'Williams'.

Augustus Daniel

Medical practitioner and Mayor of Scarborough, Daniel made daily and intense study in the National Gallery on his visits to town, and thereafter, in Frederick Wedmore's old seat by the Burlington Fine Arts Club fire, discussed pictures with Tonks or whoever of the elect might be there. He had previously, in company with Roger Fry and C. R. Ashbee, given the like close scrutiny to Florentine and other masters in Italy. His scholarship included older fields, of Greek and Roman antiquity, and he produced a catalogue of the marbles in the Capitoline Museum. This, save for a lecture betraying a gloomy view of criticism, was his only trespass into semi-literature: he remains a well, not a fountain, sealed, of immense knowledge, but also a judge of notable acumen, vouched for by the collection of paintings he has formed, with Steer for its leading ornament: Tonks contrived his appointment to the Directorship of the National Gallery by a word to his school fellow, Stanley Baldwin. Amid the jarring voices of its Board, his lips, like the Prime Minister's at an uneasy juncture, appear to have been sealed, no less than his learning, for next to nothing was acquired. 'King Log', as has been said, conserved the funds for his successor 'King Stork' in that drumly pond. Steer and Tonks, at least, could tap his learning, respected his taste, and enjoyed his nervous talk.

The Harrison Brothers

'Peter', so-called, but properly Laurence Alexander Harrison, was a son of the famous Frederic. He was tall, golden-haired, notably good-looking; wealthy also, and the additional, real gift for painting which he possessed was thrown away upon him, but for a short harvest and the inside knowledge it furnished to his excellent taste. He had shown good portraits, but astonished us all with an interior of which a large flowering plant was the motive, and then ceased to exhibit: either his interests, social and of connoisseurship, crowded out painting, or his self-criticism kept it private. His wife, a sister of Mrs. Comyns Carr, was the talented translator of Carmen Sylva's 'Bard of the Dimbovitza', and their house, at 46 Cheyne Walk, was full of lovely things, and a hospitable resort for Steer, Tonks and others. Harrison's health, for long precarious, broke down and he died in 1937. His brother 'Jinx', properly Leonard, was a close friend of Tonks and companion in his fishing holidays, a patron of Steer and welcome visitor. Here is a characteristic letter from 'Peter' who was a prime source for Steer of caustic comment and inconvenient anecdote:

12.1.09   Glen Eyrie, Colorado Springs
    I suppose you are still sitting in the usual whirl of uneventfulness, regarding your usual spring masterpiece.
    I have been in the wars of late—my belly and its unruly members have taken the appendix in their teeth and confined me to my bed. After 4 days enforced seclusion I have now got the mutineer under hatches—and tho' I can still hear grumblings and mutterings below decks am in charge of the ship once more. The winter has been fairly damnable with hot gales and snow (below zero last night).—Work out hasnt been feasible. I have tried indoors to my usual disgust and discomfiture.
    Breakfast here is beginning to tell on me. We take it in company with 5 boarhounds 2 parrots 2 white rabbits 4 children (one a baby) and others—The din is only rivalled by the smell—the early egg has a way of catching the flavour of Great Dane that is truly remarkable!
    I have read an article of Sickert's on Whistler in the 'Fortnightly' (did you see it?) 'real pâté de foie gras' with too many truffles. I can't imagine why Sickert cleaves to London: he too at bottom must be a sentimentalist. George Moore has the better taste, perhaps, in spite of his literary learning.

I hear rumours of large deficits in the budget and consequent fresh taxes—which reminds me that I am in your debt somewhat.

Love to the melancholy one and a stroke for Thomas.

The Sargents

Of all Steer's friends John Sargent had closest community with him in some elements of character, but was a puzzle, as to us all, in his seeming immunity from human weaknesses or passions, save for the arts, including an eager appetite for books in several languages and for music. He numbered among his friends players and singers—Shakespeare and Henschel were two—and himself could perform with skill and gusto on the piano during a sitter's 'rests'. He was open-handed, responding not only generously but with a grateful alacrity to any appeal, whether for money or service. Thus when Charles Furse, at a stay over a wall-painting, wrote to him from Liverpool for advice, his reply was to emerge, up the ladder, early next morning, and when a gifted young painter was fatally injured in a railway accident and other artists were colloguing and sending for Sargent's counsel, he was already, by first train, on the spot. Like Steer, he was honest of mind and downright in judgment but secretive about his private self, tongue-tied in public speech, in conversation obstructed and explosive. A vigorous trencherman, he sat, like Steer again, stiffly upright on his chair to minimise a bulging front.

His opinions were a constant surprise and matter for combat with Tonks, who wrote to me:

Sargent and his sister are the most delightful people, who are always the same. Sargent and I agree on very little yet I get to like him more and more. He is an odd fish with a curious reserve about him, which I doubt if anyone has ever broken down.

That sister, Emily, another, Mrs. Ormond, and their mother, while she lived, were equally devoted to Steer and Tonks. The table of their Carlyle Mansions flat and sitting-room, hung with Venetian crimson stuff, were the scene of many happy evenings. The ladies had the perfection of high-bred American women in solicitous yet easy hospitality, and among frequent guests were Mrs. Charles Hunter, English hostess of the same type and Henry James, for whom Tonks was an engrossing study.

Sargent's sudden death in the night after a particularly happy dinner-party was a shocking blow to his circle. Steer, in his restrained fashion, wrote to Blackwell:

18.4.35

I feel his death very deeply as he was such a good friend to me and always exactly the same.

A problem arose: how to deal with a huge accumulation of the painter's own studies and of pictures he had collected. Steer, who had previously given help to Charles Furse's widow in the like case, joined with Tonks in urging and arranging a public sale, the result of which, on the first day, was £146,000. He was, as he told Blackwell, 'flaberghasted' [sic] at a result which 'far exceeded his wildest dreams' and was 'glad for Martin's sake, as he certainly worked like a nigger'. A foreshadow, this, of what happened at his own death.

A slump in reputation inevitably followed for a man who in his boyhood had been hurried by a mother's restlessness from place to place, trained to take eyefuls of objects like snapshots and too seldom permitted or provoked to stand and stare. But *Carnation, Lily, Lily, Rose* was not a mere proceeding *in camera*, nor his Venetian *Interior* of the Curtis family, so happily disliked by them and given to the Diploma Gallery; nor yet portraits like the *James* and *Patmore*, witnesses to friendship and amazement, nor yet some of his Hebraic figures. Repaints, premature varnish and restorer's 'balsams', alas! have belied much of an originally startling brilliance and justice in values.

David Muirhead

I must forbear any attempt to complete the Chelsea circle, which included Ambrose McEvoy, prematurely cut off, to Steer's sorrow, Philip Connard, till he migrated to Richmond, close neighbours in the Walter Russells, the Gerard Chownes, who occupied the lower flat of Tonks's house, William Carter, a good critic, immense talker, and frequent visitor, numerous acquaintances and chess-partners in the Club, but the gentlest and most self-effacing of them all claims a word. David Muirhead had been one in a group of Scots at the Westminster School, pursuing art with frugal means. A comrade, the Orchardson and Whistler-inspired W. J. Yule, in the few years allotted to him, was his first leader, but thereafter Muirhead won an honourable place in the following of Steer, both as oil-painter and watercolourist: I have seen the master momentarily mistake one of the disciple's pictures for his own: but in Muirhead's there was a shy, individual tenderness deeply native. Steer genuinely liked him and his sympathy for non-human creatures was one of the ties between them. As 'The Times' obituary notice recalled:

... Pestered by mice in his Chelsea studio, he would set traps for the creatures—only to release them because of the look in their eyes. On one occasion, it is told, he sat up half the night, breathing slaughter against a noisy cat on the roof. Having enticed the animal to a skylight, he seized it—and then, because it was so thin, gave it the milk that he had saved for his breakfast.

VIII

THE GOOD UNCLE

Steer, unguessed by acquaintance and barely surmised by friends, showed himself freely to those of his own house. Here is a family portrait by his niece

'The first thing I remember was a doll he brought from Paris, when I was two years and four months old. He was visiting my parents at Headcorn, Kent, and on the morning after his arrival I wanted to go and have a look at him. With bare feet and in my nightgown I pushed his door open at 6 a.m. but he was fast asleep. I looked at him for a long time because he was so still and so beautiful and so very, very long—there seemed to be no end to him! I was so awed that I forgot my usual tactics of waking my elders by pulling their eyelids apart with my fingers and instead left him in peace.

I have no other memories of that visit, though it was then that he painted an amusing conversation-piece of two funny little heads among flower-like dabs of colour, inscribed 'Jim Jim and Do Do', but 'Uncle Pull' (to rhyme with Hull) was a golden thread that ran through the pattern of our childhood, for he had a wonderful understanding of youngsters. What a glorious and hilarious playmate he was! Our games always ended with a free fight and such a hullabaloo of joy and anguish that the elders must intervene.

I much regret how I jigged about when he was painting my portrait at Trafalgar Studios, Manresa Road. He used to give me an orange to keep quiet. It was of course difficult for a little girl to know that painting was a serious business and not one of his usual games. But alas! the portrait of my Mother in a pink dress with me sitting at her feet had finally to be abandoned because I was so tiresome. A painting of my Mother in her prime was lost through my fault.

I loved going to tea with him at the Avenue Studios. The smell of paint and magilp, the picture on the easel and the kettle boiling on the fire were all enchanting. I ought to have plentiful memories of the N.E.A.C. Private Views but alas! all my youthful attention was centred on big 'Uncle Pull'.

During school holidays I sometimes stayed with Granny Steer at 44 Stratford Road, where she was then living with her elder son. Uncle

Philip used to drop in for lunch on Sundays and generally brought a friend with him, very often Mr. George Thomson, whose black beard was awe-inspiring. That was after my Uncle started a beard, but there was such a clamour in the family over it that he quickly shaved it off. Sometimes it would be Walter Sickert. Those were the days of Sickert's dandyhood, yet he too would condescend to amuse a little girl with tales of his white mice who *always* produced a new family on *every* third Sunday morning without fail and other serious tales of nonsense.

Although Steer and his brother were utterly unlike one another there was a great bond of affection between them; the artist, who despised the frothiness of society, and the debonair young parson, the much sought-after diner-out, the charming fellow in whose veins ran the Harrison blood. Both had wit, and both warmth of heart and understanding of their fellowmen; one meditative and mentally alert, but indolent in all save his work; the other conscientious and energetic in his clerical duties but enjoying the glitter of social life. As Henry used to say, the rich need a parson as much as the poor. The love of the two brothers never waned, but as years passed Henry's respect and admiration for his brother grew, though they never ceased laughing when together alone or in congenial company. When both were over seventy we three lunched together at Cheyne Walk and they were as absurd and funny as two boys and Philip laughed so much that tears ran down his face at Henry's pranks.

When Granny Steer lived at Stratford Road, Steer had several serious turns of 'flu' or devastating toothache and he would arrive in a 'growler' and go straight to bed to be nursed by his sister. All through life he had the deepest sympathy for anyone suffering toothache, and would want to hear all the agonies of inflamed roots and horrors of extraction. During one of the illnesses Sickert called to see him and was much impressed with a painting of a sleeping infant by Phil's sister which was hanging in his room. He urged her to work seriously, but family duties precluded study save in watercolours of flower, which her brother admired and encouraged her to carry on. He told me that with opportunities of study she would have been a fine painter.

On Sunday, March 6th, 1898, Emma Steer died in her 81st year. This was a terrible shock for her son, as he had been lunching that day at Stratford Road and she seemed fairly well and bright. How stricken he looked next morning when he came round after breakfast! He was deeply attached to her and felt the parting acutely.

A new chapter in his life now began. In the following June he was best-man to his brother Henry at his marriage to Miss Maria Halse Morgan Reed, who, as niece of Sir Walter Vaughan Morgan, acted as Lady

Mayoress, since Sir Walter was a bachelor. Henry was Chaplain to him during his office, 1905–6, and in the official robes Steer painted his brother's portrait. He was godfather to the baby nephew, W. R. Hornby Steer, born in April 1899. His two nephews and niece were as unlike peas in a pod as possible, but he had no favourite. He would jeer at our weaknesses, which was more searing than being scolded, but also commended what he found worthy, adding inches to our stature.

I saw him but intermittently for some years after Granny Steer's death, as my parents had gone to live in Suffolk. He would invite me to stay at Cheyne Walk or see him there when visiting elsewhere in London. He was anxious I should take up embroidery, considering, as he did very strongly, the needle a better tool for women than the brush. He was enthusiastic over Mrs. Harrison's group of embroideresses who reproduced 17th century Italian and 18th century French needlework from rare examples she possessed and other collections. He stimulated my interest in French painting by giving me a book on François Boucher, and initiated me into the wonder of Chinese paintings and ceramics. This was a great bond between us up to the last, as it led us into the philosophy and religious impulses underlying early Chinese culture. I think Tonks only peered into the kingdom where Steer wandered so happily. Tonks wrathfully complained that 'Your Uncle would have a far greater faith in incantations written around a Chinese bowl than in any doctor's prescription',[1] but I can still see him when he came in one evening, almost breathless with excitement, to tell Steer of the Sung Wall paintings of the Three Bodhisattvas from the Ch'ing Liang Temple, recently given to the British Museum by Mr. Eumorfopoulos, which he had visited that day and declared to be the *most* beautiful things he had ever seen!

What an eye my Uncle had! he could find treasures in all sorts of unexpected places. The Yuan ink painting, circa 1280, of the Tang poet, Li Po, known as The Drunken Sage, was one of them. He would chuckle over the charming old reprobate who always was forced to return to his circle of friends and his cups because of the sorrow of the earth that overwhelmed him when he contemplated her in solitude.'

I break off Miss Hamilton's account at this point, to be resumed in a later chapter.

[1] A 'sunshine' bronze from Steer's hoard was pounced upon in a Glasgow exhibition by the Chinese scholar, Dr. Yeh, for its superb seal, enriched and guarded by dragons and engraved with the mark of the Hsuen Ho Palace collection of a Sung Emperor. In this Steer had kept his prescriptions.

IX

PAINTINGS

Yearly Outings

From 1884 to 1934 we have Steer's own list of places visited in summer or autumn for painting in those fifty years.[1] For the first eleven years the excursions were English, broken by French; for the rest English, with one return to Montreuil-sur-Mer. They were regulated, from 1903, when he was appointed to teach painting in the Slade School, by the limits of the vacation, namely from the beginning of July to October. That period was given to landscape painting; the rest of the year divided between his teaching engagement and painting from models or of portraits in his house.

A deep, exclusive love for England early asserted itself. If the Saints took pleasure in the stones of Zion, Steer had a fondness for the old bones of his country. He was pleased to find a fragment of Offa's Dyke near Whitchurch. This affection was reinforced by veneration for the Turner who had peregrinated his country as a topographic artist, but also pursued the picturesque for its own sake in castles, rivers, ports and waterfalls. Norham Castle, Turner's first popular success, was the signpost for much that followed, and Steer tracked the master to begin with in his Yorkshire travels, at Richmond (1895) Barnard Castle (1896) Knaresborough (1897) and returned to all three a second time. He liked to have company on those outings and it became the custom for Fred Brown to join him with W. C. Coles, master of the Winchester School of Art, for a third.

Miss Brown, sister of the painter-professor, has supplied me with the dates and places of this association:

Mr. Steer and my brother were at Richmond (Yorks) in 1895. The first year they were away together was in 1888 at Walberswick, but I am not sure if Mr. Coles was with them. The association continued for 21 unbroken years, except for three summers 1892–93–94 when Fred went away with me and my eldest brother, who was recovering from a very serious illness.

These dates I have copied from a list of places my brother went to for his summer holidays.

Right rooms, right skies, and a loved place all together were not, how-

[1] See p. 186.

26 (b) Poplars at Montreuil

26 (a) 'The Three'

27 (a) RICHMOND CASTLE, 1903

27 (b) THE SHOWER, 1903

ever, often easy to come by. Here, in a letter to Blackwell from Bridgnorth in 1911, is a tale of tribulation in one season's prospecting:

I dare say you will be surprised at seeing by the above address that I have settled down in quite another direction than the one I set out for, namely the Eastern counties. Brown and I spent a week exploring the various places that we had heard of, seeing the Dedham district which seemed to us rather monotonous and flat. We then saw the Ipswich district, which we liked better, and saw a really beautiful spot called Gainsborough Lane about 4 miles away but with absolutely no chance of accommodation.

We then went to see Wells in Norfolk which was absolutely a bad egg, but on our way there we passed Sudbury, which from the train we liked the look of, so we returned there and did not like it so much as we did from the train, a very usual experience, and while there we decided to take a drive to a place near called Lavenham of which I had heard a good account; however fate was against us seeing it on that day, as we had not proceeded more than about 2 miles when we were aware of our carriage shaving very close to a corner of the road, and next minute we swerved across and ran up the hedge opposite, the driver at this moment falling off his box. This alarmed us, and seeing that there was no chance of getting hold of the reins which had tumbled down we thought it advisable to descend as well as we could. The horse happily was a quiet one and was only going at a sharp trot along the road; Brown strained his wrist rather badly and I got off with only a shaking, as I failed to keep my feet. We found the driver was more seriously hurt than we were on reaching him, so we put him into the carriage which had fortunately been stopped, and sent him home. The tragic part of this incident was that he died the same evening from hemorrhage of the brain following concussion we learnt at the inquest next day. This was a decided damper and we decided we had done enough exploration for one season, and that it would be well to go to some place that we knew something of so I suggested Bridgnorth which I hope will not turn out badly. The weather, of course, since we have been here has been far too hot to get much work done. As the effects have been somewhat tame, so far, we have only been doing watercolours. It is very fine wooded country and more to my taste than anything I saw in the Eastern counties.

I hope we have had the hottest of the weather as it makes work very difficult. If you are within motor-shot so to speak of this place, sometime during the summer we should be very pleased to see you.

That is a recurring refrain about heat, as in this to Behrend:

6.7.30
. . . We are having boiling hot weather which makes it very difficult to get anything done in the way of getting things together and sometimes I sets and thinks and sometimes I just sets! ! I have just opened one of the numerous appeals which bombard me at this time of year headed—Will you give some lonely lad a holiday? Which is thoroughly a propos of the situation.

In the absence of full illustration it would be tedious to chronicle the outings year by year. If this should ever be undertaken Steer's part-impressions of each place are on record in letters, chiefly to Gray and Blackwell. I will choose, more particularly, for one reason or another, the seasons spent at Richmond (Yorks) Chepstow, Montreuil, Painswick, Chirk Castle, Dover and Brill. In two respects beside choice of pitch this pilgrim in the steps of Turner echoes the pioneer, for Chirk recalls that other great country house, Lord Egremont's Petworth; Dover and the Dogger Bank sea-fight the historian in paint of the British Fleet with the captured Danish ships at 'Spithead', the 'Death of Nelson at Trafalgar' and the 'Temeraire's' last trip. There is a third analogy: happy visits to the house of a patron, Geoffrey Blackwell, like those of Turner to the Fawkes at Farnley Hall.

Richmond (Yorks)

Of the well-established routine I was a witness when, on Steer's second visit to Richmond (Yorks) in 1903, my wife and I, as well as Tonks, were neighbours of the Three.

Steer was the still centre of a trio in which the other two were complementary figures. Brown most looked the artist with his picturesque, deeply carved head. Spare of frame, severely upright, slow to speak, but revolving problems in a singularly honest mind devoid of humour, he pounded the roads or piers and chased golf-balls with a determination to keep himself in trim. W. C. Coles was all rotundities and lazy good nature, a talker and jester; at one moment the polished host ('Can I assist you, Madam, to another slice?'), at another the abandoned rake, frequenter of bars, and constantly engaged in little plots to take a rise out of his companions. Steer had a liking for 'holding hands', as he put it, when painting, and the three took station together at each chosen spot.

On Sunday there was no painting. The ritual was a morning walk, prospecting for subjects, a big midday meal, and after repose and tea an evening stroll. Once snooze and tea were sacrificed; Tonks and I joined the party for a long tramp and climb to discover a point from which the indefatigable Turner had painted one of those topographic views of his, which had been a good deal obscured by a growth of trees. We reached the spot, a pub-less, tea-less desert, and a dispirited band sat dutifully down to sketch. Steer, throwing up the sponge for once, declared who 'took the cake', but so poor was the pretender to a phantom prize that its author tore it up on the spot.

We had rooms looking over the market-place and church. The Three were on the other side of the river, where Steer had converted a disused chapel into a studio, from the vantage-point and shelter of whose high steps he painted the stormy *Richmond Castle* at the Tate and *The Shower* in Blackwell's collection. Tonks was elsewhere in the town. It was a dour and wet season. The Three went forth carrying, as well as their other tackle, little platforms to keep their feet dry, for Steer had not yet given up painting a big canvas in the open. Tonks, on a memorable day, defied the heavens. He sat in a downpour, going through the motions of painting a water-colour, and carried home his sodden portfolio with a gloomy satisfaction. I was driven to take cover in a draughty entry, commanding the market-place and church.

On a middling good day a picnic was plotted. The rest of us bicycled; the Three chartered a carriage and set off. At the first hill Steer was 'heated' or became conscious of a 'draught', and the carriage was closed. We picnicked in a glade, not without anxiety. When we had downed our victuals and sherry an improbable incident followed: *Brown unbent*. Poising himself on a low bough, he swung backwards and forwards and vacantly smiled. 'No sound of joy or sorrow' was heard: 'dumb surprise' held the onlookers; the fatuous moment passed, and our friend was his grave self again. We pushed on to Leyburn, ransacked the great shop of antiques, and returned. Alas! Tonks was called in and had to diagnose *intracostal rheumatism*.

Of an evening the day's production of our three friends was stood up, considered and criticised, or Steer and Tonks would come round to us to draw and talk. Tonks had decreed that at nine o'clock precisely, and not before, the whisky bottle should be opened: once he forgot the time and gave no signal, but time remembered his masterful will and the cork leaped out to the second. It was there that Steer began the portrait of my wife, by a lodging house lamp. It was completed in Chelsea, with a Whistlerian night-background of river and bridge and lights. He unearthed a full-size study for it many years later.

In addition to my wife's portrait Steer made a wash-drawing of myself, which I had forgotten till, in 1939, with his absurd excess of modesty, he asked Gray whether he thought I should care to have it. I sent, as small change for gold, a little profile I had drawn of him that same summer, and got in reply this culmination of self-depreciation:

2.10.39
It is very kind of you to have sent me such a charming record of my early days, when the world seemed such a pleasant place.

It has been very much admired by all who have seen it, especially by Ronald Gray, who came in for a few minutes last night.

Personally, it appeals to me, being a pure line drawing, a thing which has always been a closed book to me, but which, none the less, fills me with admiration when so successfully stated.

A drawing by Steer of Edward Stott, dated 1894 and reproduced on page 36 gives the lie to such over-modesty.

What we called 'Number One' subject, as the most obviously inclusive, was the view on the other side of the river embracing the bridge and Castle piled up behind it. Steer's view of this was, under pressure by Furse, bought by Lady Harmsworth, and is the subject of the following letter to its painter from Roger Fry.

17.1.09   Chantry Dene, Guildford

At last I have succeeded in buying for the Metropolitan Museum of New York one of your pictures. It is the one that belonged to Lord Northcliffe. I think it is Richmond, Yorks. You will remember it from this very rough memory sketch; at least I hope you may in spite of the horrible tricks my memory now plays me. It is one I admire very much and which fortunately pleased those Americans who saw it over here.

I want to write a notice of it to our Museum Bulletin and should be immensely obliged if you would tell me (1) whether it is Richmond, Yorks, (2) in what year you painted it. Also you might tell me the absurd and irrelevant fact which I have quite forgotten as to where you studied, as I ought to mention it in introducing you to America. I hope this may lead ultimately to some recognition of English Art in America.

I hope you like my American friend A. B. Davies's things at the International. He is one of the few men there whose work interests me.

Another warm tribute to that season's painting came from George Clausen:

10.12.03   Widdington, Newport, Essex

I was in at the New English yesterday and *must* write a line to say how much your works delighted me—all of them, but especially the *Shower*.

I don't know when I've seen anything that gave me more pleasure; it's so fresh, and easy—like nature. (I mean of course that it looks to have come about easily and naturally).

I hadn't time to look in on you.

For sites following the Yorkshire group Turner was again a safe lead. At Bridgnorth, Ludlow, on the Severn and the Wye, at Corfe and elsewhere he had blazed the track, and Steer carried always with him on his excursions a miniature edition of the 'Liber Studiorum' for reference and inspiration, as an Authorised Version of English Landscape. As time went on the choice of a place, with attendant complications of accommodation and latterly of nearness to London on account of the old nurse, began to worry the Slade teacher as summer term advanced: there was an anxious tension among the 'Cronies' while guide-books and letters about quarters were discussed, and when first impressions were reported.

Mr. George Charlton, one of Steer's colleagues at the Slade School, describes the change from the comparative trance of teaching to the tense activity of painting.

28 MRS. D. S. MacColl, 1903-4

29 (a) P.W.S. by D.S.M.

29 (b) D.S.M. by P.W.S.

Steer's leisurely attitude was, I imagine, reserved for London. In the summer of 1929 he came down to where I was, at Long Melford, to see if he would like it. It was a very hot summer, and at 3 o'clock on a blazing afternoon he and David Muirhead arrived by car from London. I was postponing further work to the cool of the evening, but not Steer; we were off for a tramp of the surroundings, he having given me no time to change my carpet slippers. After a hour of this I began to talk about tea in my apartments. But, oh dear, no, a hurried Council of War was held outside my door. Steer was for staying, but Muirhead 'didn't like willow trees'—and their car was dashing them to Harwich for further reconnoitring. I remember Steer's stiff collar becoming completely limp.

Chepstow

Severn and Wye have, time out of mind, been holy ground for English poetry. Milton summoned Geoffrey of Monmouth's nymph Sabrina from her river to free the Lady from an enchanter's spell in Ludlow woods; Pope, yes Pope, took up the song with

> Pleased Vaga [Wye] ecchoes thro' it's winding bounds,
> And rapid Severn hoarse applause resounds.

A letter of the poet Gray, the month before his death in 1771, is less stilted.

The very principal light and capital feature of my journey was the River Wye, which I descended in a boat for near forty miles from Ross to Chepstow. The banks are a succession of nameless wonders.

Chepstow Castle, he adds, was among his acquisitions, 'no bad harvest, in my opinion.'

In the previous year the worthy William Gilpin made the same river trip under rain, sketching the castles as he went, to illustrate, in aquatint, his 'Observations on the River Wye and Several Parts of South Wales, *relative chiefly to Picturesque Beauty*'.

The 'Picturesque' was thus launched on its fashionable course, meaning, for Gilpin, simply 'pictorial',[1] but the adjective became attached to the picnicker's growing interest in rocks, caves, waterfalls, ruined castles and abbeys. Like 'Impressionism' later the epithet was rationalised, becoming the modest third in a trinity with the Sublime and Beautiful[2] when taste had recovered from the first shock of mountain 'horrors' to call them 'pleasing', reassured by the 'daring pencil' of Salvator, the 'dashing Rosa'. Gilpin had put 'Nature' gently in her place, 'too vast in her scale' to attend always to the 'front-screen' and 'side-screens of the winding river area', but Goodrich Castle won high marks as 'correctly picturesque',

[1] Pope is quoted by the Oxford Dictionary for 'what the French call *very picturesque*' in 1712; Steele used the word in 1703.
[2] Sir Uvedale Price, 'Essays on the Picturesque', 1794.

G   W.S.

giving 'consequence to the scene'. Usually 'something or other', Gilpin hints in his gentlemanly way, 'is not exactly what it should be.' In fact, as Steer put it in his ruder workman's lingo, there is apt to be a task of 'filling up the corners'.

On the heels of literary explorers the indefatigable Turner, from the age of sixteen, had toured the West, as so much else of England, Wales and Scotland in pre-railway exploration, often on foot. Ludlow, Monmouth, the Severn, the Wye to Chepstow and beyond are all noted in his earliest and 1798 sketchbooks; but that same year Poetry, in the neck-and-neck race, struck its profoundest Landscape note with Wordsworth's 'Tintern Abbey'.

In early days, he recalls:

> The sounding cataract
> Haunted me like a passion: the tall rock,
> The mountain and the deep and gloomy wood,
> Their colours and their forms, were then to me
> An appetite; a feeling and a love,
> That had no need of a remoter charm,
> By thought supplied, nor any interest
> Unborrowed from the eye.

Now that was doubled by

> a sense sublime
> Of something far more deeply interfused
> Whose dwelling is the light of setting suns,
> And the round ocean and the living air,
> And the blue sky, and in the mind of man.

That interfusion of the entranced mind with the excited sense is what stirs behind visual 'consequence', like a muted counterpoint, in the painter's image of a mouldering castle or monastery.

Steer's first reactions to Chepstow were not all favourable. The country-side was too much cut up by walls and hedgerow trees, 'vegetables', he called them, borrowing, I think, from Sargent, who snorted the word explosively at all trees and adored Thomas Seddon's *Jerusalem and the Valley of Jehoshaphat* for its nudity. Steer was to find his account this time, not in a wide prospect, but in cliff-like immediacy. His search for a place and early impressions are recounted in a letter to Tonks:

We are beginning to get shaken down here and have been so far only water colour-ing. The place is beginning to shape better than I thought it would at first, but it is not easy to get good points of view as there are too many vegetables and high walls. Before settling here we went to North Wales, starting with Carnarvon, which has points but not enough. From thence we went to Llanberis and Beddgelert, Harlech, Aberdovey, Machynllch, Welchpool and then here in desperation, so you see we have seen a great number of beautiful places as Coles put it. He is now peacefully sleeping on the couch with his watch chain reposing on his stomach, the result of a long walk which Brown took us this morning, when we got a magnificent view of the Severn looking back to the Stroud hills. We have not been lucky in our studio accommodation this time and have only been able to get some rooms over a shop, not at all ideal. I wish we were nearer to you and Gray it would have been very nice. Brown is exceptionally young and active this year, and rejoices in the fact that there is no level ground about, so we have to drag about up hills at an angle of 45. I like the drawing of the arrival of Coles very much, especially Brown's legs; also the historical party at Loseley. Tell Gray I had a most dreadful dream the other night so bad I can't write it. Brown and Coles both send kindest regards to you and Gray and hope you are comfortable in your 7 foot room. We have bed rooms 30 feet long and 25 ft. wide. Coles wants to know where you are going to place your 'secondary dark'.

Steer's ultimate judgment of Chepstow is given in a letter to G. L. Behrend:

5.6.32
Thank you for your interesting letter about a part of the country that I have known in my boyhood as we lived at Whitchurch for 17 years so that I know more or less most of the places you mention and I therefore have a sentimental feeling for it and I think Chepstow is really the plum. . . .

The up-and-down of his spirits is reflected in a letter to Gray, one of his rare efforts to be facetious as a correspondent. On paper he 'jocked wi' dee-ficulty', and another example, a letter to Tonks, is too cryptic in its fun for quotation.

Wyecliffe House, Chepstow
The melancholy of a summer's afternoon, the melancholy of many summers' after-noons, weighs on my soul, and the dismal gloom of the summer holiday is strong within me, for perhaps you don't realise that we say and do the same things in the same way and at the same time every blessed day of our lives? No, this is not quite true, there is one thing that I alone don't do every day which I would tell you if I were not afraid that you might inadvertently read this dirge to Tonks. However I must not be-come domestic. When we take our customary walk in the town the elder of my com-rades always keeps twenty paces ahead. I have often pointed out to him that if he would only start twenty paces in the rear we might manage to walk together, but without avail. Needless to add that the smothered smile which greets the advanced guard develops into loud laughter by the time that I and that worthy fellow Coles are reached; hence our elder companion, not observing the smothered smile, concludes that we alone are the objects of female derision. We are all suffering from colds, Coles has had one, I have got one, and the Professor thinks he may have one. . . .

An account follows of a breakfast conversation in which Brown be-trayed his astonishing innocence of sexual experience, an immunity which must have been a rare safeguard for the teacher of so many charming and adoring girl-students. The letter ends with a change of key:

Since starting this epistle, I feel much more cheerful, in fact I may say I have not had a single dull moment this summer. Tell Tonks we have taken his advice and drink cider made on the premises, also we have taken his advice with regard to dropping the evening whisky; we drink Hollands instead. I hope you are having better weather, we are having worse if possible.

I have reproduced one of two 'Elegant Pastorals' in Turner's 'Liber Studiorum' devoted to what he calls, in a sketch-book note, 'My Chepstow.' A comparison of the former of these with what Steer made of the subject is an excellent lesson for the grudging critics who think (if that is the word) that strong 'influence' excludes 'originality'. The margin here is narrow, but decisive. In Turner's admirable composition the light is of evening, from the side; the tide is high, and the castle, while giving 'consequence' to the scene, is a background for the vigorous foreground, with its silhouette of cattle and bushes which repeats the Castle motive with Turnerian subtlety of variation. Steer's is starker treatment; the Castle more centred and confined, the foreground 'corner' accordingly reduced and simplified, the light Constable's midday sun, raking down the cliff almost vertically and striking glistering reflections from the mud uncovered at low tide.[1] This, the best of three pictures, is the Tate Gallery version, that in the Windsor collection a good second, the more extended view in the Liverpool Gallery comparatively dull.[2]

I have unluckily never visited Chepstow, and was puzzled why Steer had not also tackled Turner's second and adorable view of the Castle from above with the great stretch of Wye and Severn beyond. The Town Clerk of Chepstow, in answer to a question whether that view is still obtainable, or ever was, quotes the opinion of a local artist to the effect that the scene, as a whole, never existed: the point from which the Castle might be painted is thickly wooded with sturdy oaks.

Steer was later (1909) to treat the windings of Severn at his ease from a window elsewhere;[3] but more quintessential is the 'Rainbow' view of the year before at Ludlow, now in the Tate Gallery. Ironbridge and Bridgenorth in 1910 and 1911 were rich fields for him, and the smouldering sunset over the latter in the Daniel collection is one of his colour-miracles.

A letter to Gray from Ironbridge is one of Steer's more lively summer reports:

1910   Tontine Hotel, Ironbridge
Many thanks for your letter and I am glad to hear you have been having such a gay and festive time with M . . . and other members of the aristocracy. I suppose you have suffered from bad weather much as we have, but I think now it has taken a turn

[1] When the picture was before the National Gallery Board this feature completely puzzled even Mr. Heseltine, himself in early days something of a landscape artist. Lord Plymouth happily came to the rescue and won a grudging vote from the aloofness of Lord Lansdowne.
[2] The three are reproduced in the Phaidon Press volume devoted to Steer.
[3] Pictures in Aberdeen and Manchester Galleries.

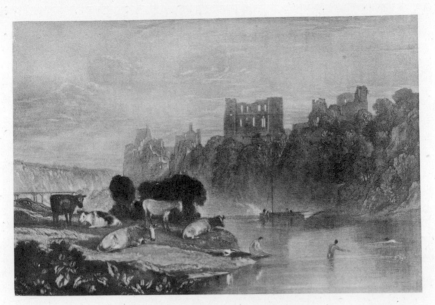

30 (*a*) CHEPSTOW CASTLE *by J. M. W. Turner*

30 (*b*) CHEPSTOW CASTLE *by P. W. Steer, 1905*

31 (*a*) CHIRK CASTLE, 1916

31 (*b*) LADY HOWARD DE WALDEN, 1916

for the better. Brown has been very downhearted about it and has done a good deal of cussing; happily there are a hundred and twenty steps near the hotel leading to the church and when he wants to let off steam he runs violently up and down them thereby expending his superfluous energy. Coles is in excellent form, and is driven to his work in a wagonette; consequently he is getting no thinner, in spite of which he places his secondary dark with the regularity of clockwork. He has a leaning to the barmaid, and in the furtherance of his suit absorbs numerous gins and bitters which Brown in an unromantic vein terms 'bar loafing'. Coles assures him however that his intentions are strictly dishonourable.

We are very happy in this sweet spot apart from work, and have the use of a large room 40 ft. long, with five windows, in which we all work hand in hand. I heard from Tonks some time ago from Wemmergill. He appeared to be pleased with things in general, soaring on the wings of Mrs. H. to the empyrean (I never thought of her before as a biplane), from which giddy height he sees us mortals including Count Osberg pursuing our mundane avocations. I understand he has now returned to earth and is arranging his new studio. Brown and Coles send their kindest regards and are glad to hear you are able to work. Please remember me very kindly to the Hammersleys. I had a letter from Mrs. Rothenstein who tells me that Will starts for India on Oct. 15th.

Montreuil

It is not surprising that Montreuil, of all foreign places, should tempt Steer to a second visit since it has many attractions for the painter. Montreuil 'sur-Mer' is withdrawn now from the sea, but rises, an old stronghold, above the mill-stream at its base over a plain of farms with fortified yards.[1] The bastions of Mauban, the great military engineer of Louis XIV, encircle it, and a boulevard, shaded by tall trees, follows their course. In the shelter of those earthworks lies a delightful little town, whose alleys yield glimpses of half-hidden gardens and whose great market-place is swept, on one side, by a terraced-up pile of shops and houses. The main hotel, with its memories of Sterne and other English travellers on the road from Boulogne, became headquarters for Haig and his Staff during the 'Great' War, an old coaching hostelry with central court galleried above and draped in huge festoons of creepers over an airy salle-à-manger. This was occupied; but near it Steer pitched his summer tent. He was prejudiced against much French landscape, Picardy views, for example, with bunches of foliage at the tops of endless road avenues of poplar—'dam silly' he swore—but in Montreuil he found, on a height recalling our own Shaftesbury, a growth of old, unpollarded trees that might have been English. These he painted on a greater and a lesser canvas, entitled *Outskirts of a Town*. The 'Grande Place' also he attacked and his picture of it, shown at the Goupil Gallery after Judge Evans's death, brought

[1] A picture surviving from Steer's first visit is of poplars and stream, recalling the subjects of Monet on the Epte.

from Roger Fry a tribute which I am glad to reproduce. His early admiration had been followed by silence from the date of Steer's declining to leave the 'New English' for the fresh secession he was organising. The boycott spread among obsequious followers and culminated in Fry's article, 'The End of a Chapter.' Steer did not greatly mind, but it went against his sense of behaviour that a colleague as lecturer on the Slade School Staff should attack one of his fellow-teachers. He was the more pleased to receive Fry's warm letter about the Montreuil picture:

17.11.18

As I know you feel that I've sometimes been unjust to your painting—though never consciously so—it is a pleasure to me to tell you how wholeheartedly I admired a landscape of yours which I came across the other day at Marchant's. It's a great empty '*place*' in some French or Belgian town with a great space of sky above.

I expect I've seen it before, but it came to me with a new sense of delight, which shows that one grows new perceptions. I thought the relation of the sky to the buildings and the foreground one of those discoveries of proportion that only very real artists make and the colour and handling altogether beautiful.

Don't bother to answer this, which I write merely for the sake of acknowledging a debt of gratitude. Good painting isn't so common that one can afford not to be grateful for it when one comes across it.

In the summer of 1907 another notable figure in English painting, Frank Brangwyn, was lodged in Montreuil with a following of pupils who filled the great inn. The two leaders were on nodding terms, but did not coalesce. There was an episode, however, alarming to Steer's watchful friends. In the Brangwyn party was a charming American girl who, having made Steer's acquaintance, volunteered and was permitted to carry part of his painting tackle to the daily pitch. There was growing anxiety on his behalf as the season went on; but it ended without any declared renunciation of bachelorhood. The testing-point came later, when Poppa and Momma arrived in London and Steer was summoned to dine. He shied: 'was out of town', and sent his regrets. Chelsea breathed again.

The inseparable 'Three' were joined at Montreuil by Ronald Gray and shared a house run by the typical 'bonne à tout faire', Marie, whose sharp eye and tongue were a delight to Steer. She appears in his view of the house. In that season's surroundings, so much more sociable than those of the customary English outing, there was dancing and practical joking, such as Coles loved, to fill the off-hours. Coles, this time the victim, was persuaded that a fair student had fallen for his charms, and paraded before the window of her lodging in his finest array. An earnest seance of table-rapping was stimulated from without by the whiz and bang of fireworks attached to the windows, and I came in for ocular evidence of one 'morning after' the ball.

Deceived by the seeming nearness of Montreuil to Ambleteuse, my wife and I accepted an invitation to lunch with Steer's party and set off at a godlessly early hour on a railway line that ambled, with frequent pauses for introspection, along the convolutions of coast. As hours went by the memory of roll and coffee turned prehistoric, and it was ravenously that we sought our friends when the customary hour for solid food had already passed. We found them, alas, somnolent, after a night of dancing, and even the excellent 'Marie' seemed to have revelled and lost count of time. An apéritif was produced: lazy discussion of the night's events fought with yawns; figures of Harrington Mann and others loomed in the hunger-haze, and it was after two when we were summoned to recall the nearly forgotten practice of eating. Then we took our places for the interminable saunter back.

When the Montreuil party broke up Steer made a dash for Paris, his first visit since student days, and his last. He captured some excellent watercolour views of Notre Dame from the river-side, and a letter from Francis James speaks of a 'stunning' watercolour of St. Cloud. He saw, on this visit, the memorial exhibition of Cézanne's work, five years before the enormous 'Post-Impressionist' fuss in London over a painter who, as one of the 'Impressionist' group, had a true gift of colour, but by defect of eyesight progressively lost a never secure sense of form. Steer told me the picture that struck him was the early still-life of a black clock, shell, and other objects. It is an exquisite piece; was shewn at the 1933 French Exhibition in London at Burlington House, but disdained there by the hierophants of toppling jugs, botched and bashed apples, bodiless clothes, muddled perspectives and the rest, thought to illustrate the cubical nature of the sphere, the geometry of colour and other brave profundities. The excitement had behind it a dealer's ramp: collectors were foreign, rarely French, and the liquidation of the Swedish Consul's Parisian collection would have brought, but for the War, peace to the fever of the shops in Paris and London. At the height of it Steer and Tonks determined to by-pass the perpetual yapping of the patriarch's name by calling him 'Mr. Harris'.

Painswick

Of the Painswick outing in War year 1915 Steer's brother-artist, C. M. Gere, has furnished the following memories:

9.9.43

One morning in the early summer of 1915 there was a knock at my door and Wilson Steer appeared. He had found his coast resorts impossible under War conditions, and had come down to ask if I could recommend rooms at Painswick for the summer

months. I found him quarters at a small stone house standing on the left of the Chelten-
ham road just beyond the 'Adam and Eve' Inn. It was then the highest house in that
region close to the upper slopes of Painswick Beacon, which is where he wished to
paint. He liked the hill with its quarries and pine woods and the distant prospect over
the Severn vale to the Malverns, Dean Forest and the Welsh Hills, and he worked
there very happily but hadn't enough light to paint indoors, so I helped him to get a
room in one of the iron sheds by the quarries. He got permission to put in an extra
window there, which made the place into a possible studio, with subjects at its door.
There he painted the series of his Painswick oils. I often joined him on the hill, where
his rotund and almost immobile form, on his low heavy stool, became a recognised
landmark.

The oil *Quarry among pines* was painted looking South from the ridge, but for its
background he crossed over and used the view over the Severn facing North. He
missed water and buildings, and would probably have moved on elsewhere but for
Wartime difficulties.

John Kemp, former head master of the Gloster School of Art under whom Steer
had his earliest instruction, had retired to live at Clevedon, and I wrote to tell him that
his distinguished pupil was at Painswick and would be much pleased if they could
meet. So one day Kemp made the journey to my house and Steer came down to see
him. I can't remember the talk: I know that Kemp had found it difficult to understand
Steer's work of that period, his own being strictly traditional; but he was a man of
character and charm and there was evidently real affection between the two.

Later, Steer was joined by Brown and Ronald Gray. Years before Steer, accompanied (I think) by Brown and Tonks, had been to Haresfield Beacon and thought it
the best painting ground on the Cotswolds; so we all had a picnic there and Steer did
a drawing which may still survive though I've never seen it again.

Chirk Castle

In 1916, on the invitation of Lord Howard de Walden to paint his
Denbighshire castle, Steer had a change from stuffy lodgings or cramped
hotel rooms and their monotonous fare to the luxury of spacious quarters
and the other amenities of a great house, but also to thoroughly congenial
company. Attached as he was to his fellow painters, he often wearied of
professional talk, and only came out of his shell in less strenuous company,
especially of larky young people. In his letters to Blackwell and Gray he
says 'he has enjoyed living above his station very much, and it is wonderful how soon one becomes accustomed to the best of everything'. In those
letters, discreet as ever, he says nothing of the high jinks customary in
English country house parties, but he entered into them with spirit. Here
are notes about his work and surroundings in two letters to Blackwell:

31.7.16.
    Just a line to report progress, which up to the present is slow as the weather, although
fine, has been very trying and close, and there is no going out here unless up and down
a hill; in fact most of the good views of the Castle are rather far away, and to put it

quite plainly I am not in for an easy job as things are on such a huge scale; for nearly a week I was quite alone, which was rather depressing, but I think soon there will be some people staying here. There is a good room which is at my disposal when I start oil painting, which I hope to do next week. I am writing to Newman for the necessary equipment. Brown wrote to me that he has had an unexpected invitation to Scotland and Cole, I understand, is moving from Yelverton to Lynmouth.

I was very glad to hear of Holmes' appointment to the N.G. I think it quite right that he should be promoted. . . . So far I have seen nothing of his lordship, who is with his regiment in Suffolk; but her ladyship, who I like very much, has been here on two occasions for a short time; there are three children, very fine samples, a boy and girl (twins) rising four and a little girl of eighteen months. The secretary who is here at present is a nice man and does all he can to make me comfortable.

August

Thanks for your letter. The weather for the most part, as you say, has been too fine, but lately it has become more broken and there have been some fine skies, but difficult to nail down. I have got a number of canvases started, but cannot tell how many, or if any, will come to anything, and at the moment I am not feeling at all happy about them, but such as they are you shall have second choice. The Castle itself is a tough nut to crack; I am trying a near view and a couple of distant ones. Apart from work, life passes like a pleasant dream; many nice people staying here and games and music after dinner. There is a very large organ with a pianola arrangement which renders all the finest masterpieces; a great treat, I assure you.

A letter to Gray adds some details:

I am enjoying myself very much in a quiet way. There is a very nice man called Captain Oppenheim staying here; he has got phlebitis in his leg and we have great chess contests, besides many other people who come and go. As for work, I have got a good deal in hand, in fact I have probably bitten off more than I can chew, but I have a nice room to work in with a top-light, so there is no excuse, and the weather on the whole has been good. I find most things rather difficult to coax into a canvas as it is all on such a vast scale and the castle is quite a change from my ten-foot square room of last year.

With his sympathetic host and hostess Steer quickly became a fast friend. They have been good enough to draw on their recollection. Lord Howard de Walden writes:

I remember asking him very shyly if he could give some helpful hint to an amateur struggling with water-colours; to which he replied, 'There is only one hint I can give you. A water-colour is nearly always a fluke. If you go on doing them flukes will happen a little oftener.'

I have toiled a good deal since, and am still waiting for the flukes to happen. I think he was quite happy here: even though the company was rather young and riotous and far from artistic. Nevertheless they were all devoted to Steer, although they did tease him a little about his great coat. In fact he joined very heartily in one or two little practical jokes at the expense of some of the party.

I do remember asking him (again with a good deal of diffidence) about the price and value of pictures. It was soon after his *Bend of the Severn* had been bought by Aberdeen for a large sum and some huge prices had been paid by America for various English pictures. He evaded the question for some time and then said suddenly, 'I don't think any man ever painted a picture worth £2,000 I certainly never did.'

When he had finished his several pictures of Chirk and its surroundings I was again compelled to approach him nervously about the price. I was well aware that his pictures were then fetching four to five hundred pounds in the ordinary market, and I could only afford two or possibly three. I was therefore startled when he said, 'Take what you like of them for £50 apiece.' I was very much taken aback. I could not very well say anything, for it is as impertinent to tell an artist he is charging too little as it is to tell him he is charging too much. It was a very great kindness on his part which I very much appreciated, although I was embarrassed. However, shortly afterwards, I was able to buy a picture of his at the New English at the market price. I hope he understood my feelings in the matter, I think he did, for he was a very understanding sort of man. At any rate he told my wife he was very glad I had bought it.

It was very interesting to me to watch his method of working. He used to go to his chosen spot day after day to do a quick watercolour of the effect at a given hour. After that he retired to my workshop and with the sketches pinned around him proceeded to do a synthesis in oil.

I daresay many other little details will recur to me especially if and when I can discuss it with my wife (who was devoted to him).

I don't know if these oddments can be of any value to you but it is the best I can do at the moment. I had the greatest admiration and respect for him myself both as a man and an artist. There was something monumental in his absorption with his own art and his indifference to the general scuffle of opinions.

Lady Howard de Walden adds the following notes of a happy episode for hosts and guest alike:

We all loved that dear Mr. Steer. He would enter into any discussion in his slow quiet voice, always amusing and wiser than anyone, with an all-round knowledge and cleverness. Evan Charteris, for instance, fancied himself at chess. I suggested that I knew someone who could beat him. This he doubted, and I brought Steer to his home one evening. It was fun to see the shy modest man making havoc of Evan's chess, for of course Steer won! We had at that time lots of young people to stay. He was always ready to join in the fun and dressed up as a brigand for dinner one night, in long stable boots, and other odds and ends we found for him; large curtain rings on his ears, a wig and an old Cromwellian hat. He looked splendid and enormous and suddenly took on a violent personality. His was a remark which came out as a 'Punch' joke in another setting. The young men present tried to persuade him to walk with them up on the hills and not always 'just potter about the grounds' as they put it. He asked why should he, and they said 'Well! to keep fit!' He looked slowly round the table, with a gentle twinkle and said 'Fit for what?' They were duly humbled without being snubbed and we all laughed. He disliked trees; said they spoilt the view. He never wanted to go abroad as England was beautiful enough for any artist!

Once a man said how ugly the slag-heaps near the mines were, and how they ruined the scenery from our terrace. He was a man Steer disliked very much and he thought the best way to show it (politely of course) was to do a picture from just that spot. It is lovely, one of his best! He wrote to me frequently—always with affection and wit.

We have two fine full-sized Coromandel Screens that he found, and showed me when we went for a ramble round antique shops. His taste and knowledge were inestimable. He says in 1917, 'I had a strenuous time at Mrs. Hunter's as I attempted to paint 3 children, which involved 3 sittings a day. I quite felt I was emulating McEvoy' (the latter was having a great social success at the time).

I can only add that he had charm and gentleness. How shy he was and yet always ready to join in any fun and nonsense. He was sincere and wise with a lovely sense of humour: a perfectly delightful friend.

Steer's letters to Lady Howard are no perfunctory compositions. Here are some passages:

I have written you three letters and torn them up, they all seemed so foolish and inadequate to express my feelings about my most delightful visit, which when I look back seems like one long and pleasant dream.

I enjoyed the stunts and I enjoyed the souls, tupy, tufy, but far more the first part of the time when we were arranging the room and the peaceful sittings in the Bow drawing-room.

I wish you had put on that black velvet dress you wore last night for Coburn. I liked it so much but perhaps you had not got it at Chirk.

I hope to have one or two frames here by to-morrow afternoon to try round the portrait.

5.10.16

Chelsea seems a little dull after the delightful time I spent at Chirk, and my house seems to have contracted, but I got a warm welcome from my Nanny and the Tom cat. I met Augustus [John] yesterday who took me to his studio and showed me an enormous canvas 40 feet long, filled with gipsies, ruffians and children. He told me it had taken him seven days. I thought to myself, quite Biblical.

No date   Chelsea

I suppose two continents are awaiting with impatience the publication of G.M.'s new book, so far I have not subscribed as I feel doubtful as to whether I am sufficiently grown up to read this kind of literature.

No date   Chelsea

I was most interested to hear from M'Evoy the account of his visit. He appears to have had a lovely time, although he did not go into detail quite as much as I should like. I gathered the unfortunate saloon had been subjected to another raid; how sad, after all our exertions of last year, but no doubt it is a better winter sport than a summer one. I remember how heated I used to get dragging sofas about. I'm sure if I had been there I should have been so heartbroken that I should have retired to bed for the day, but apart from this regretable incident my soul is filled with disappointment at not being able to have accepted your very kind invitation. It was most tiresome that the New English took into its head to be hung at that time.

Dover

A change from river-scenes to coast began in 1912 with Portchester. Most seaside places were ruled out by their lop-sidedness in composition, but harbours, estuaries and muddy inlets with stranded craft gave rich material for pictures and unnumbered watercolours. Portchester was followed by Harwich (1913 and 1929), Bosham (1914), Alum Bay (1919), Maldon (1920 and 1933), Southampton Water (1921), Shirehampton (1922), Shoreham (1926), Whitstable and Sandwich (1931), Greenhithe (1932), Walmer (1934).

Dover Harbour in 1918 stands out in this series as the subject of a public commission. During the 'Great War' painters were employed by the State to illustrate its aspects and events, abroad and at home, for the collection to be housed in a War Museum. The assignment to Steer was a happy choice, not only as material for a picture, but one near his heart. He was critical of our old Army Command, but had a profound love and admiration for the Navy. War restrictions and the winds hampered the execution of his task, but he summoned all his obstinacy to cope with them. Here is a letter to Blackwell from the 'Hotel National', Waterloo Crescent, on 12th July:

For the first few days I put up at the chief hotel, which was anything but satisfactory being both depressing and rather sloppy, but here in this private hotel I am quite comfortable, the food being excellent and it is quite likely that ere long I may regain my lost figure.

With regard to work I see great difficulties ahead as the place is so vast, for instance the end of the Admiralty Pier is a mile and a half and another point called the Eastern arm is about as far, and then when one gets there it is almost impossible to get shelter from the wind which today is blowing almost a gale, however, although at the moment I am feeling heavy hearted, hope springs eternal and I must try and stick it.

I think if there were no war on this would be quite a good place, but all the permissions and restrictions seem to have a paralysing influence and at times I feel I cannot bear it, especially when I have done a bad water colour which occurs too frequently.

I have come across a man here that I can't have seen for thirty years, the master of the School of Art; he was very kind and offered me the use of his studio, but I had already taken a room overlooking the harbour, it was pleasant to have a talk about the old Walberswick days when I met him.

Another is to Gray on August 12th:

Congratulations on the Collison bequest. You are lucky to have something to warm you during the coming winter, as from the accounts I read I don't think there will be much coal. I shall look forward with pleasure to drinking your health in some of the choice vintages on my return, which however I don't think is very near at hand as work does not seem to progress very rapidly: in fact I am feeling pretty downhearted as there is not only the usual difficulty of doing the job but whenever I sit down to sketch some blighter comes up and wants to see my permits, which is very upsetting just in the middle of laying in a wash; in short I am regarded as a suspicious character; in fact the landlady of the house where I engaged a room to work in told me that after she had let me the room she had a sleepless night thinking she might be harbouring a

32 (a) RAINBOW LANDSCAPE OVER SEVERN, 1901

32 (b) DOVER HARBOUR IN WAR, 1918

33 (*a*) JAMES HAVARD THOMAS, 1895

33 (*b*) DAVID CROAL THOMSON, 1895

spy. However, on going to the police station to make enquiries they set her mind at rest as I had previously reported myself there. I find the whole situation very unpleasant and I look forward to the time when I can shake the Dover mud from my feet. If it wasn't for the infernal restrictions it would not be half a bad place, but they sort of put me off work.

I think we ought all to be extremely grateful to Tonks for the way the war has been going. No sooner did he take over the command than things at once improved and have gone on steadily doing so ever since. You call him Lord Tonks. Pooh! When he returns he will probably be created the Duke of Vale Avenue.[1]

There has been as yet no serious raid here, only a small daylight one which did not amount to much. I am told the Huns call Dover, 'Hell corner' and give it a wide berth unless there is a good chance, which I am afraid there may be one of these nights.

In a third to Blackwell on 25th September he writes:

I don't quite know when I shall be able to return home, it all depends on how the picture goes, I think after many struggles it is beginning to shape, but ships and boats are very obstinate customers to deal with, and after spending much time and labour in putting one in, one finds one has got it in the wrong place. I am doing the harbour from the end of the Admiralty Pier, looking back to the castle and cliffs, and spend most of my time in the studio now which is more agreeable than sitting out on a three-legged stool and being regarded with suspicion; however they have got accustomed to me now at any rate on the Admiralty Pier, and don't bother me any more.

He had fought the gales on the exposed pier to some purpose. His Dover Castle, town and cliffs are spread out between a windy sky and troubled waters with a converging movement towards them contrived from the defensive nettings and boats that point inward and the launch with its wake that rushes out. This is accurate history and beauty well married and one of the few works of permanent value as pictures in a well-meant but mostly weariful company.

Steer inevitably discovered a delightful secondary painting-pitch at Dover, chiefly for watercolours, in the little back bay and shipping behind the great harbour. Both in 1918 and on his second visit in 1920 he had a rich crop from that source.

Related to this commission was a private one from Admiral of the Fleet Sir Cecil Burney for a picture of an incident in the Battle of Jutland. Steer was at infinite pains to get the perspective and details of his subject correctly set out, and obtained from the Admiralty models for the ships, but modern sea-engineering and fighting afford little of the old close-set engagements, and no brave show of wooden walls, towering masts and sails such as rewarded Turner's brush. In the end Steer was so dissatisfied that he offered the picture to his patron for the price of its frame, and the offer was accepted.

[1] Tonks had gone out as an artist with the British force attached to the White Russian army

Incidentally, however, an investigation at Rosyth took Steer to Scotland for the first and only time. Miss Hamilton writes:

During the Great War No. 1, Steer became a Special Constable, but I rather think he had to discontinue because the bronchial attacks which beset him were aggravated by patrolling his beat at the Power Station on cold nights. His work for the Admiralty eventually brought him up to Rosyth on a visit to Sir Cecil Burney, Commander in Chief. Owing to my brother, then Major Hamilton, having a Staff Appointment as War Department Lands Agent in the Scottish Command, Mother and I were tenants of a Georgian flat in India Street, Edinburgh. One day in February Steer unexpectedly arrived at breakfast time: his train had come in very late the previous night and the only hotel he could get into could give him no more for a meal than Bovril, golden syrup and bread! He had not advised us of his coming. That day he went on to Admiralty House, a visit he much enjoyed. He loved the Navy and the Navy seemed to love him! He used to say how much he liked the visits of the Naval experts at Cheyne Walk in consultation over the paintings which followed his Rosyth visit.

Upon his return to Edinburgh he stayed for a few nights at our flat. He was out all day looking at the City, searching for coins and so on. He came back enthusiastic over the beauty of the pictures at the Scottish National Gallery; considering it of the highest quality and most complete collection outside London. He liked the maroon walls as being the best background for pictures and would refer to them in after years when he expressed an horrific fear that the National Gallery in London would eventually have tiled walls in the zest for whiteness!

He was quite startled with the clear-eyed beauty of the Scottish girls and remarked the loveliness of their complexions and their sensible shoes!

He was full of fun while he was with us and laughed until he was speechless over some good Scottish stories my brother recounted at dinner. Steer always wept if he was roused by wit. He complained to me with sadness just before his death that wit no longer existed—he had no tolerance for what he called the silliness of the B.B.C.

As usual he went fast asleep on one of those Edinburgh evenings when some friends came in after dinner and one of them explained to him what art was, but I did not wake him as he sat by my side on a sofa, and told them it was the sea air!

He was glad, after all, to return to London, and at the Waverley Station could not resist the Johnsonian remark that it was the best view he had yet seen in Scotland! Years after he would refer with horror to a war-time train journey from Scotland to London.

Major Hamilton had tried to tempt Steer by the view of Edinburgh from the high place of Calton Hill, but he was recalcitrant.

Steer's handing over to Admiral Burney for nothing a picture he was dissatisfied with, after spending great pains upon it, was characteristic of the unexacting attitude in such affairs to which Lord Howard de Walden has been a witness. I experienced the like openhandedness in the matter of my wife's portrait. The windfall of a little legacy allowed me to ask for 'a sketch', which he priced at £50, but to satisfy himself he abandoned the sketch, which long afterwards he sent as a gift, when I had forgotten its existence, and completed the picture, for which he refused further payment. He never could bring himself to dun a customer, and one noble owner of an important landscape, doubtless by an oversight, remained his debtor. He came to the conclusion, however, that gifts of paintings were seldom valued, a not uncommon experience of artists, whether in friendly transactions or in the calls which organisers of charity sales lightheartedly make upon painters, musicians and actors.

Nor was he at all eager to extend his practice overseas. Nettled by local criticism of his pictures at Melbourne, he rebuffed an offer from the National Art-Collections Fund to represent him in Queensland. He had resented the apathy of Pittsburgh and other cities to which he had sent without result, and my attempt to introduce Duveen as a gangway for his pictures to the States came to nothing as will be told later, in face of his indifference.

Maldon and Hythe

I will interpose here two letters to Tonks, one from Maldon in 1920, the other from Hythe, Southampton Water, of 7 September, 1921:

I am very glad to get your most interesting letter and to hear that you have struck such a delightful spot, which in spite of some discomfort must be a land of enchantment and eminently suited to the gentle art of water colour painting. I expect you are able to discard subjects which if they were here we should gulp at, however in a small way this is not altogether a bad place; the chief interest so far as I am concerned being the river which at low tide is a tiny meandering stream but at high tide, almost like a lake with plenty of barges and a fleet of small fishing boats which are extremely graceful in shape and very interesting when they manocuvre the sails except that they do it so quickly that it is heartbreaking to get hold of. . . .

In our lighter moments we sometimes indulge in a mild form of excavation which consists in overhauling earth thrown up from the digging of the foundations of a house and we found several pieces of a Roman urn and some bits of bone. I need hardly say that Brown gets restive while this folly is proceeding and eventually when he can stand it no longer goes for a solitary walk.

Drummond Arms Hotel

I am afraid you will think I have been a long time in writing you my annual letter, especially as you sent me so many kind messages through Gray when I was ill and I much appreciate your thoughtfulness in putting many people off writing, of which I have had an exceptionally heavy dose what with my illness and my domestic affairs, which have been a source of worry, but happily my niece came to the rescue and in several of her letters she has told me how extremely kind you have been to her, for which both she and I are equally grateful. Mrs. Ormond and Miss Sargent also seem to have treated her with much kindness thanks to your introduction, and she was delighted with them both. Gray has been a perfect brick, and has done for me all that any human being could possibly do. All I regret is that I am afraid I have made him waste a great deal of his time, but latterly we have got to work and are beginning to find out the possibilities of a not too promising place which affords nothing in the way of landscape, as this country is far too bunged up with trees, so we are entirely dependent on the large ship-building yard where we also have a good place to work inside. We can also boast of a pier nearly half a mile long on which Brown disports himself, as he says it does not wear his boots out and he also knows exactly how many yards he has done, a kind of measured exercise which seems to give him much satisfaction. The hotel luckily is very comfortable and the food excellent and not too rich; it is chiefly frequented by yachtsmen, but at present we are the sole occupants. I don't think the fishing here would interest you as it is done with a lot of worms and a lead weight which they throw out a long way and now and then catch a tiny flat fish. There is a ferry-boat to Southampton where we occasionally go to shop, and the other day I fell to a Dutch sea-piece which I, the fatuous owner, attribute to Van der Velde, but perhaps it is by a lesser master! ! I hope you like Godstow and find plenty to interest you. A man I met here told me it was a delightful spot. I had a very nice letter from Child[1] who seems to have found an ideal spot. I wonder if there are 'kiddies' there. Moore seems to have fallen foul of dear Edmund [Gosse], who seems to have said that G.M. does too much re-writing. It was rather a scathing letter in the 'Sunday Times' to which I have not yet seen a reply. We are having very fine weather here just now which looks like lasting, and I think we must have had less rain here than in most places as the country still looks very parched. I don't remember a summer like this since 1911. I suppose most people like it but, as you know, I don't!

Brown and Gray who have just returned from a handicap on the pier join me in love.

P.S.—Brown has just shattered my hopes by pronouncing that the sea in the alleged Van der Velde is 'woolly'.

Thame: Brill: Long Crendon

After the summer partnership with Brown and Coles broke up, Steer's chief companion was G. L. Behrend, a pupil of A. W. Rich, the prolific and successful watercolourist, whose systematic method was said never to fail in his own hands and was imparted to troops of summer students. In 1923 and '24 Steer and Behrend were together at Brill and Long Crendon, and also at the neighbouring Thame, where John Fothergill, a brilliant Slade student, had diverted (in more than one sense) his talents into equally shining inn-and-diary-keeping. In reply to a request for memories of Steer he sent me a letter which hammers some nails so firmly in their place that I will quote the greater part of it, including, by his permission, a passage which has already appeared in 'The Diary of an Innkeeper':

... I didn't really see much of old Steer, either shy of him or too fidgetty to bear easily his Olympian peace. He was always attended by Tonks, who directed the conversation or rather did it and kept it prettily obscene and away from art-shop—I mean art-theory, which was unintelligible to Steer. It's true he went to sleep always after dinner, guests or no guests, but two minutes of theory sent him quite suddenly to sleep. Genius, it seems to me, is not the capacity of taking pains; anyone can do that, char-

[1] C. Koe Child, secretary of the Slade.

34 (*a*) AMINTA, 1899

34 (*b*) THE BLUE GIRL, 1909

35 Mrs. (Violet) Hammersley, 1907

woman or bank clerk, but infinite capacity for being selfish. . . . As Steer didn't
invite people to dinner, he was thought mean. It was simply that he didn't think or if
he did he wanted to be alone and untroubled; so his worldly wealth was useless to
him. Others would have thought it might be spent to some good purpose. But I
remember a very kind thing from him. I bought at a show one of his water-colours for
£30, and a week later he found out who had bought it and sent me £15. I did not
see much of him at Thame because I was occupied trying to make the place go.
Behrend was there at the time and I like to think that there started a very long painting
friendship between them. B. I hope will tell you lots. He has nothing to do but count
over his thousands of (some beautiful) watercolours. Steer used to smile indulgently at
B's Trollopian method and output. . . . He wrote to me from Bridgnorth [here I copy
out of the 'Diary'] ' . . . Behrend has just received a letter from Balmoral couched in
these terms:

Dear Mr. Behrend,
The King has heard with much pleasure and interest of your unique achievement in
painting 12,700 water-colours, thus exceeding the number painted by the late A. W.
Rich, and also attaining a further record of 1,400 water-colours in one season.
His Majesty warmly congratulates you upon this remarkable feat, whereby you
have established a new and greater record in the history of our national Art.
Yours very truly
Stamfordhambridgnorth

N.B. Whilst B. was doing his last two water-colours at Bridgnorth he was in possession of a four-leaved clover sent him for luck. And yet it was Steer who got the O.M.
later and not Behrend. [Still quoting Diary]. Steer came to stay for his summer's
painting, and Montie Pollock sent George Behrend here for the same purpose. Without one another's company I don't know what they would have done, because there
are no subjects here and the weather was worse. Anyhow, in five or six water-colours
Steer created grandeur for this open town and market-place, a few months after he had
immortalised the rather nasty horse-pond in the Town. Was it by coincidence or out
of spite that the Council filled it in? One evening to relieve the monotony, I told him
that we'd had a baby born. He looked frightened at first, then asked, 'Is that really
true? I didn't know it could be done so quickly.' God knows what he expected. It
was done cheaply as well as quickly, for when Dr. S. sent his bill of £7, I told him
that he had acted under false pretences, for if I'd known it was to cost only that I'd
have had twins. It was cold, and Mr. Hawkins opposite did a brisk trade with Steer
in waistcoats. These he would take off and put on again several times in the morning:
the temperature was never right for him. Behrend wrote to me from Shoreham, 'we
have no news for you as we have barely recovered from grief at the failure of Steer's
recent attempt to swim the Channel. He started, full of buck, and was in the water
exactly two seconds when, owing to the excessive choppiness, he regretfully returned
to the beach, where he partook of a hearty meal and redonned his waistcoats.'
Draughts were the chief bug-bear of his life. . . . Once he came to me and said,
'Fothergill, I've found the ideal place to live in—a Diving Bell'.
Referring to my modification of the definition of genius though neither one nor the
other defines it at all, but only the conditions for its growth, Steer seemed always perfectly happy about his work. If you said to him, 'Steer, that's a most lovely picture of

yours,' he would quietly reply, 'Yes, it is.' Tonks was never satisfied, he was always talking of the one really great picture that he would do before he died.

As for Steer's teaching . . . there ought to be a sort of All Souls for geniuses to protect them from that necessity, a distracting and futile thing. . . . He talked very little. What little he did say was as rich and clear as his painting.

Long Crendon Steer and Behrend had seen when at Brill and had luck there in lodgings. The latter writes:

Steer wrote to me in the early summer of 1924, evidently in some trepidation, that he had taken a house (between the two of us) for 10 weeks, at Long Crendon from an advertisement, without having seen it. He went into Newmans' for colours and turning over the 'Studio' noticed the advertisement and replied. After agreeing he went down to look at it. He found its description was not exaggerated, for it was modern but constructed with beams taken from an old farm and there was a studio, a comfortable parlour, a panelled dining room, and a garden which had a wall peach from which we had a couple of dozen; there were also 2 Jersey cows. Everything else was convenient, so we had a good summer there. The arrangements were amusing. A young but capable village girl arrived about 7.30, tidied up and prepared breakfast and did the bedrooms. The 20-year old cook from the village turned up about 10 o'clock, prepared lunch and went off when she wanted, returning for tea, and again for supper. My knowledge of housekeeping is nil, and in London Steer left it all to his housekeeper. Our only effort was on the first day when, passing the butcher's, we invited a suggestion for two not very great meat-eaters, and accepted 'a nice neck'? When we returned we found a curious joint of apparently several feet long. That was our first and last effort at the butcher's, or at any other of the trades-folk.

Steer was here, as ever, the friend of cats:

The house adjoined a farm where there were a number of cats. The farmer apparently did not feed them—no doubt thinking rats and mice were sufficiently nourishing. They were always hungry. One stormy evening a small thin famished and halfgrown cat jumped through the two or three inches open casement of our room, and retreated under the raised stove. It was weak and ill from hunger. Steer tried to tempt it with bovril. Eventually it began to take food and in a day or two went out of doors again, but returned daily, and soon after seven every morning I would find Steer in his dressing gown outside, feeding it. Eventually he walked two miles for some liver. From a half-starved tigerish little animal it grew to be a plump cat, and when he returned to Chelsea at the end of our stay the cat went with him, in an attractive early Victorian woven basket he had picked up in Thame. I state these facts as an illustration of Steer's kindliness and humanity. Even when I swatted house flies he said it was a pity to kill them, as they were pretty things.

Another of Steer's prospectings, to an old-fashioned dancing-ground that would attract him, was not so fortunate:

He proposed to W. T. M. Hawksworth and me that we should go and have a look at Gravesend as a possible painting ground. On the way back, approaching the once famous Rosherville Gardens which had been derelict for years Steer suggested going inside and exploring them, because the main entrance gate happened to be open.

After wandering about for a bit we came to the entrance of a dark stairway, and Steer, leading the way in his usual slow way, descended into the growing darkness, but suddenly stopped, with an exclamation, for he had come to the end of the steps and there was only an invisible black, deep cavity. He naturally got a bit of a shock. Some time subsequently he wrote to the mayor of Gravesend about this danger, but got no reply. In any case we were trespassers!

Steer the collector is the subject of another note:

It was his custom to buy something wherever he might be, and if there were no antique dealers he would go to a general dealer's, and assuredly picked out the only thing worth having. He never came home without something, if only a single Georgian spoon, or a coin. At Harwich there was no antique dealer and hardly a general dealer. He managed to find an immense and heavy bronze tuning fork weighing pounds, which he gave me for a paper weight. When struck, it booms like a lightship's foghorn, and makes the room vibrate.

Behrend adds to the legend of the Yuan Chinese find, bought for a trifle, this note:

When a young man, Steer and his friends used to go to dances at Walham Green run by a certain J.S. and frequented by models. J.S. was a general dealer in old music, books, and other things. Steer asked him if he had any Chinese or Japanese things. 'Only one' said he, and produced a rolled-up painting on silk. Every time it was unrolled bits of silk used to crack off, so Steer had it opened and framed under glass.

This companion of ten summers adds his testimony to the unbroken good-fellowship of his painting-partner, his easy humour and kindly attitude towards all acquaintances discussed. What did disturb him at times was the kind of demand that came from unknown correspondents:

A lady once asked him to go to her place in Scotland and paint a picture of it 'with the sky black with grouse' and Mr. X asked him, during the last war, to go up in an aeroplane and paint a picture looking down on the clouds.

The view of them from below was task enough for their lover.

Winter Work

Portraits: Models: Subjects

Steer was in largest measure a landscape painter, but he combined with that figure-and-portrait-painting, inversely like Gainsborough, who was famous for his portraits but had his house stacked with unsold landscape pictures and drawings.

In faculties and tastes the two had much in common, though Gainsborough was fiery in temper, Steer solid, and to the outside observer even stolid. Both had a turn for trenchant colloquial phrase, but neither was bookish. Gainsborough's master-passion was music, and his description of what a painting ought to be is borrowed from the structure of melody. 'One part of a picture ought to be like the first part of a tune, that you guess what follows, and that makes the second part of the tune, and so I'm done.'[1]

In early days I had judged Steer impervious to verbal poetry. George Moore, to a group at the Hogarth Club, had delivered one of his pet diatribes against Browning: his single devotion was to Shelley, of whose 'Sensitive Plant' he was one among few persevering readers. I flung in to convince him of Browning's quality, citing a number of pieces, lyrical or dramatic, including that most tremendous crescendo in literature from 'The Ring and the Book':

Abbate, Cardinal, Christ, Maria, God—

then, with a gasp of shame and despair,

Pompilia, will you let them murder me?

and I ended with the line:

Eve also has her one, supreme, forsaken star.

Steer to rescue Moore, cut in with 'I suppose that was Sidney Starr'. I had personal grounds later to realise that he was by no means deaf to poetry, though meagrely acquainted with its masters; best, perhaps, with Byron, and could be moved by lines like those from a play of Yeats sent him by Lady Gregory 'extraordinarily apt in their resemblance to [Hugh] Lane', who, he said, was the only saint he had known:

> I choose for the championship
> The man who hits my fancy. And I choose the laughing lip
> That shall not turn from laughing whatever rise or fall,
> The heart that grows no bitterer although betrayed by all,
> The hand that loves to scatter, the life like a gambler's throw;
> And these things I make prosper, till a day come that I know,
> When heart and mind shall darken that the weak may end the strong,
> And the long remembering harpers have matter for their song.

Steer, though in a less passionate way than Gainsborough, loved great music. Both men brought into portrait and figure scenes a landscape element, texture 'all a-flutter, like a lady's fan' or like the throb of light upon flowers. Lord Howard de Walden recalls that his wife had been bewailing her fate, in that she could not get a satisfactory portrait of herself:

---

[1] Letter to Jackson of Exeter.

36 (a) THE MUSLIN DRESS, 1910

36 (b) THE MIRROR, 1891

37 (*a*) PILLOW FIGHT, 1896

37 (*b*) THE SURF, 1924

John had ruined a perfectly good portrait for no particular reason after seventy-odd sittings. McEvoy had given her up in despair, and so forth. Steer said, 'I am not a portrait painter, but if you like I wi¹l do a small landscape of you,' which he did.

His landscape backgrounds to figures do not necessarily mean out-of-door study. G. L. Behrend notes:

At Greenhithe he received a letter from a curator, saying that his committee had purchased a portrait by him of a lady seated in a garden, and wished to know who the lady was and the place. Said Steer to me, 'I painted it in my room. She was a model. The garden was a rhododendron in a pot, which I happened to have.'[1]

Steer offered me for my 'Artwork' article a photograph of his earliest portrait, that of a gardener, Theophilus Morgan, now reproduced. It has the intense application, with some of the clumsiness, of unpractised talent. A portrait of himself at the age of eighteen is, on the contrary, easy and accomplished, with a romantic swagger very different from the straightforward Uffizi figure of his middle years. The portrait of his teacher, John Kemp, preserved in the Gloucester School, is in a deeper vein, an intensely expressive rendering of the man. To his own portrait came to be added other members of his family; his mother reading and asleep in two swift sketches on small panels; his niece, Dorothea Hamilton, in an admirably direct, unaffected notation; his clerical brother also, in more official style.

Out of school, but still learning from contemporary masters, he painted, under Whistlerian leading, the delicate small portrait of Sickert now in the National Portrait Gallery, the full-length, less successful *Lady in Grey* (Mrs. Montgomery) and the exquisite *Jennie Lee*. A curiosity in perspective grouping, traceable to Degas or Japanese design, marks the *Mrs. Cyprian Williams with her Children,* of 1890, and the studio scene in which he appears as the painter, beheaded, a little later. Family groups for patrons followed, the Cyril Butlers and Geoffrey Blackwells, and the Lawton children for Mrs. Charles Hunter.

Two figures of men from his immediate circle in their forthright vigour and spontaneity, those of Havard Thomas, the learned sculptor and exorbitant character and of Croal Thomson the dealer, make one regret that Steer was too preoccupied with the lovely sex to spend time upon the masculine. A filmy, small portrait of Lockett Thomson, a son, measures the change from the painter's youthful attack to the old man's lingering, gentle touch.

Another man's portrait, the head of W. P. Ker, was commissioned by his University College students in 1923. That great scholar and humorist was a mystery at first to his colleagues, Steer and Tonks. I do not think

[1] Evidently *Summer* in the City Art Gallery, Manchester.

Steer ever got on free speaking terms with a man whose tight-lipped taciturnity could excel his own: the sittings must have passed in silence or even sleep. The sitter always described his portrait as 'The Blue Boy', but it is a good one. Tonks also was disconcerted when Ker sat as a guest at his dinner-table without a word, but had a rapturous revulsion when he was treated, as the Professor's guest, to a week-end at All Souls.

Commissioned portraits occupied more of Steer's studio hours than I had realised: he did not display them. He perhaps felt that in the elaboration of some among them he had indulged himself at the expense of first and better impulses. Two accounts of the pains that went to the design and revision of such works I am allowed to give. First, from Sir Kenneth Clark:

I went to see Steer when I was at school. I had been given some money by my parents, and my first thought was to go and buy one of his pictures. I got an introduction to him from Charles Sims, who was a friend of the family and gave me occasional lessons in painting. All this must have been in 1919 or 1920. Steer was rather put out by this unusual visitor, and we had a, for me, somewhat embarrassing interview. He said he had nothing at all which he could offer me, although he afterwards relented and produced the Nude of a very fat girl seen from behind which is now in the Tate and did not appeal to me, as well as being somewhat beyond my purse. I was bitterly disappointed, but at the time genuinely supposed that Steer had no pictures there. I afterwards realised that his back room was full of pictures, including a number of small sketches of exactly the kind which would have gladdened my heart; and I have often speculated on the strange combination of laziness and defensive machinery which led him to send me away empty-handed.

After my marriage, when we came back from Italy, I wanted to have Jane painted, and although I knew that Steer was by no means always successful as a portrait painter, he was so much better an artist than anyone else I thought we might take the risk. I forget who it was re-introduced us; perhaps Tonks, whom I used to meet at the Burlington Fine Arts Club. Steer was rather less alarmed at the appearance of two young people than he had been by a school boy, but he looked with dismay at Jane, who at the time wore her hair in an Eton crop, and said 'I am afraid there is nothing to paint'. However, he finally agreed to do so, consoled by the sight of a yellow silk dress with a full skirt. He began a small oil sketch, which after a few sittings became extremely beautiful, and on the basis of this he was about to start on a large picture when by an evil chance Tonks persuaded him to finish up the sketch. I suppose the idea appealed to Steer's natural laziness, although as a matter of fact it involved him in an immense amount of work. At this time Tonks was himself painting his small conversation pieces. The scale and manner suited him, but I doubt if it would ever have suited Steer, and he set himself an impossible task in trying to turn a picture conceived as a sketch for something large into a finished miniature. He certainly took immense pains. Sittings went on for over a year. The yellow dress got very dirty, in spite of the fact that it was carefully folded up by Flo after each sitting and most conscientiously aired in the kitchen before Jane came in the morning. Steer might have stopped painting the picture at any time during the year, and it would have been as good as it is now, perhaps better; the face is painfully over-painted, but the dress is beautifully done and the still-life enchanting. I am glad to say that it includes the concave painted side-table, some of the gold splash bronzes and the Japanese toad. As sittings went on, Steer lost all his suspicions. He talked to us on every topic, and his traditional wisdom and humanity was a very useful offset to the adventurous intellectualism of Roger Fry, who played a great part in our lives at the time.

Steer always struck me as one of the most catholic and unprejudiced judges of painting I have known. I was at that time still involved in the ridiculous science of connoisseurship, and it was interesting to see how Steer came immediately to the conclusions which connoisseurs only reach after years of laboriously shuffling photographs. He liked all things which were not allowed in Bloomsbury—French colour prints, late Chinese and even Japanese bronzes, Chelsea porcelain, etc., and I was always grateful to him for encouraging me in my own taste at a time when it seemed almost immoral to like anything which was not ugly.

Another account is kindly furnished by the sitter, Mrs. Thomas Lowinsky. In this case, however, the particularity of treatment accorded well with her taste and that of her painter-husband:

Steer had just abandoned a very interesting portrait because his sitter had twice sent him a note postponing her visit. In consequence he said that he would paint me on two conditions: that I never put him off at the last minute and never asked him when the picture would be finished. These promises I kept. I sat to him three mornings a week from ten to half past twelve for about one hundred times, not once failing him, in spite of catching bad colds during the winter from my proximity to a window which touched both the ceiling and the floor and let in the wind from the Thames. Steer worked between me and the gloomy grate and thus blocked the only warmth.

In the beginning he had no preconceived plan and I realised that he could not decide what he would like until he had tried it on the canvas provisionally. The background, thinly painted, was changed again and again, and only became gradually as elaborate as it is now. It started by being a flat brown wall. Soon, over a corner of this, he sketched part of an Italian picture of a ruined temple, which later was to serve as the landscape for Mr. Lockett Thomson's portrait. Then came an empty room and finally Steer's own drawing-room crowded with bric-à-brac. The long reflecting mirror and the oriental shawl thrown across the back of the arm-chair were still later additions, whilst the occasional-table with the opened letter on it appeared after I had imagined that all the still-life was finished.

The clothes presented even greater difficulties. Steer loathed the fashion of that moment and went through my wardrobe in despair, begging me to wear one of some Victorian dresses that he had found in King's Road. I said that I would let him choose any material and design that he liked and have a gown made, but that I would not put on second-hand clothes untouched, and he would not have them cleaned lest they should be spoilt. At last, in one of my trunks, we found an old white muslin frock spotted with black, which Steer could tolerate. After some while he arranged a lace shawl aslant one of my shoulders, at the same time scraping out a pearl necklace that he had suggested with great skill. The skirt, which had been originally of the same stuff as the bodice, became orange and green and was done from a model, while I was on holiday in Italy. Thinking that I should have on my return to give quite twenty more sittings, I was astonished to find that in my absence the picture had been completed and was being exhibited at the New English Art Club. The reason for the change of skirts, Steer later told me, was because so much white low down in the composition detracted from the head, which in a portrait should be the focal point. Steer was delightful to sit to, as he was most considerate and gentle and loved gossip and jokes. He did not, however, seem to get pleasure from painting, for he never came up to his own high standard and was always dissatisfied with his efforts. If I asked him on leaving whether he had done a good morning's work he was quite annoyed, and if I was tactless enough to inquire during the rest, 'How is it going?' really upset.

My husband and I consulted Steer about the hanging of the picture in our house. He advised that we should place it on the wall of the room where the prevailing light came from the same side as that depicted in the picture itself. He further instructed us to avoid white or light walls. To stress this point he declared that picture-dealers, who knew their business, invariably displayed their wares on deep red velvet or damask.

This last point of a red background was a cardinal one with Steer. He lamented the supersession of the old ruddy flock-paper background at the National Gallery, and thought Holmes, whose appointment as Director he had welcomed, had in this gone astray, 'turning the place into a lavatory.'

In one portrait, commissioned by the painter's affection, elaboration of study certainly justified itself, that of Steer's old nurse, already referred to. The background was part of the memorial, being that of her habitual station as an invalid. Steer, so often the capturer of lovely surface aspects, in that good sense 'superficial', was here profoundly intimate.

Only once or twice did he apply himself to something more ambitious in scale and manner, recalling the *Mrs. Sheridan* and *Perdita* of Gainsborough. The outstanding case is that of Mrs. (Violet) Hammersley, seated on the ground, and placed, in eighteenth century fashion, against an out-of-door landscape background. It is, with no conventional use of the words, 'in the grand style'. Mrs. Hammersley has been good enough to write of it and of Steer as follows:

It was in 1902 that I first met Steer at the Grove, Hampstead, where my sister-in-law, Mrs. Hugh Hammersley, entertained a small group of artists and literary men on Sunday afternoons.

Steer, Tonks and Ronald Gray formed the nucleus, for they seldom missed a Sunday, but Augustus John, Sargent, the William Rothensteins and MacColls, Max Beerbohm and Sickert were of the company.

Steer seemed a static figure, seldom moving from his seat, always a small one, on which his ample figure overflowed, but he must have preferred it to an armchair. He mixed little in conversation, but listened intently, occasionally putting in a shrewd remark or sally, cocking his head on one side, and raising his voice to a falsetto. He chuckled with joy when other peoples' foibles were on the *tapis*, for he was amused by the weaknesses of his fellow beings, though without malice, especially when they related to matters of sex. He adored a joke, and the more rabelaisian the better, always with due respect to the company.

In the Autumn of 1906 it was decided he should paint my portrait, which was to be on a grand scale. Mrs. Hugh lent me a wonderful oyster-coloured satin dress made by Jean Worth, but not in the fashion of the day. It had blue velvet bows on the bodice, but after making a sketch he decided to replace them with white. I sat to him all through the winter and spring and into the summer of 1907, and we had near a hundred sittings. These took place at 109 Cheyne Walk, and I sat on a sofa at the end of his charming drawing room with its three French windows facing the river. I used to drive down in a small pony-cart, and I can see his tall figure at the window, standing expectant. The sitting lasted about three hours, and I do not remember ever being bored for a moment. The fire crackled pleasantly; the light in the room was lovely, whatever the weather, we chatted of persons, politics and things, and I suspect I did most of the talking. One of our subjects was finance, in which he took an interest, and as I had occasion to hear a good deal about such matters he would speak of investments and companies, fall and rise of markets. Considering that he never was a fashionable portrait-painter (how he would have hated it!) he died leaving a remarkable fortune, and I conclude he was both shrewd and lucky in the matter of investments.

Once I induced him to come and see 'Ghosts'. He was immensely amused at Thorpe's masterly performance of the mad son. He loved telling the story of poor Thorpe on his way from performances in the States, losing in an Atlantic storm the false hand he wore, which fell on Grossmith, sleeping below. As Steer 'did' Grossmith saying: 'Thorpe's hand fell on my chest' he would shake like a jelly.

When I was still sitting to him that summer (1907) we had arranged he should actually come and spend a week-end at our house on the river. Preparations and packing went on all the week, for how could one tell what the weather might be! All must be prepared for. Thick and thin underclothes, suits of varying weight went in and out of trunks. Tonks joined us at Paddington, and all went well. The weather was heavenly, and we sat out under a great chestnut tree in front of the house. Steer wore a straw hat; kept a finger in his shirt, and from time to time went into the house to remove a garment or put one on according to the moisture of his skin. He was afraid of catching cold, and I now think it was a huge compliment that he should have ventured on the risks of week-ending in a strange house.

On Sunday he came out in our gondola, an imposing figure in the high black seat beside me. No effort need be made; tea was passed on a table over our heads by the gondolier, and he could observe the busy scene in Maidenhead Lock with acute concentration, making, one was sure, mental notes of everything.

Steer, as a wise man, enjoyed good food and greatly esteemed good claret. Once when a lyrical eulogist of wine dined with me a very fine claret was offered. When I asked how he liked it he answered 'quite a pleasant little wine', upon which Tonks exploded and Steer, though more restrained, never forgot the crime.

For many years I was in the habit of dining frequently with Steer or Tonks, alone, or someone made a fourth; often it was George Moore. Steer would say: 'I've told Moore he must be careful what he says before you, and *not* to insult the Catholic Church'. All went well for years, but in the end the restraint was too much and he burst out into an obscenity which distressed Tonks and Steer a good deal, though no doubt they were much amused. After that when G.M. came round of an evening he always called out to ask whether I was there before coming in.

When Moore, and even when Tonks died, he resented any expressions of sympathy, or the idea that he could not do without his friends. G.M. had become rather a worry and a bore, he said, and Tonks very strange and unaccountable the last years and 'so terribly sensitive about his work'. He himself, though he would take up the cudgels in defence of the school of painting to which he belonged, did not mind any personal attack. When he met Roger Fry one day at my house he whispered: 'I see I've come into a hornet's nest—shall I come out alive?' None suffered less from vanity or inferiority complex, and he shewed his great detachment when he grew old and lost his sight. He seemed to have no self-pity nor wish to batten on anyone. He enjoyed a visit, and the last time I saw him I read out some extracts of Jacques Blanche's 'Autobiography', which amused him. But I think he needed no one and it was wonderful that a man so nervous about disease and accident should have endured the Blitz as he did. But he was *sui generis*.

'Subject' Pieces

Between Steer's portraits proper and his few 'Subject' pieces there is an indeterminate group, portraits and portrait sketches of models. One of these, the early *Aminta*, a portrait of the lady who became Mrs. and later Lady Walter Russell, has a masterly breadth and vigour. Others share with it the fortune of a charming subject, like the early lamplight studies of Rose Pettigrew, or the intensity of colour and character that render the version of a favourite model, Miss Montgomery, in the Dublin *Blue Girl*, so enchanting. There are slighter studies also, that have grown from the brush like flowers, and remained unvexed by afterthought. An example is *The Black Bow*, p. 116.

Steer's properly 'Subject' enterprises were few, emerging from a borderline plenty of models dressing, undressing, or nude, with vague titles like *Bathsheba*, or *Susanna*. With Autumn days came in their season. As might be looked for from a man with small compulsion towards dramatic expression, his early tentatives in incident or studied motive are clear borrowing. The *Signorina Gozo in 'Dresdina'* (N.E.A.C. 1890) and *Prima Ballerina Assoluta* (1891) are a trespass on Degas-Sickert territory, not successful and not pursued; the later canvas of a model dressing combined with the headless painter in a mirror reflection is an example of cutting in the Degas-Japanese, or photograph-accident fashion, as had been the Cyprian-Williams portrait group of floor perspective without the regular sitter's 'throne'. The *Molly Dickson* (N.E.A.C. 1891) is a far echo in pose of Whistler's *Little White Girl* standing by a mantelpiece and mirror, as *The Alps at Earl's Court*, close under Maclise Mansions, is a loan, without interest, from the same Master's 'Nocturnes'. In the matter of borrowings a false scent, the art of Albert Moore, has drawn off the hounds of criticism. Moore had made of Whistler an accountant of colours in 'harmonies' of one or another 'chord'. That preconception was never Steer's, still less the marmoreally fixed 'classic' shapes elaborately draped in damp 'butter-muslin'; very well in their way but looking as if they would split if they fell over. The only property in common was a sofa, an inevitable furniture when seated or recumbent figures are painted, and Steer found an excellent new motive for these in the two pictures *Hydrangeas* and *The Muslin Dress,* where a girl is playing with a pussy, thus occupying the model and introducing another of his interests. The first of the 'sofa' subjects was so named in Steer's 1894 exhibition, a thoroughly original and beautiful piece, notable, like others, such as *Rose Pettigrew* on a sofa and the same lovely model in *Jonquils,* for the broad simplicity of light and shade artificial illumination provides. The snag in its use is a tendency to over-yellowness in flesh-tints, a danger easily by-passed by substituting burnt siena for ochre or other yellow pigment.

Models in a Japanese gown before a mirror followed and others undressing or undressed. These, and the rather pert nude, with a far-away family-likeness to Manet's *Olympia,* were Fulham Road Studio pieces. Another much studied nude, called *Sleep,* was spoiled by a clamorous background as I have already noted.

A promising departure of the same period was the experiment in Old Master methods of laying-in the subject as a monochrome and glazing colour over it. This, I think, was due to the example of Charles Shannon, ardently espoused by Charles Furse. A recumbent nude in my possession, dated 1896, with a background of sea between faintly rosy curtains, was painted in that way and may have been the germ of a *Danaë* in the Hesslein Collection: a rare mythological sublimation. In the Daniel Collection is a *Three Graces.*

A more ambitious project in the glazing technique was the study for a *Rape of the Sabine Women,* which went no further. Here was a subject of strenuous action, involving men as well as women, that would have made an unexampled call upon the painter's powers.

The *Toilet of Venus* (1898) was evidently to be a translation of the undressed model to a rococo Olympus: it bordered on monochrome so far as it was carried. I cannot count the Cupid, occupied with the spectator and not with his job, happy, but again there were possibilities, abandoned halfway, here.

Most memorable of Steer's double-figure compositions were two. The earlier, Sir Augustus Daniel's *Two nude Women with a Mirror* (1901) uses the mirror ingeniously to abolish 'unresolved duality' by introducing a reflected third, but, as I have already noted, it is characteristic of Steer's disinterest in event that neither the girl holding the looking-glass nor the one reflected is occupied with the act. The later picture, *The Music Room*

(1905–6, Sir Cyril Butler and Tate Gallery) has another solution, a pyramid of standing and squatted lute-players, half dissolved in a shimmer of radiant light and precious colour. Here is a Steer unheralded by previous masters.

A solitary study, the *Pillow Fight,* marks what might have been a departure into action such as Fragonard broke the path for in his enchanting *La Culbute.* I sent Steer a reproduction as an incentive, and he loved it, but, cautious husbander of his energies that he was, he never repeated the freedom of his promising romp. There was, however, a gentle culbute from a see-saw, and other groups of figures, all of them girls, in a set of grisaille panels between others of rose silk, painted to decorate the drawing-room of Cyril Butler's house at Shrivenham; girls fishing below a waterfall, playing Badminton and the like, a far cry from the Antony and Cleopatra subject of schooldays in the Whitchurch house.

My conjecture, in the 'Artwork' article, of an influence from Tonks in the pictures, *The End of a Chapter* and *The Muslin Dress* was, I learn from Gray, well justified. It was characteristic of Steer to bear with nagging for a considerable time, but in the end to revolt sharply, as in the childish affair of the hoe. In the same fashion he endured the flouts of Coles and Brown about his laziness, but finally challenged them at Corfe to outwalk him. He led them over hill and dale till they wilted and cried for mercy. So again he bore with Tonks's exaltation of 'finish' and Rothenstein's preaching of 'probity' till he was tired and determined 'to show them.' These pictures therefore were painted somewhat in the spirit of a wager, and are marked by that impurity of origin. The invention of the figure and rendering of detail are in either case excellent, but the surroundings have not the instinctive subordination which gives value to intensity of portraiture in the *Blue Girl* of the Dublin Gallery, the concentration of *Hydrangeas* or the transmutation of models and scene into a fabric of sun and air in *The Music Room.* Critics have seized on this lapse, due to a challenge from Tonks, to imagine a much greater influence than ever existed. Steer's attitude to the Professor was one of affectionate amusement and wonder as to what hobby he would mount next, and he spoke of his going on and on 'finishing' a picture already finished.[1] It seems to me that a subtler influence than Tonks's was at work in the endless sittings for and repaintings of certain portraits and their backgrounds, namely Steer's affection for his 'things'. In the days of the blitz, when friends pressed him to take refuge

---

[1] Mr. Daryl Lindsay, now director of the Melbourne Gallery, who had studied under Tonks, found him once worried about what he could add to a picture to 'finish' it. Steer sitting over the fire with his back to the speaker, interjected, 'If you can't think of anything, perhaps it *is* finished.'

38 (*a*) GOLDEN RAIN

38 (*b*) RECLINING NUDE, 1905

39 (a) GIRLS FISHING

39 (b) THE QUARRY, 1915

out of London, he refused, saying he would rather perish 'with his things' if they must go. A portrait could be an occasion for poring over his furniture and treasures, regardless of his sitter's time, the expenditure of his own, or even the integrity of the picture.

Steer did little still-life painting, save for flower-pieces to fill up rainy days in the country and one notable canvas, *Windfalls*, on a large scale, which completely puzzled critics in the 'Anonymous Exhibition' at the Grosvenor Gallery in 1921. In the same collection was a ravishing models portrait in a red jacket, the finest thing there, called *Reverie* and now in Lord Blanesburgh's Collection.

Oil Technique

Steer's technical methods were simple and straightforward. His canvases were mostly half-primed a near white, with a 'tooth' to them, from Newman's. Later, he was more promiscuous, picking up bargains, odd in size and character. 'Turps' and linseed oil were his staple medium, with occasional poppy oil for quicker drying; hence there has been little cracking of his paint; one unfortunate instance of a portrait so affected was due to repainting in a 'tacky' condition. He was never, I think, seduced into using the fatal asphaltum, with its seductive initial depth and lustre, to be paid for by a future of pigment never dry, slipping about and cracking. It is strange that the tragedy of English painting in the eighteenth and early nineteenth centuries, whose painters sloshed happily with the treacherous medium, seems not to have reached the ears of Tonks, the Slade Professor. Much of his work has suffered from that ignorance. Steer's faith was in the main for thin fluid paint, but this was varied, in some early work, by Monticelli-like jewellery of leafage, and by overpainting when the first trial called for correction. The over-painting, completed occasionally with the palette-knife, reached at one time such thickness, with projection at points where the palette-knife had been withdrawn, sucking up the pigment, that Steer jokingly claimed to know by its weight when a picture was finished. There was one Chepstow scene, promised to a Japanese patron, which underwent desperate over-loadings in the studio and was finally given up, to reappear in the 1943 sale at Christie's, a monster of rehandling. Blackwell thought the studio re-paintings were always unfortunate. I saw less of them than he did, in his frequent visits, but I question his judgment. In one instance, the *Painswick Beacon* at the Tate, Steer told me he had rehandled the whole, land and sky, and the result is excellent.

He was wise in using panels for sketches in one painting only, without rehandling; and in the early 1894 exhibition series the cedar wood supplied a pleasant coloured ground.

In the 'Studio' for 25 December 1909 Mr. Collins Baker reproduced the list of colours filled-in and signed by Steer on a palette form; one of a series. This gives a surprising number of pigments and must represent the total battery from which he selected for a single painting.[1] He believed, however, in an ample range, and counselled Gray to that effect in 1939:

I was saying what trouble I was having with the background of a portrait I was doing of the Master of Charterhouse, Mr. Schomberg. He asked me what the yellow wall-paper was like and I found a stripe of inlay in a commode in the sitting room much like it. He asked the colours I was using and I said 'Black, Golden Ochre and Yellow Ochre'. He said: 'Of course you can't get it with those. Don't use black; try deep chrome and ash blue, and glaze it down. Why on earth you will try to paint with about four colours when there are so many! Deep chrome is a good colour and dries well, I sometimes used it in flesh colour. If a wall is yellow you must make it look yellow and luminous.' Years ago, however, he used to say the fewer colours one used the better.

His strict views on brushes have already been quoted; he made large use of sables latterly and had reacted against the fashion among Paris-trained students for square touches with flat hogshairs and the evil devices of 'wet cat' and the like some of us remember in the eighty-nineties. A filmy delicacy was his last, but no one is bound to accept it as his best, word. It is one variety in a constant and never-satisfied research.

The economical habit, however, seems to have spread to his use of brushes. Another note of Gray's reports:

Steer today (Feb. 3rd 1939), talking of brushes, said he couldn't think why fellows used so many. He found washing them such a nuisance that he only used two, one for light and one for dark colours.

The brushes would have to be frequently dipped in turps or petroleum and wiped clean. Perhaps he wanted to save work for Flo.

Collins Baker adds these notes:

Mentioning my own insufficient practice in painting I once said that I supposed he, with all his experience, found no difficulty in handling his work: the paint did what he wanted it to do: it didn't get intractable, etc. He replied, almost in these words. 'Not a bit: every time I start a new picture (in oils) I feel it's like learning to swim all over again.'

I recall his shewing me a large oil he was beginning: some castle (? Framlingham).

[1] Here is the list: Flake White, Chinese Vermilion, Permanent Crimson, Rose Madder, Venetian Red, Indian Red, Strontian Yellow, Chrome Yellow, pale and deep, Yellow Ochre, Brown Ochre, Burnt Siena, Cappah Brown, Emerald Oxide Chromium, Cobalt Blue, French Ultramarine, Cerulean Blue, Blue Black.

He pointed to a particular passage in it and said: 'I always have some bit in my pictures that gives trouble from the very start. They never go well. And this passage, here, is the one in this picture I shall have the devil of a time with always.' As I remember it was a piece of trees against the sky, at one edge of the canvas, about 5 or 6 inches long.

Muriel said to him she noticed that Reynolds never gave the hands of his sitters (or hardly ever), the individuality they should have. Steer said 'Well, with a fashionable portrait painter it's merely a matter of giving his sitter the right amount of points'. M. said 'Points?' 'Yes,' Steer insisted, 'points; like a horse, you know.'

Oh, I recall one more tiny straw: he was showing me a little nude, and said that it would not be finished (I thought it was) till nothing in it asserted itself by catching the eye above its fellows.

As you know he bought odd minor pictures: seeing something in them which was not apparent to me. If he felt he couldn't have painted them (e.g. minute Dutch marines with rigging and masts neatly drawn) he was drawn to them.

Some further notes by his Slade pupils will be given in a later chapter.

Baker, in his 'Studio' article, speaks of the heavily impasted canvases as the climax of Steer's painting. Rich as they were in succulent pigment they came about rather by dint of correction than by first intention, and like all such work, have considerably quieted down.

X

WATERCOLOURS AND OTHER MEDIA

The short entrance wall of the Dudley Gallery, shown in the photograph of the last 'New English' jury there, was given to watercolours, drawings and prints. From that small space spread a revolution or return to the watercolour *wash-drawing* as opposed to watercolour *painting* at the Royal Societies, a bastard form which aped, as far as it could, the elaboration of oil-painting, helped out by gilded mount and heavy frame. The trouble had begun with Turner, who, from his rapid notes, not always coloured on the spot, elaborated 'finished drawings' for his patrons. In 1890 the practice persisted: when I went sketching with Alfred Hunt, President of the Old Watercolour Society, he made what he called 'blots' to serve as the foundation for carefully 'finished' works. The 'New English' artists have, since then, invaded and transformed the 'Old' Society as completely as the Academy, and the heavy frames, gilt mounts and much of the 'finishing' or tickling-up process have departed. Beside those transparently-washed drawings Hercules Brabazon introduced another variety, based on one usage of Turner in sketching, *gouache* or 'body-colour', i.e. colours made more solid by a mixture with Chinese White. Brabazon had reached in this mode a rich brilliance of rendering: when he opened his portfolios for the first time, the effect was dazzling. One or two had been shown at the Dudley Gallery, and convinced that here was the most original talent next to Steer's on its walls, I urged an exhibition on Croal Thomson. He obtained a preface to the catalogue from Sargent, who had known and admired Brabazon's work; there was a huge success, and the portfolios have been emptied to the dregs since then, with ill effects, of late years, on the dead artist's reputation. Steer greatly admired his work.

In the early years he did not himself practise watercolour, and my impression had been that he began in 1903, when we were at Richmond in Yorkshire, and the three comrades, equipped with Newman's sketching folios, went forth to 'wash-in', at first somewhat in the manner of early De Wints, with a foundation of pencil. Steer, however, said he had begun at Knaresborough (1900). This was true of the manner of working he had, by 1903, adopted and stuck to throughout. Seated on a sketching-stool he held the folio well away between his knees or feet, and from a colour-box of hard cakes on his left thumb and an ample fully-charged sable in his right, he spread the tones and struck in the accents that became broader and more decisive, with emptier scenes, as time went on: an affair of atmosphere and space, mass and umbrage of clouds and trees, horizontals of sea, punctuated and given recession by a few barges or other foreground shapes. He won what I have called a 'Chinese-like' control in the placing, shape and subtle modulation of the wash, between damp and dry of the paper. More 'busy' and definite subjects there were occasionally, as in the Dover drawings. A noble example of architecture and river dates from our summer at the Yorkshire Richmond, the *Castle and Lake,* so-called, in the 'Phaidon' reproduction.

Previous, however, to this real beginning there had been something of a false start. J. L. Henry, who was a kind of shadow-Steer in Dudley Gallery days, told Gray that he had given Steer some first aid about water-colour at Swanage in 1890: he was again Steer's painting companion at Boulogne in 1894. Here comes in a concatenation I had not realised till I received from William Rothenstein a letter in which Steer wrote, after his generous fashion, 'MacColl's exhibition looks stunning, I and Sickert helped him to hang it.' Sickert, I remember, helped, and we lunched to-gether: Steer must have looked in afterwards. It was he who had first encouraged me to exhibit. On the visit to my studio I have already men-tioned he spotted on the wall a drawing of market umbrellas round the fountain at Perugia in 1887. He said, 'I thought Francis James was the only watercolourist.' James's master, Brabazon, had not then exhibited. I had practised since the seventies, but never shown. On this hint I sent those *Umbrellas* to the 'New English' spring exhibition of 1892, where it was bought by the Scottish dealer, Alexander Reid. The exhibition of which Steer wrote was the opening one of the new 'Goupil Gallery' at 5 Lower Regent Street. It took place in the winter of 1903-4, and was followed by that of Brabazon. Incited, apparently, by both, Steer had taken up watercolour and returned from a summer at Boulogne and Rye to arrange his, the third, Goupil exhibition in December, 1894. I am tempted here to extend a somewhat personal parenthesis so that I may recall David Croal Thomson's gallery, one of the pleasantest for propor-tions and lighting of the many belonging to dealers in those times, before a rise in rents drove most of them to poorly-lit back shops or attics and cellars. It was entered through the Boussod Valadon office and that firm used the upper floor also, from which a balcony commanded the gallery at its inner end, and furnished a useful spot for a private-view tea-party, with chairs commandeered from the offices. Thomson hung his gallery with a rich crimson material highly approved by Steer, who threatened never to set foot in the place when in the subsequent Marchant tenancy it was proposed to substitute a lighter ground more to the taste of the young. The red was retained and the substitute pinned over it when requisitioned.

The watercolours Steer showed in his 1894 exhibition were unlike anything he did later and only one was sold, to Dermod O'Brien. They remained on his hands, were to have been exhibited at the Barbizon Gallery along with small oil-panels of the same date, when in 1939 War intervened. They reappeared, with puzzling effect, in the posthumous sale at Christie's. In my show, chiefly of two summers' work at Whitby and Varangeville, there had been an admixture of architectural and lively beach scenes and portrait sketches in a technique of part-body-colour over a linear foundation on smooth or slightly tinted papers: also a strong admixture of local colour, a part cause of which was the shortness of holidays for completing oil-paintings. That inclusion cost me, however, as many, sometimes, as half a dozen trials for a subject. Steer's passing phase[1] was marked by such subjects as crowded streets and harbours, by strong local colour and admixture of gouache. All these he dropped when he had found his way to a more congenial choice of simpler matter, local colour minimised but for sky-blues, and transparent washes. One feature of his otherwise admirable technique I could not abide, the use of blue pigments, tempting in themselves, which granulate as they dry; but he did not seem to mind. In the earlier days Steer described watercolour as 'whoring' in contrast with the 'married state' of oil-painting. Daniel had been influenced by that view, but was solemnly warned by Tonks to repent and sin no more in a letter bursting with various topics:

5.2.31

You make my mouth water telling me of Degas who was a wonderful artist. Never again in this civilization will such drawing be seen; he and Keene were the outstanding draughtsmen of our time with John occasionally. People simply won't draw to-day; the critics are all against it. They talk the most horrible muck on the subject and know nothing. L.'Hôte in the N.R.F. thinks Matisse better than Degas. I suppose you have 'Lettres de Degas' prefaced by Daniel Halévy. I am just about to read it; there is a divine picture reproduced of a lady sitting by a sick girl's bed. Get it if you have not got it. It is a relief to be able to tell you that Steer's water colours are better than ever. They are the outstanding feature of our world of art. His oils of course are remarkable, but his water colours, as one can certainly say of Turner, reveal the mysteries of space for a moment. As in water colours themselves, description of them can only hint at what they are, so you must interpret my words as you will. Anyhow accept the idea that they are very very wonderful.

[1] I am unable to say what part J. L. Henry's practice may have played, since I cannot recall any examples of his watercolours.

Steer is most alone in his transcripts of foreshore bounding stretches of sea under a windy passage of clouds or the quieter bars of sundown; but he abstracted, with that same sleight-of-eye and hand, the intricacy of trees, and his interiors of boat-building sheds are lessons in where to leave off in discovery of the dark, without overtaxing paper and paint. Even when the result was over-wrought for the coy colour-medium half-successes come well in a black-and-white reproduction.

Steer relented from his original flippancy so far as to break into a discussion Behrend and others were engaged in with 'Watercolour is like a cow eating grass, oil-painting like a cow chewing the cud'. When he abandoned his practice of finishing a big canvas in the open, with frequent revolutions of effect, watercolour became his means of exploring for a subject and noting its variations of chiaroscuro, leaving final decision and full colour to the oil. There is an example, in the Daniel collection, of one early oil-painting done from memory with the aid of a pencilled scrap of paper, the *Ermine Sea*. Finally, with growing physical inertia, and a ready sale of watercolours at a handsome price, he gave more and more time to this short-hand art.

It inevitably disconcerted a public still faithful to the neat detail of a Birket Foster. Connard tells of a Lancashire painter who asked him, 'How much does Steer get for a watercolour?' 'Forty guineas.' 'Forty guineas! and for a mere nowt', complained the man who doubtless gave his clients much 'loving detail' and 'faithful labour' for a lesser sum. Steer chaffed Behrend for lingering to put in 'added truth' (Ruskin's word for detail).

Many were the successes, but no one knew better than Steer that miracles, in the conjunction of the exactly right degree of humidity, absorption and superposition of touches, proportion and weight of accents and general absence of worried afterthought must be rare. It was inevitable that alongside of the exquisite miracles, 'flukes', Steer called them, a vast number of merely respectable pieces should accumulate, and he himself was often dubious about the viability of his offspring. He would invite the opinion, which to license for exhibition, of his mount-maker, Lewis, or of Flo. Many he destroyed, but a sore problem faced his executors how many of the survivors to preserve.

A strange trick of the hoarding tendency affected his use of paper. Newly manufactured watercolour papers of the old descriptions are so imbued with size that they call for years of storage before they will be readily absorbent of the wash. Steer had quantities of good old paper in his cupboards, hunted out of colourmen's stocks or old account-books, yet he had recourse, like the rest of us, to using the French 'Michallet' paper, not intended for that purpose, subject to buckling when wet and inapt for elaboration. To counter the buckling he had two sheets pasted back to back by the skilled Mr. Lewis, who had mounted for Ruskin.

At the risk of occasional repetition I add a fuller account of Steer's practice that Mr. G. L. Behrend, Steer's painting companion for ten years from 1924, has generously put at my disposal:

Many a time on a summer's day I have seen Steer in an undecided mood wander about, sitting down first here and then there, unable to decide upon a subject owing to lack of effect, and finally after a little waiting and rumination, doing a monochrome in Payne's Gray or something else, but generally Payne's Gray. On one such morning he said 'This is the sort of day when the less you get it like, the better.'

But it might happen at times there would come a change and an interesting effect. Then he would begin to use colour and the result would be a thing of beauty, for the slight and varying monochrome undertones would give a quality which only he could get. When he had chosen his subject he sat down and quietly looked at and meditated about it, making his mind up as to composition. Very occasionally he would hold up his right hand and make a rough circle with his thumb and fingers, to frame his subject. Then he started off with a big brush full of colour. Most rarely did he use a pencil, even in a topographical, architectural or shipping subject.

In bad weather, during the summer when I was at Shoreham with Steer, we worked in and about the premises of a friendly builder of yachts, whose biggest building was almost cathedral-like in its pillared loftiness. I spent the mornings of a week making a detailed, intricate tinted pen-drawing of this interior and its great pillars, beams, timbers, boats and general clutter. One morning Steer wandered in, had a look round, and sitting down near me, worked for a couple of hours at the same subject. It so happened that his watercolour and my own drawing were both in the New English exhibition of that autumn. I was not in the least surprised when the assistant secretary said 'Mr. Behrend, I hope you don't mind my asking you if Steer's subject is the same as yours?'

Frequently Steer would put his board on the ground in front of him or slightly to the right and bending forward on his stool, complete his watercolour that way.

He was fixed in his habits. He started off in his leisurely fashion, a loose, large, imposing figure, at about ten o'clock, and after looking at the sky and observing where the breeze was coming from would say 'What about such and such a pitch this morning?' and off we would go at a saunter of two miles an hour or less, for he tried not to get overheated. Once arrived at the spot he would, if there were an effect, begin almost at once. If not, he would take a long time to decide, or leave and look for something else. In the afternoon he made no move until at least five o'clock and preferred nearer six. Often when leaving off about seven-thirty on a summer evening he would bewail the fact and say the effect was then beginning to be at its best, for detail had become less and things were 'all together.' For this reason he did not like 'summer time.'

Often on summer evenings he would begin by putting a wash of warm tone over his paper. He preferred it to dry before beginning to paint, though there were evenings when it wouldn't. He used hard cakes of colour. At the beginning of each season when he opened his paintbox of japanned tin, the cakes looked pretty well all alike, for he had put the box away at the end of the previous season without cleaning it.

40 (a) THE BLACK BOW

40 (b) HYDRANGEAS, 1901

41 (a) PROCESSION, BOULOGNE: *watercolour, 1894*

41 (b) BOAT-BUILDING: *watercolour*

He didn't use a wooden board or drawing pins. He used his standard quarter imperial portfolio with metal frame, containing paper of varying sizes, mostly smaller than the frame. He just put his paper on the frame. If it happened to be windy he pushed an end or the top of it under the frame. Much of his paper was old. It didn't seem to bother him if it became uneven when wet.

On a gusty day his watercolour more than once blew away and he retrieved it with a remark somewhat stronger than 'tut-tut', but soon regained his equanimity. In reply to any question why he so seldom used a pencil he said that drawing fatigued him.

He had a good collection of old paper, which he preferred to paint on, but he also used Michallet, and now and then David Cox paper—not old, and approved of it, but said it would have suited him better had it been cream-coloured. He had some old toned Creswick paper which had a deeper shade than he cared about. He told me that he had spent time before coming away for his summer-painting in putting a slight wash of diluted Chinese white over some of it to lighten the tone.

As to colours, Steer told me that whenever he put a new cake of colour in his box he found himself using it more than usual, and when a colour was used up and he had omitted to replace it he seemed able to do without it and to use some other instead. He used transparent golden ochre a great deal, and several blues, including cerulean, cobalt, French ultramarine, real ultramarine, and a small cake of indigo. He told me that he found difficulty at times in getting a wash of his deepest tone sufficiently dark on one application. Now and then when buying a few cakes he would try something new, recommended by the colourman. Thus he began to use, and used moderately 'Mars violet', which I know nothing about. Though particular about using transparent colours he used yellow ochre.

On the suggestion of a friend who told him that moist colours were pleasanter to paint with Steer brought away with him in 1924 or thereabouts a new paintbox containing pans of moist colour only, but not once did he ever use this box and all his watercolours have been painted with hard cakes. He may have felt about it what a golfer would feel who contemplated playing with a complete set of new clubs.

He told me that when he returned home and went through his work he occasionally reduced a tone with a piece of india rubber.

In a letter of 6 October 1924 he wrote:

. . . I wonder if you or H. have ever heard of adding sugar to the water you paint with, I am told the old painters did it, in the proportion of a small lump to a gill of water or about eight to a pint and half. Hayward tells me he has tried it recently and was very pleased with the way it went on, you might give it a trial and report when we meet. . . .

The 'H' of the above letter was the excellent but little appreciated watercolourist, W. M. Hawksworth, who was Behrend's friend and fellow-townsman at Rochester. He greatly tickled Steer, who admired his work, by speaking once of 'latreen' sails. He never, Steer ironically put it, 'realised the advantages of publicity.'

I make no excuse for adding other notes from Behrend's devoted Boswellising of his comrade:

On our annual trips, if I had to go to his room for something in the afternoon, oftener than not I would find him with his watercolours spread out round him on the carpet, meditating about them, may be, also, thinking out some picture composition in oil. When I admired them, he would bewail their general 'muckiness', as he called it. This was not a pose, but a genuine humility. When in his own house he showed his summer watercolours to buyers he displayed them in the same way, merely putting them down unmounted and unframed, on the floor in his painting room.

He said of Rich's book on water colour that you might think it the most delightful and easy occupation; you took your things out and sat down comfortably in charming surroundings, drew in your subject, and painted a successful watercolour with no tribulation. He said he would like to see a book setting forth the other side, and among one's bothers would be the disappearance of the sun when painting a sunny scene; its appearance when painting a gray landscape; rain coming on and spoiling one's sketch; or wind getting up and freezing you; how flies would worry you; or you would upset your water over your paper and paintbox, or inquisitive spectators would annoy. How in some seasons you might have only cold or gray or rainy weather, or constant threatening of thunder, or long periods of featureless blue skies.

In Wensleydale (Hawes) a farmer ordered Steer and his companions out of his field saying 'I won't have anyone making merchandize out of my property'. They wanted to do a subject from inside the gate of a meadow. The farmer mowed the small piece necessary and charged them 5s. for doing so. But speaking generally, farmers are obliging folk.

When going out painting he carried, in addition to portfolio, painting bag and stool, a light overcoat, in case he arrived hot (which he generally did) at his painting pitch, or in case a breeze got up. Passing a young mother with her child in a pram he remarked in his plaintive, joking manner, 'I've often thought a perambulator would be excellent for carrying one's things in—excepting of course for stiles and gates.'

He wore collars measuring 19 by 3. They were 'all-round' stand ups, such as were worn by the Gaiety theatre 'mashers' when I was a youth in the eighties. He continued to wear them because, having become accustomed to something high round his neck he feared taking cold if he left them off. At times, sitting painting in his black soft hat, he was taken for a non-conformist parson. At Maldon, when waiting for the traffic to pass at a crossing, a holiday maker started chatting with him, and asked if he was a bishop on holiday.[1]

Seaside places being so over-crowded in summer he tried to pick out what he termed the 'mucky' places, that is the unfashionable ones. Amongst these was Whitstable, where the crowds frequented only a part of the shore away from the fishermen's quarters, which were chiefly old wooden buildings and huts, mud, pebbles and boats.

In 1926 we spent the summer at Shoreham, which at first sight appears to be a collection of bungalows. But it was quite a good painting spot, for there was the tidal river where he made several lovely watercolours, and the shore, though, to be sure, his difficulty there was the people round about (and the complete absence of a lavatory or anything of the sort). There was also pleasant country at the back in the neighbour-

[1] He found it convenient, in railway travelling, to have his painting-kit in a cricketer's bag, winning greater respect from the porters.

hood of a spot known as Buckingham (or Buckingham farm?) which Moore wrote about. But I believe all is now obliterated by modern 'development', the building of small property. One of our most successful outings was at Greenhithe. Going through Greenhithe by the main London to Gravesend road, it appears merely as a busy place of cement and paper works, but old Greenhithe still had and possibly has its village street, and excellent pitches where one could get subjects looking both up and down the river, and where occasionally for a change we could sketch in the Ingress Abbey grounds, belonging to the 'Worcester', or go to Northfleet and other spots. Our difficulty at first was to find quarters, for nobody wants to spend the summer at Greenhithe. Yet five minutes from the main road brings one into quiet and pleasant country and from the higher ground are many subjects of the distant Thames, with perhaps an old overgrown chalk quarry here and there. We eventually got adequate rooms in a large house which had a garden and belonged to the skipper of a Thames barge. It was homely and comfortable. There are a good many well built old Victorian houses there. A school master of the 'Worcester' came to stay in the same house with his young family, and one had the satisfaction of seeing Steer painting [?punting] a football on the lawn for the small folk.

There was a summer when we could not decide where to go, so we packed up and went to Ramsgate. We went out to explore, and walked along the promenade below the cliffs, for Steer always made first for the waterside. All was cement, even the cliffs being cemented. So we packed up and next day went off to Sandwich, which was better, though not very good.

Connard, who often joined us, used to say that Steer's requirements when painting were, in order of importance: (1) Shelter from wind, (2) Proximity to a lavatory, (3) Shade from the sun, (4) Protection from children, (5) Subject.

Though Steer taught oil painting for many years at the Slade School, he frequently declared how impossible he would find it to give a lesson in water colour painting.

Two scraps from Tonks's letters to Steer may end this chapter:

25.8.32
I hope and feel sure you are doing fine water colours. I may as well confess I am jealous of your gift; never the less this evil feeling does not prevent me admiring them. You seem in a different world to us clodhoppers.

15.9.25
Please give all kind messages to B[ehrend]. I wonder if he has tried the wash of chinese white, I was very interested to see his water colours, which are in the right tradition of that art.

He talks more than I do, and I felt at 11 o'clock at night absolutely exhausted mentally and in my chest from excessive speech in answer to him. What a lot you gain from remaining silent.

Other Media

Two pastels only by Steer are known, one of them of a girl sewing was shown at the National Gallery. Of the other I wrote to him:

15.5.1935

I was delayed the other day, in getting to your show, but it was a great satisfaction when it came. There was one thing that surprised me a good deal, a pastel of a girl on a sofa, dated 1887, I think. Was this right? It seemed very mature, as well as good, and I thought it might be well worth your while to take up pastel again, since it has the advantage, with care, of being unchangeable in colour and tone, neither darkening nor cracking.

He replied:

16.5.35

Thank you for your very kind letter about my show. The pastel you mention was done for an exhibition of Pastels, either at the old Grosvenor, or the New Gallery many years ago, I remember my difficulty in never finding the tint I exactly wanted and the sticks used to get rubbed together and looked all alike, at the same time I admit all the advantages you speak of and even now, I sometimes find them useful in trying some alteration in a painting.

I think you are probably right about the date being too early and when Thomson asked me, I evidently made a bad shot but I am certain it would not be later than 1893.

Steer, in early days, had not narrowed his activities as he came in middle life to do, but took a normal part among fellow youngsters in this or that experiment. We have seen him reading a paper on 'Impressionism'; he had several of his paintings reproduced in 'The Yellow Book', executed lithographs, one *The Nursemaid* for the short-lived 'Albemarle', another, a portrait of the author for Le Gallienne's 'Prose Fancies', the pencil drawing of Edward Stott for an article on that friend by J. Stanley Little in the 'Studio' and a crayon profile of Fred Brown for my article in the 'Magazine of Art' (where, by a mishap, it was attributed to Sickert).

The most unlikely of those extra turns by the Steer now remembered were 'assignments' such as Muirhead Bone might now accept, to draw London scenes for the 'Pall Mall Budget' in 1893. These were two:

(1) *The New Light in the Clock Tower; the House Sitting;* a wash-drawing or watercolour.

(2) *The Thames from the Ball of St. Paul's Cathedral;* showing Waterloo and Hungerford Bridges, the Houses of Parliament and St. Thomas's Hospital; the original apparently a chalk drawing.

A younger generation who knew only a lethargic figure may well gape at this evidence of a Steer who could make that steep ascent and not be too exhausted to draw the panorama when he got there.

XI

RANGE, LIMITS AND AFFILIATIONS

'They said I was wild'—*Steer to an Interviewer*

It will be expected of a biographer that he should attempt an indication, so far as is possible to a contemporary, of Steer's claim to originality of gift, to a place as master in the chain of painters, English and other, and of the limits within which such a claim is arguable. Much of this has been asserted or implied in the previous pages and in those appended from periodical reviews in the Press; but I will set down some general considerations and their application to my subject. First, let us clear away several critical obsessions that obstruct the view.

1 It is a strange though a common practice to complain of an artist that he gives what he can instead of what, with another constitution of mind, eye and hand, he might have given, and to belittle him by inapplicable measurements and confrontations. Language is but a teasing, refractory medium for coping with visual sensations and an artist's practice: criticism is therefore a difficult and fallible business at the best, but its first duty is to define, as clearly as may be, not what its subject ought to do, but what he can and does; with allowance for points at which the habitual fence is broken and excursions made into the no-man's-land of unsubdued and undemarcated territory. Writing to Tonks from Greenhithe on 28th August 1932, to Tonks who for once had found some satisfaction mixed with habitual despair over one of his own best pictures, Steer said:

I think painting what one cannot do, as you put it, is, although paradoxical, the only thing worth doing, and I am sure the labour you have expended on the *Lady at her Toilet* will repay you in the long run.

2 A second fallacy haunts the opposition of 'Derivative' to 'Original' art.

It is difficult to have patience with the nonsense which clots the handling of those terms. Steer has been run down as 'derivative'. It is one of his titles to honour. Every one of us is 'derivative', as the son of father and mother, forefathers and fore-mothers more or less luckily combined: our deficiencies arise from the absence, not the presence, of choice congenital strains. 'An original' is the kindly name given to the mentally deficient, but in its proper and favourable sense it means come from deep wells and roots in the past. There is 'original sin' as well as original virtue, a name for any profound defect of inheritance, and the unfortunates who exploit the presence in their make-up of that 'originality' are repeating a divagation from the strait path by those who have gone astray in the past.

At this late hour in the now ancient history of painting our fathers in the art are a mighty host, the possibilities of tolerable novelty in matter and manner ever more restricted, fine increment or fresh combination rather than revolution the way to perfection, the would-be 'solipsist' condemned to rake the dust heaps for discarded rags to cover his nakedness, or to abolish the whole convention of the picture by assaults on its integrity.

Artists vary, naturally, in the range of their knowledge among fathers and uncles consciously adoptable, and it is well they should not be overwhelmed by knowing all. The museums make us contemporaries of all time and all masters and the load of knowledge and emulation may well prove crushing. Chardin the elder was wise in sloughing the top-dressing of an academic training for his natural taste in Dutch scouring of pots and pans, in French bread and wine, and, cautiously, in children at play or bound for mass, or their mother at tea. With that modest baggage he won a ticket for eternity. Chardin the younger, more pompously brought up as prizeman-pensionnaire in the 'School of Rome', overstrained his powers and in Venice of towering masters and too-handy canals, drowned himself.

3 There is, however, what may seem a contradictory side to this affair of 'gift' and its applications. The artist has his instinct, his 'talent', but not necessarily the mind for turning it to usury. Mr. A. G. B. Russell, in a recent lecture[1] has an excellent passage on this subject, pointing out how Botticelli, ineducable in reading, writing or accounts, was inspired to his greatest work by the poetic stimulus of his patrons, the Medici; but illustrations abound. The doctrine and guidance of the Church inspired and regulated mediaeval sculptors and painters, classic myth and legend those who followed. What did not Handel owe to the genius of his friend Jennens, who extracted and arranged for him the biblical text of 'Messiah' and threw the musician into a three weeks' rapture of composition. That wizard of sound depended on stimulus from the visual in paintings no less than in fields, woods and storms: he possessed a Rembrandt in his collection, and blindness left his music thirsty at one of its lively sources. Nor did he scruple to plagiarise when he could better what he borrowed.

[1] 'Hellas and a Renaissance', Batsford, 1943, p. 10.

So among poets: Burns the song-writer was heir to a boundless patri-
mony of old ditties, whose fragmentary charm he could work into his
own fabric, controlled by the tunes humming in his head which he
'soothed' while he composed. So again Tom Moore, who can be sung
because he wrote to traditional tunes or composed others like them.[1]

No such inspiring element came Steer's way. His painting comrades
were honestly but sluggishly minded and the early New English atmosphere was suspicious of literature, Old or New. For the greatest things in
painting, as in the other arts, direction, collaboration, interchange are
called for, a constructive and discursive mind matched with the painter's
eye for the likeness of men and look of things. Both elements may be
present in the same person, as in Blake, prophet, poet and painter, but on
the empty road of the strictly single imagination lurks danger of wild
solitariness or its acme, madness: what the Greeks called idiosyncrasy,
and we more bluntly term idiocy. Blake himself had his forebears, Gothic
and Italian designers, and literary sources, Indian and Swedish as well as
English. The course of human thought cut away the mythical springs of
the greatest painting, first the Christian, then the Pagan, and across the
everyday life of the Low Countries painting reached its finally emptied-
out scenes in Landscape, peopled at first by departing myth and history,
then by everyday traffic, then chosen for associations, then as empty of all
these as Crome's superb *Slate Quarries*[2]; finally without 'cause' other than
anonymous 'effect'.

Beyond that point in painting lies Nothing, however plausibly dis-
guised. 'The Times', on the sixteenth of February, 1934, regretfully but
honestly admitted so much, speaking of 'the lapses into representation
which no painting can really avoid'. The lapse surely is into the widow-
hood or divorce from the 'marriage' of the painter with nature, of which
Steer spoke, into practices which are no better than artistic masturbation.
Of these we have seen enough and to spare.

Towards that blind alley, with ears shut, and skirts drawn tight against
contamination, 'Independent Art' hastens or titubates. There is, however,
as well as solitude, the other danger of bad company. An artist of original
gift may be likened to a man who carries a vessel of precious spring water
or stronger drink for the thirsty: it may be across the hazards of a battle-
field, like the 'Three Mighties' who fetched a draught from the well by
the gate at Bethlehem for King David, or those others who fought through
to Philip Sidney at Zutphen, or more often merely from joggings of the
elbow and trippings of the feet by careless passersby. Worse, however,

---

[1] 'The Masters', indeed as I have put it elsewhere, ' are Master-thieves.'

[2] Or Steer's, in Sir William Jowitt's collection, which Tonks thought his finest landscape.

than those accidents that spill or upset the pitcher are the drugs and sugars that may be added to the spring water by well-meaning teachers or trusty friends, kindly poisoners at the well-head. The water, if only it remain pure, may be carried in make-shift vessels, a helmet, a hat, or a pail, or resin from a wine-skin taint a headier type of drink and have to be disregarded as an accident.

Inventors and Discoverers

Such are some of the enemies who lie in wait for the artist and the critic. Now let us come closer to our subject with a broad distinction of kinds.

Painters may be usefully, if not too sharply, divided into Inventors and Discoverers. Musicians must be inventors, or nothing, because there is no world of ready-made creatures of sound for them to adopt and modify, but the painter who has not the divine gift of semi-creation, of the grouping, 'out of his head', of human and other forms in action, verified, not ready-made, in models, the painter even for whom memory of shapes and colours is uncertain, has the resource of finding in a scene presented to his eyes the half-made material of a picture. It is a fallacy of ignorance that there is no 'imagination' in such an act, dividing, as it does, the painter's activity crudely into 'natural effect' and 'technique'.[1] Out of the camera-image a picture-image must be detached and moulded, and seen in picture terms before the brush begins its work. For the camera there is no discovery beyond the initial act of choice and direction of the lens, but 'imagination', which means 'image-making', is in action when the hunt is up for a picture in the outer, visible world; exalting, reducing or suppressing features, determining and rendering lucid the governing lines, so that they shape into a design, reading tone and colour into answers and contrasts not fiddled away towards infinity, but vividly singled and developed.

This occupation and entertainment of the eye, present, more or less, in anyone's sight-seeing, this day-dream, was what remained over and became 'independent' in the latest of painting's preoccupations, landscape nearly 'pure and simple', a foraging of the vision that accompanied a taste for sociable or solitary commerce with 'Nature'. The mediaeval sculptor who carved the Labours of the Year month by month, from pig-sticking to threshing and wine-pressing, was contented with a symbol hung up instead of a view, and would be scandalised to see humanity take so secondary a place, or none at all, and the background he omitted

[1] This is a root-fallacy in the introduction to the Phaidon 'Steer.'

42 (*a*) THE POOL, HESDIN: *watercolour, 1905*

42 (*b*) THE MILL: *watercolour*

43 (a) DOVER (*study for war picture*): *watercolour, 1918*

43 (b) GREENHITHE: *watercolour, 1932*

come forward to usurp attention. So too the demi-gods of painting who displaced his art and did evoke a harmonious counterpoint of water, hill, tree and sky, might also have been scandalised to witness an 'exit all' for the actors from the stage, leaving only its scenery behind. The art of land-scape as Steer took it over did not ascend into the high heaven of inven-tion which the saints of painting inherit and its rebels storm: still less did it descend into any of the hells. It occupied the middle earth of England in sunny or troubled weather, ignoring man and his toils even in the fields.

Instead of excursions to 'orra' countries of the mind Steer set up his 'moving tent' in pleasant scenery such as it had become the habit of his countrymen to seek out for an annual holiday, bringing a new eye to what, for most of them, had been stereotyped and academised by more popular painters. So Pope, whose ordinarily unsentimental temper, and the habit, for his poetic purpose, of seeing under ticketed epithets, melted for once in 'Windsor Forest' to a soft ecstasy of lines that could be sung:

> Where'er you walk soft gales shall lend their aid,
> Trees, where you sit, shall bend into a shade.

doubled, in their loveliness, by the music Handel created for them.

If Steer could have organised all his forces for attack he might have peopled such scenes with the 'nymphs' who remained mere models in his studio and added 'swains' in the manner of Watteau, whom he adored. Tonks did export 'nymphs' into his holiday work, taking models into the country or finding them there, but was incapable of rendering out-of-door sunshine: its brightness turned, under his inquisition, into a tired, yellowish grey. Steer probably shrank from the worries of transferring to the scene, arranging and controlling subjects for 'conversation'. That avoidance of worry may have been one motive, but another was probably decisive, that his scenes, to give furniture and motive to their skies, usually demanded 'bad weather', clouds at least, if not wind and rain; nor does the British climate often provide unbroken spells of idyllic sunshine or British propriety the needful freedom for posing 'gallant' scenes; in France it is more possible. There are however, woodland and other settings that he peopled with girls and children very happily.

Gainsborough, who rarely painted a 'nymph' from literature such as Thomson's *Musidora,* and only once was betrayed into a mistaken attempt upon 'high art' and deep significance in the 'Parish Clerk', amusingly hits off, in his shirt-sleeved letters, the proprieties for an unhistorical land-scape painter:

I admire your notions of most things, and do agree with you that there might be exceeding pretty pictures painted of the kind you mention. But are you sure you don't mean instead of the flight into Egypt my flight out of Bath. Do you consider, my dear maggotty Sir, what a deal of work historical pictures require to what little dirty subjects of coal horses and jackasses and such figures as I fill up with. . . . But to be serious (as I know you love to be), do you really think that a regular composition in the Landskip way should ever be filled with History or any figures but such as find a place (I won't say stop a gap) or create a little business for the eye to be drawn from the trees in order to return to them with more glee. . . . But I talk now like old Square-toes . . .

The lugging in of objects, whether agreeable to the whole or not, is a sign of the least genius of anything, for a person able to collect in the mind, will certainly groupe in the mind also; and if he cannot master a number of objects so as to introduce them in friendship, let him do but a few, and that, you know, my Boy, makes simplicity.

Then follows the admirable phrase about picture and tune I have already quoted.

The task, even thus simplified, was hard enough for Steer. His early idol and ultimate master, Turner, was a man endowed for all troubles of outdoor study with the contempt for ease and rest of a seasoned campaigner and the toughness of a hill-shepherd or a sailor. For sleep he could lay his head on his arms at a table in some crowded inn and be out at dawn to watch the sunrise or study the wrinkles of water in a stream. When others were helpless with sea-sickness he perched in the bows and made notes of waves, and in a memorable blizzard was bound to the mast so that he might study the driving snow. His nerves were so steady that when a heavy gun opened fire from behind his head 'it was to him as the sound of lutes and viols'; his curiosity and alertness so constant that he nipped from the diligence at every slow-down or stop to jot the surroundings, and can be tracked from landing stage to the home-bound packet by a diary of pencillings; as a guest he appears to have contrived those entries even while waiting for dinner. He must have carried all baggage on his person; had a tiny colour-box in his pocket and spat in it for moisture when no water was at hand, to the disgust of Sir Walter Armstrong.

Steer, follower in the tracks of that predecessor who had modulated a topographer's task into a painter's creations had no such physical independence of times and seasons, baggage and tools. Painting for him was 'a job to be done between meals'; these regular, beds comfortable, change of underwear and provision of tackle ample. He did not rise with the lark to anticipate the sun. As the season wore on and evenings shut in there was the concession of a shorter nap and earlier tea-time, so that, as sun-down neared, the previous dinner-hour effects moved back, and the ethereally flushed or burning register of his master or the tremulous ambiguity of a moonrise could be captured. I remember how, standing before Sargent's remarkable war-picture of gassed and blinded soldiers lifting their feet high for fear of stumbling, with a moon overhead, I said how fascinating was the effect of early moonrise in moist air. 'But', he replied, 'the moon could not produce any change of quality in the light against the sun,' and would not listen to my protest that I should know it was up behind my back. There was the capture of such a conjunction in the Steer sale, wisely secured for his birthplace, Birkenhead.

The defensive habit adopted by Steer of going out into a world aired and warmed so far as the niggardliness of English summer permits, was countered by his preference for weather not fine nor cloudless, but broken by dramatic cloud and thunder shower. He thus narrowed his range very much to the habitual effects of Constable, noon-day light, white clouds upon blue or black, skies rainbow-struck, greens absorbed by dazzle, a general silveriness with spots of intense brilliance, the famous 'snow' that outraged academicians on varnishing-days. In the splendid *Chepstow Castle* at the Tate light, as we have seen, is nearly vertical, just skimming the walls and rock to glisten on wet mud laid bare by the ebb. A contrast is the rich smoulder of day burning out at Bridgnorth in the Daniel collection. I know nothing like it.

The special trouble then for Steer was that weather must be not only not too bad, but also not too fine. Pouring and drizzling rain or dull grey skies were useless, but the spells of bright east wind characteristic of English 'good weather' were also unwelcome, because clear skies had no composing features of cloud-shapes lighted and shadowed. What he prayed for was the south-west wind with broken weather and changing skies. 'Perfect weather', he wrote from Long Brendon, 'under trees, I find quite endurable,' but not in the open.

It is easy to scoff at Steer for his careful ways, fear of cold and heat and other precautions. There was something obstinately stouthearted, not to use a big word like 'heroic', in a man whose life-long danger was of colds and bronchitis confronting, as he did, the hazards of English summer. That it was English, with breaks and conjunctions of glory, was charter enough for him: a cloudless Italy or Southern France he would have detested.

Sprung though he was from a yeoman strain, he was strangely unconcerned with field-labour; unlike Clausen, whose subject has been peasants in landscape, under the successive tutelage of Bastien-Lepage and J. F. Millet. Gainsborough, in one of the dashed-off letters, already quoted from, is excellent on this point.

Such were his limits. His early affiliations in Landscape embraced Monticelli for the 'powdering' of light upon trees, as well as contemporary French masters, but he staked out a domain of his own, and I see no reason to withdraw the claim I have made for him that he was our greatest landscape painter since Turner and Constable. That reasonable claim was grumblingly disputed[1] when it was reproduced in the catalogue of the Steer Exhibition at the National Gallery, but none of the grumblers put forward another name. Buxton Knight, I think, came nearest in the Constable line. One critic was so bold as to challenge the direction of shadows in the great *Richmond Castle* with a rainbow, not understanding that the painter had to switch his direction to the left and render the shadows accordingly, as all painters had done, from Rubens to Millais. Only in a hieratic picture could a rainbow be central, with sun behind the painter's head.

Steer was more than a landscape artist. Like Gainsborough, who counts among his landscape-uncles, he was a painter of portraits as well: not so prolific as the man who could send fifteen or twenty works to a single Academy. Photography had reduced and perverted demand, and with the lesser demand went a less systematic painting, but here too, and in rare 'subjects', are peaks also in the count of Steer's rich legacy.

He is no mere copyholder, therefore, in an old estate. 'Windy, silvery and delicious' like Constable, ethereally glowing like Turner, lover of the graces like Gainsborough, and going back to a father of them all, Rubens of the Rainbow Landscape and much more, he added to that heritage his own conquests of light and capture of flower-like loveliness in flesh.

Gainsborough had more than enough of portraits; he wrote to Jackson:

I'm sick of Portraits and wish very much to take my Viol-da-gamba and walk off to some sweet village, where I can paint Landskips and enjoy the fag-end of life in quietness and ease. . . . Others ride in the waggon . . . gazing at green trees and blue skies without half my taste.

He is a warning, too, against the traps of ancestor hunting. Who would have guessed that his secret worship went to Pietro Francisco Mola, if Desenfans had not caught him in the act at Dulwich. 'It is this manner of painting' he confided 'which I shall never attain, for Mola appears to have made it his own by patent.'[2]

Artists are apt to be like the plover, distracting the attention of inquisitive intruders from its nest by misleading indications. That is one of the pitfalls in the track of critical birdnesters. The general danger, however, from which none of us altogether escapes, is *categorising,* the failure to enjoy the work of art for itself, without diluting its appeal with glosses from a reference-library of history, biography, Schools and Kinds; labelling, in

---

[1] See my pamphlet, 'In Memoriam Philip Wilson Steer,' printed by Shenval, Old Bailey, 1944.
[2] Whitley, 'Thomas Gainsborough'.

effect, and putting it to sleep upon a shelf. One of the category-mad among us, notably equipped with knowledge of events and dates and schools, carries the practice to absurdity when a fumbling attempt at mythological composition by Renoir is treated as a 'Classical Renaissance', and Sickert condoled with for being out of step with his contemporary, Seurat. Let us be as undistracted as may be when we are out, not to overhaul the works of the Time-machine, but to enjoy the time of day.

Against the inclusion of Steer in one of the slippery categories I have already argued; the ticketing of him as camp-follower of French 'Impressionism'. It remains to insist on two cardinal features in which he contrasts with Monet's group.

1. *Design,* or Composition. In respect of this Monet was uncertain, too often indeed chaotic, and Sisley weak; Pissarro entirely wanting, for perspective of his scenes is deplorably photographic, the placing of buildings, trees and figures awkwardly accidental. Sickert, in spite of the chance-seeming but cunning contrivance of a subject by his master Degas, seldom got beyond a slice of material. Steer, after some early floundering, turned to the great master of landscape design in Turner, as we see him in the 'Liber Studiorum', where the rhythms of stream-erosion and cloud movement are profoundly understood and every part rhymes with the rest and obeys the whole. Let anyone who has forgotten turn to the *Solway Moss* and consider how the herdsman's gesture with his staff, struck vertically at a key-point, is like a conductor's baton not only to the train of cattle but to a vast orchestra of stormy cloud, plain and mountain. The greatest things in art are never done twice, but the lesson was fruitful.

2. *Chiaroscuro*, ('its the loight and shide that counts', as Steer jokingly chanted on a return from Dulwich), was the organ of composition to which Constable was faithful through all his adventures in natural effect. As I write a Bond Street firm is showing a series of landscapes entitled 'From Constable to Cézanne', and the moral of it is that in spite of fine discoveries of colour two little pieces of the English painter, by dint of their light-and-shade constitution and concentration wipe the floor with the French succession. Constable encouraged his engraver, David Lucas, to emphasise this feature in what was his 'Liber Studiorum', the 'English Landscapes' of over a hundred years ago. The lesson stands, and was learned by Steer, along with the glitter of silver or green, if more quietly applied. 'They said I was wild', he threw out: he was of the centre, with variations of a fresh eye, enriching the norm.

Steer, then, belongs to that lately despised variety of artist, the English, acclaimed as chief by the leading painters of his generation and worthy heir to the greatest landscape painters of the early nineteenth century in Europe.

K   W.S.

With the well-known love of our race for self-depreciation critics have for thirty years humbly adopted the perspective of Herr Meier-Graefe, and recited it at second-hand. The pre-Raphaelites are not 'in the main stream of European painting'. Out they go; they 'are not artists'. Whistler is no great shakes. And into the dry watercourses and weedy ditches of that 'main stream' whose real name is the Rue de la Boétie, the form-and-colour-blind, who 'look at pictures through their ears', have been conducted. Steer is as insular as the French, as much a spring in the waste as Manet or Degas. The wind blows where it lists and carries, in a single picture of Constable, an unsealing of the eyes to Delacroix; so with Steer; the food convenient filtered through, was absorbed and transmuted. But the Napoleonic blockade behind which Turner grew was a better nurse of art than our unremitted exhibition traffic. 'Speed-cops' are badly wanted.

It is a good omen for the future of an artist that he should be little known in his own day. It is only in the last few years that the fashionable press-boycott of the Meier-Graefe period has been by sudden consent relaxed in the case of Steer. He is unknown to the Luxembourg and other European galleries, except the Uffizi, scantily known even in his birthplace, Liverpool. It is true that, as Sickert once said, the connoisseurs of good wine contrive to find it, and they have not failed to lay down this vintage. At the Tate Gallery, also, under Charles Aitken, a series of his paintings was steadily built up and has been enlarged and even diluted.

That is the kind of thing which is going to survive from a period in which the picture has been evacuated to death. We have been asked to believe that salvation lies in thin abstraction, independence from subject, freedom from representation, arbitrary distortion, and persuade ourselves that when an apple has plainly lost shape and equilibrium it triumphs as a demonstration of three-dimensional space. Why three dimensions should be a virtue in the non-representational world is left obscure.

We have seen the result of this pedantic 'slimming'. 'Bombinating in a vacuum,' the picture-chimera has lost even that which it set out to separate, design, 'construction,' colour and its tone-values, and any preciousness of quality in the paint. These elements, for their richness, for their very existence, depend on vision excited by an attitude towards the subject of affection or irony, of a wrestling interest at least that will not let it go without a blessing of beauty. To such affection and absorption, so fatuously termed 'literary', to such discovery of beauty the painting of Steer belongs, and therefore will not be emptied out with the slops of our time.

XII

TEACHING: THE SLADE SCHOOL

1893–1930

Art Schools, like academies of every sort, are at once a public danger and a necessity. In the dead centre of the eighteenth century the least likely of men, one would have thought, Edward Young, author of the bland 'Night Thoughts', launched, in nicely balanced and alliterative prose, the most radical claim ever made for untutored genius: 'Conjectures on Original Composition,' in a Letter to the Author of 'Sir Charles Grandison.'[1] Even William Blake, who terrified the great Whatman pages in an edition fifty years later of the 'Night Thoughts' with images that belied its Pope-inspired text, if he came near to Young's dream of solitary inspiration, had his own sources of schooling, and against the ultra-romantic claim for complete independence it must be allowed that there is a place for discipline, traditional lore and the other classic curbs on unlicensed genius.

In the eighteenth century, when the Royal Academy and its school were founded, Gainsborough and Reynolds were perfect examples of intuitive genius over against the academic. In our day Steer and Tonks were as complete representatives of the complementary types: Steer the instinctive artist, hater of theory; Tonks, the academician *in excelsis*, who ought, of course, to have been President at Burlington House:[2] but Tonks, in place of Reynolds's rather fearful and grudging attitude towards Gainsborough, had a reverence for his friend's powers and judgment, though he essayed the schoolmaster even with him.

From 1893 to 1930 Steer was Teacher of Painting at the Slade School, first, as we have seen, under Brown, and afterwards under Tonks. The

[1] I owe my knowledge of this to Nikolaus Pevsner's 'Academies of Art, Past and Present'. The author refers to 'Young' simply, perhaps not recognizing the poet and coiner of a famous line, 'Procrastination is the thief of Time', too famous, since procrastination may be the thief of everything else but is the saviour of Time. Dr. Pevsner's knowledge of academies in the British Isles is scrappy, but his review of foreign institutions has much of interest.

[2] He failed in an attempt to win the professorship of anatomy at the R.A. His appointment might have changed many things in official history.

advantage for him of the appointment lay no doubt at first in a steady source of income; intercourse with colleagues and the young further counted throughout: for his pupils there was the incitement of working under the eye of so notable a painter, with useful hints and interventions, if with scant critical analysis or direction, for Steer was no professor. His usefulness extended to reports and consultations with Brown and Tonks about promising students and decisions about prizes, a matter in which even Tonks bowed to his judgment.

In the later years Steer was held to his post less for his uses as a teacher than by Tonks's sense of the added prestige his presence gave to the School. This is confirmed by a letter of the retiring Professor to the Provost, Dr. Allen Mawer:

9.3.1930.

You will probably receive from P. Wilson Steer, about the same time as this, his letter of resignation from the Slade School when I leave. As you have only lately come here, I think I ought to tell you something of him and his relations with the Slade School. When Brown was made Professor, he suggested to Steer that he should teach one day a week until he did well enough as a painter not to make it necessary. That was, I think, a little over 37 years ago. Gradually Steer has made for himself a position as a painter second to none. He stands quite alone. For many years it has been quite unnecessary for him to teach. His pictures are bought privately and for Public Galleries for very large prices. He has disregarded this and continued to come to the Slade, and though his health has been by no means good, particularly lately, has remained to help me, and what that help means to me I can hardly explain to you. So you see his resignation is a great event in the history of the School.

He is so modest that unless I tell you about him you might never know.

The Professorial Board minuted the above letter and placed on record 'its appreciation of the thirty-seven years of unbroken and untiring service which Mr. Steer has given to the School'.

Tonks was determined that so long as he himself remained at the Slade, Steer also must be there, but was ready to make things easy for him. He wrote:

24.9.26

This is merely a senior's protest against your conduct in daring to answer my letter, I see what it all means; your pen is becoming your method of expression, and you also will bring out Memorials of your Dead Life, and will drag out into the open such a picture of the latter end of the Victorian era that our poor old friend will become green . . .

For God's sake do not answer this, though your last letter was a gem. You write the best letters I receive; they really make me laugh . . .

I want you to remain at the Slade as long as I do, *but* never to look upon it as something you *must* attend. If you want to go away in the winter we can settle that easily.

Tonks was properly jealous of the days reserved from Slade teaching for his own painting, and held that all teachers ought to have the like chance of renewing their freshness by regular practice. Steer was amused by the extremity of the Professor's ban upon interference with his seclusion. He told Vernon Wethered:

Two students from the Slade called at his house and rang the bell. Presently the door opened, Tonks appeared and asked, 'What do you want?' They answered, 'We have come to see you.' 'Well, you've seen me', and he banged the door.

He would put himself out tirelessly for pupils in Gower Street, but at the Vale he was peremptory in shutting out the school.

In the legend of the Slade it is Steer of the middle and later periods who chiefly figures, grown lethargic, and not polysyllabic when he criticised at all. Thus his colleague Mr. James Wilkie describes the oddity of his arrival:

On entering one of the life-rooms Steer often would yawn quite audibly. He would then look round for a chair, and drag it along the floor to a student's easel; carefully look at the chair again and say, 'Do you know if this chair is safe?' He would look at the work for some time, then say, 'Well go on.' The student might say, 'I'm in a muddle.' Steer's reply was, 'Well, muddle along.'

Mr. Wilkie adds that:

His interest in the students' working from the Antique was very marked. He regretted that so little study was given to this part of the training; Steer felt that more instruction could be given and more use made of the school by practice in painting the light upon a cast.

Another colleague, Sir Walter Russell, who had been one of Brown's most gifted students at Westminster and returned to teach under his old professor, writes:

I was not fortunate enough to receive instruction from Steer, but I met him at the Slade on his visiting days. I have memories of him dragging a painting stool from student to student. When comfortably seated, he would quietly criticise the student's work, very frequently working on the study. Knowing him, one might have expected that teaching would bore him, but I believe he enjoyed his weekly visits, and no doubt the intelligent students learned a lot from his kindly criticism. There were no tears after his lessons.

There are, of course, tales of the agony for nervous students of awaiting a lesson from the great man seated behind, and turning round at last to find him asleep. My own recollection of the earliest days, when I did a little painting for practice from models at the Slade, is of a Steer still active on his feet and in comment, though he passed me with a nod. I add some accounts I have been able to gather from pupils who won his interest and profited from his advice. First, from Mr. Thomas Lowinsky, the well-known painter, who became a friend of his teacher:

In contrast to Tonks's method of teaching, which combined vitality, eloquence, sarcasm and facile demonstration, Steer's was of gentle understatement. He would slowly enter the lofty and somewhat cheerless painting-room and before the canvas of the first student he came to seat himself in complete silence on a high stool, hands clasped between wide-spread knees. For a long time he would look alternately from the work in front of him to the model. He might at last make a few remarks, or confine himself to one sentence or pass on to the next easel without a syllable. If he did this it was not that he wished to be unkind, or even thought the study bad, but simply that he had nothing to say. When he did speak his criticism was well-considered and sincere, his praise or censure mild. By chance I have a record of two of his conversations made in the year 1913. The first was a retort to G———, who was attempting to explain away a false relationship between blouse and neck by asserting, 'Blue is a difficult colour to manage.' 'No colour is easy' was Steer's reply. The second he made to me. 'Nasty colour', he explained, 'never becomes nice colour. A picture has to be nice colour from beginning to end.' At the school Steer concentrated solely on painting and left drawing to others. For this reason he seemed to be blind to faulty construction and proportion. It was a constant source of surprise to me that Tonks, who had a complete command of the English language, should invariably emphasise his point by making drawings and paintings on the edge of the pupil's work, whilst Steer, who was almost inarticulate, should rather teach by word of mouth.

Steer probably realised that the great majority of students being, for purposes of painting, colour-blind, it was futile to interfere. When he detected symptoms of perception he said, 'I should go on with that.'

The next witness is Mr. Hubert Wellington, afterwards right-hand assistant to Sir William Rothenstein at South Kensington, and Head, later, of the Edinburgh College of Art.

I was painting a portrait head at the Slade in 1900 when Steer on his rounds looked for some minutes without a word, then said, 'Let me have your palette and brushes.' I was using the square-cut hoghair tools then fashionable in most art schools, and was asked 'Haven't you any small round brushes? No? Oh well, you'd better get some. You will never become a colourist without small round brushes.'

I was amused at the time, but later I saw the drift of the comment. With those large square things it was all too easy to cover a few inches of paint without really examining or 'making' the change of colour in the area involved. I have since realized what valuable advice it was for a student and constantly used it in teaching.

Miss Beatrice Bland's testimony may fitly follow. Her sense of colour and of paint grew, under Steer's guidance, into the flower-and-landscape painting we know, and her close neighbourhood to 109, Cheyne Walk allowed much friendly intercourse with her teachers:

As regards Art teaching he said little, just took the brush and showed one, and perhaps remarked, 'Lay it on like a breath', which I have never forgotten but have not often succeeded in doing.

Next is an account from Miss Margaret Legge of teaching that also ripened into friendship.

In my early days at the Slade School I saw little of Mr. Steer. He taught the painters and gave lessons to the students who were doing charcoal drawings of the model only if he had time left over. Those drawing lessons were not very inspiring. He was always kind—soothing after the stimulating ferocity of Tonks, but gave one the impression that he was bored. My surprise was all the greater when I had my first painting lesson from him. I wish my memory were not such a sieve and that I could recall what he actually said during that wonderful half hour, but though I cannot bring back the words, he left me with a wider, clearer view of what painting is. Then he took my palette and brushes and began to paint. I was fascinated. He held the brush as if he were going to drop it and lightly, with slight, decided touches, went over the whole torso. Suddenly he put down the palette again and said 'Now go on with that.' Like a fool, I did!

Not long before his death he said to me 'Tonks was a great teacher; I was no good at it', and gave me the opportunity to thank him for one of those moments in life when one consciously takes a step forward. My period at the Slade was 1894–98. Though we students had a most respectful admiration for Steer as a great artist, we also had a good many jokes about him, his terror of getting into a draught being the chief source of merriment. We were so sure that he went about in a dream, looking at the work here and there, making quaint comments on the model and so on, that we felt quite safe in our laughter. Later I heard him give killingly funny imitations of Slade students and their behaviour. He missed nothing!

I imagine that ours was the only house into which Mr. Steer ever gate-crashed! It was at the end of my four years as a Slade student. I wanted a studio of my own and thought one of the rooms of my father's house in Montagu Square would do. Mr. Tonks, with whom we had all made friends by then, kindly offered to come and advise me about it. One Sunday afternoon we were all sitting at tea, when the door opened and Mr. Tonks walked in, followed by a patient-looking figure, and said 'I've brought Steer.' That was the first of many visits. He used to dine with us, and also attend riotous parties in the studio, where he sat with a smile like a contented cat's on his face while we chaffed each other and him too. So long as he was not expected to make conversation he was perfectly happy. He was very much disappointed when illness prevented his coming to a Bran-Pie party I gave one Christmas, but we chose a toy, for him, a green crocodile, and sent it by Mr. Tonks, who told us afterwards that Steer was so delighted with the colour it quite consoled him.

One very snowy day I met him at tea in another student's place. His usually good figure looked like an enormous sausage. Someone remarked upon the severity of the weather and Mr. Steer said 'Yes. I looked out of the window this morning and saw that there was snow, so when I got up I put on two of everything.'

It is a pity that in writing one cannot convey his way of speaking. He never spoke quickly or raised his voice.

One very characteristic evening I remember, when my sister and I dined with Mr. Tonks. Mr. Steer came in later. Mr. Tonks was in one of his most exuberant moods, brilliant, delightful, absolutely Tonks. Mr. Steer sat in the quietest silence I have ever heard, and as the talk went far above my head, I joined his silence. The others got on to perspective of the most complicated kind. My sister kept going brilliantly, but then she was unhampered by the smallest knowledge of perspective. They discussed the curve in the floor of the Parthenon and its relation to the curve of the world's surface; they seemed to me to have flown into the higher mathematics and became, so far as I was concerned, most impressive but quite incomprehensible. Suddenly Mr. Tonks stated that he always did such and such a thing in certain conditions of perspective. He became more and more didactic; beat time more decisively with his long, flat hand, and then exclaimed, 'Everybody *must* do it like that, I *know* it's right, you *can't* do it any other way, you *all* do it, I'm *certain* you all do it—*you* do it, of course, don't you Steer?' A sleepy voice from the corner of the sofa: 'I think perhaps I sometimes do it by mistake.'

A fellow-student and friend of Miss Legge, Muriel Alexander, now Mrs. Collins Baker, adds these notes.

When I was painting in The 'Life' at the Slade, my lessons were mainly from Professor Brown. Mr. Steer then taught more in the 'Little Life Room'—a Holy of Holies where some eight or ten of the special and advanced students worked—Winnie Matthews, Jane Grey, Mary Hogarth and others. Mr. Steer would come into the big life-room once a week, usually towards the end of the model's six days' posing. He would say little, except, perhaps 'You need to see more Black and White!' He might repaint the head and then say 'Now go on with that'; leaving one feeling much as might a schoolboy, had Shakespeare suddenly reached over his shoulder and penned a perfect couplet in the middle of the smug essay on the page. I think that the Black and White remark must have coincided with Steer's own phase of that tendency—'96–'97. I remember vividly an occasion in winter when a group of us, including Margaret Legge, went to tea with him. Timidly, after tea, we asked if we might see what he was painting. Lamp in hand he led us to another room where *The Toilet of Venus* was on the easel. Far too shy to utter words, we made vague noises of admiration, Steer standing behind and holding up the lamp. Suddenly he said 'That's enough I think', and walked firmly away with the light. What stood out for me, and I think for all struggling students who knew Steer, was a confidence in his kindness, a sort of comfortable glow that made many a bleak day warmer. He had an amazing memory for people's needs, and it never failed at the moment when a contact would be helpful. An instance of that was his mention of C.B.'s name when the 'Studio' needed someone to write a Steer notice. That was in very early and difficult days. Mary McEvoy once said to me 'I think Mr. Steer is the kindest person I have ever known'.

One evening at the 'Vale' we were discussing the post-war tendencies of the youth of that time. Tonks and C.B. had both said much—Steer had sat silent on the green couch. Tonks turned to him with 'Well Steer—what do you think?' Steer said, 'I think that all the time we are young we wish that something would happen, and when we are old we wish it hadn't.'

. . . Steer did not see in line. At the Slade School, in the nineties, when, under the influence of Fred Brown and Henry Tonks, the expression of form by line was almost a cult, I once sat behind Steer as he drew the model's head for another student from the end of the semicircle about the model's throne. The girl's head was a delicate projection from cast shadow and penumbra towards the light. Steer said, 'Why all this line? there is no line.'

Miss Grace Wolfe, by marriage Mrs. John Wheatley, writes:

To-day I have tried to go back to those days when Mr. Steer was a god, one that had little foibles, but still a god. How well I remember painting in the Life at the Slade;

the door would open slowly for him: instantly we all turned to smile—hoping he would come to our end first. If he did, we immediately fetched a high stool. He would sit down and perhaps not speak for five minutes. I well remember one morning I had put on the model a little old blue shawl and when Mr. Steer came in he walked to my stool and looked at the shawl. Then he held out his hand for my palette and brushes (I was very careful always to have the kind he liked and very clean) and he painted for an hour without saying a word. It was a breathless experience. When he rose I couldn't think how to thank him. He taught much but said little.

Later, when I was married and we lived at No. 1 The Vale, he came in almost nightly.

We used to spend delightful evenings upstairs in Professor Tonks's flat. Usually Mr. Steer was there, perhaps George Moore as well, and sometimes our little daughter Elisabeth with us. Mr. Steer was very fond of her and gave her many a charming toy. He used to ask her to visit him and show her his china. When she married he gave her an engraving after Fragonard.

He said it was a bad plan to give away one's work. He had once given a water-colour to a young woman and the same evening he found it left on a seat by the sea; it made a deep impression on his mind.

One day he came to see our R.A. pictures, and he had a wonderful new hat. When he left his hat was found to be missing—only a small one in the hall which he perforce wore perched on the top of his head. It cost my husband more than a pound in taxis to retrieve the hat, which had been carried off by Sir George Clausen, who said when he discovered he had worn it, 'I thought I was becoming a good colourist.'

Professor Wheatley stereoscopes his wife's portrait:

When I was about ten, say in 1902, for some reason the Lord Mayor of London paid an official visit to Abergavenny, and had tea with us. He brought with him his Chaplain, who was interested in my boyish efforts at painting and said, 'When you grow up you must go to the Slade and study under my brother, Wilson Steer.'

The first time I met Steer was in 1913. I had married a Slade student, Grace Wolfe, in 1912, and we decided to bust the fees for half a term, as I wanted to know the meaning of all this to-do about drawing. Mr. Koe Child, the secretary, told me I must present myself to the Professor, with works, to gain admittance to the sacred precincts. I arrived one day at two o'clock (the appointed time), with a self-portrait in oil and a charcoal drawing of a woman and child, to find a very thin, tall man sitting at a table, and a very stout man leaning on the mantelpiece and smoking cigarettes. The thin man (Professor Tonks) on seeing my painting, started a tirade against Watts (thereby shaking the foundations of my soul) and I was ordered never to look at a 'Watts' again. Of the charcoal drawing Tonks said it should have been put in a bottle as a medical specimen! However, I was admitted and allowed to proceed directly to the Life Class. Next day Steer came up to me and said 'I shouldn't worry about your painting—I thought it was very good.'

In 1918 I met Steer again at the Chelsea Arts Club, to which he proposed me as a Member, and from then onwards we became close friends. It was his practice to call at our Studio every night on his way to the Chelsea Arts Club when he examined and criticised the day's work. Anxious as I was to learn I found it difficult to reconcile his teaching with his practice. For example, he was a very abstract painter of landscape, but he seemed to be absorbed in getting it what he called 'right'. Then there was the question of 'Tone'—I could never find out whether he meant realistic imitation of nature, or some artistic convention. When I thought I had done a particularly good bit of painting he would say 'Well—you will go on with that'. On other very rare occasions when I had done something I thought indifferent, he would say 'I should leave that, it has come off'.

I remember once we planned an expedition to the Dulwich Gallery, and spent a very exciting afternoon there. The whole way back in the train Steer kept on repeating in Cockney 'It's the loight and shide that counts'. Another saying of his was 'Forty years of a wasted life—forty years I have painted thick and I ought to have painted thin'. One evening when he came to the studio he said 'They have decided I must have an Assistant at the Slade and I have chosen you, but Tonks will be coming to tell you about it'.

Steer's own work grew apparently without effort: he was the perfect example of the Chinese tradition that all artists should be amateurs. Though he had a good studio in his house, he never painted in it to my knowledge; he always worked in a corner of his drawing-room. Though he didn't know it he was a Zen Buddhist. He even unconsciously adopted the correct position for meditation, seated upright with his feet crossed and his hands clasped, thereby completing the circle.

He was always much relieved when Tonks had finished his picture for the time being. He used to say, 'That's off our chest.' He was full of curiosity about the R.A., which he described as 'a body of men elected to keep other people out'. Every varnishing day I was expected to go straight to his house and give him an exact description of work by people he knew.

Towards the end of his life I was in his room when he was selecting a watercolour for the R.A. He explained to me that MacColl had ordered it, so it had to be done, but for the next three weeks we all suffered agonies of apprehension in case it shouldn't be accepted.

He was always much amused at the antics of the non-painting Art Critics, calling them 'Art Boys'. He put his friends into two classes, one of which was the 'donkey class'. One day, when crossing the road at the World's End to avoid a taxi, he sprained his ankle, whereupon Sickert wired him 'Do be careful—I have no desire to be the greatest living painter'. When Sickert was elected to the R.A. he rushed off to Steer and said 'I should like my first action in the R.A. to be to nominate you', to which Steer replied, 'Because you are a . . . there is no need for me to be one.'

At the Chelsea Arts Club Steer was the most popular member; every one loved him; indeed he was the uncrowned King of Chelsea. At the Club he dropped all his little affectations such as holding a handkerchief over his nose, a relic, Tonks told him, of medieval enchantments.

He liked to have artists round him to go out and find views to paint. Another amusement was to buy pictures by inferior artists and finish them.

Mr. Franklin White, another Slade student and eventually Assistant, adds these notes, including a tale of Steer playing on his simplicity:

I had very few lessons in oil painting from Steer, as I spent most of the five terms as a student at the Slade, drawing; but, the few lessons I had from Steer, as a student, always left me with the impression that either I was completely off the track, or I was going the right way about things: I cannot remember Steer showing me anything about how it should be done, but, I do remember that as soon as he came into the room, one hoped he would come and look at one's work, and if he did not one was bitterly disappointed.

From 1919 until Steer left the Slade I was on the teaching staff with him, and during that time, to listen to him quietly was to learn something, and I always became keener on my own work. And I think I learnt more from Steer's kindly interest in whatever I was doing, rather than from any technical hints.

Steer once suggested I should go with him to buy gramophone records, as my wife was a musician. He said he knew nothing whatever about music or where to buy records: we started off; he did not listen to a single word I had to say, and I found I was walking in the opposite direction to the one I tried to suggest, and without speaking to me again he went straight into 'Maples', walked to the gramophone department without asking the way, went straight up to an assistant and asked for the records he required. On the return journey his only comment was that his housekeeper would be very pleased, as he had got some solemn but mostly gay pieces.

Mr. W. L. Clause, another Slade student of the middle years, recalls an instance of Steer's very unofficial sympathy. A pupil, Miss Jean Inglis, was up before the dread Professor's tribunal for judgment of summer work. Tonks scolded her severely. A tear trickled and fell; then a second; but a great warm hand got hold of hers under the table and squeezed it. The third tear did not fall.

To these accounts of the unprofessor-like teacher at the Slade I am able to add the following note of an out-of-school lesson given to the eminent novelist and critic, Mr. Charles Morgan.

Tonks described to me Steer's method of teaching at the Slade, and I think it was confirmed by some student, I can't remember which. He almost never taught verbally, but came up behind the student, watched for a time, shouldered him or her out of the way, took the brush, painted, handed the brush back and departed.

The other story is personal. For several years I had made a habit of working every Saturday in the studio of a painter-friend, Fred Stratton. We shared a model and drew the figure. I used pencil and refused to attempt paint until I could be sure that I had the elements of drawing. I even refused charcoal, because I thought that allowed a margin of error and so (like red chalk on tinted paper) would allow me to flatter myself. Of course, from one point of view, this was wrong and made me draw too 'tight'. I knew Tonks well and often supped with him on Sunday nights. I concealed from him, for obvious reasons, the fact that I ever used a pencil. George Moore told him that I drew and Tonks asked to see my work. One Sunday night I brought a portfolio of drawings. They were left in the studio while we had supper and then returned to the fireside. He had begun to look at them when a man walked in whom I had never seen before. Tonks introduced me, giving my name, but not that of the newcomer. I sat facing the fire, with Tonks on my right and the newcomer on the sofa to my left. They handed my drawings to and fro between them. While this critical process was going on, I discovered to my horror that I was between Tonks and Steer. They completely disregarded me, took out pencils, and began to draw sections and God knows what wherever there was blank space and sometimes where there wasn't; anyhow, it was a joy and excitement to me. At the end Steer and I left together. On the way down we paused to examine the early pencil drawing of a draped woman by John which hung on the stairs. I was living in Cheyne Walk at the time and we walked down the Vale together. For a long time Steer said nothing. Then, suddenly, 'I was interested in your drawings. Of course, they are not good drawings, because they are too tight, but there are passages in them (and he reminded me of a particular shoulder) which are as deadly *accurate* as any drawings I have seen.' Then, after a pause, he added, 'But you know there are other masters beside Ingres. I suppose Ingres is your master.' When I had acknowledged this, he said, 'Do you remember that drawing by John? It was done at a time when he drew with many lines and many of those lines were superfluous or even wrong, but then, at the last moment he would select among them and emphasise those which were right, and so, by an act of genius, save a drawing which, in the hands of any other man, would have become a mess and a failure. You must learn to let yourself go, and that is what I mean by letting yourself go.'

It would be silly for me to be brought in as a draughtsman which, alas, I am not; I tell it as probably one of the few occasions on which Steer positively uttered anything.

I confess, for my own part, to grudging the time taken by Steer from painting and given to desultory teaching at the Slade, once he was independent of the post as a source of income: but it is difficult to judge the pros and cons from outside. Visits to the Slade had become a habit, and to watch the growing snowball of his fortune another: to that the Slade income contributed. Tonks's letter to the Provost, however, was no mere official tribute: in one to A. M. Daniel, in which he speaks with deep feeling of the break with his students he adds:

Steer, particularly taking into consideration his natural inaction, has, in his conduct to the school, been remarkable. It has counted much for making the place what it is, and making him what he is.

A colleague at the Slade, Mr. George Charlton, in a letter to me confirms this tribute:

... The point I should like to see recorded (and only his colleagues, perhaps, really were aware of it), is that he was very largely the 'Brains' of the Slade. Tonks certainly deferred to Steer's opinion, as you know, most of the time, especially so in the School. I imagine Brown felt much the same, though he had retired just before I joined the staff. Steer had a large say in most of the prizes and other awards. He was very useful behind the scenes ...

Steer's own word, in a letter to the Secretary of University College, was of 'services in the past which have always been regarded by me more in the light of pleasure than work'.[1]

[1] It is wholesome to remember that the French reform of English school-practice introduced at Westminster and the Slade had itself the seeds of academic petrifaction, namely drawing to a standard scale, independent of the student's distance from the model. At Westminster, for my own part, I dropped the regulation 'Ingres' sheet and charcoal for pencil and paper of a natural size and Sickert's introduction of the same practice in his Chelsea classes led to its adoption at the Slade.

XIII

OBITER DICTA

Unless questioned or roused by discussion Steer volunteered little about his artistic preferences. At the time of the National Gallery Centenary celebrations the 'Manchester Guardian' sent round to various painters for a list of the five 'pictures that please me most' in that collection (2 April 1924). To this summons Steer replied dutifully with:

1	Rembrandt	*A Jew Merchant*
2	Velazquez	*Philip IV*
3	Michael Angelo	*Entombment*
4	Correggio	*Venus*
5	Piero della Francesca	*The Nativity*

Of these, if not his deepest homage at least his strongest affection went to Correggio for the 'silvery' quality in his voluptuous flesh painting. Another picture for the same reason attracted him, the *Venus, Cupid, Folly and Time* of Bronzino, and amused him by its variety of amorous appeal. About one virtue in the bust portrait of *Philip IV* Mrs. Wheatley questioned him, 'What was the secret of its extraordinary dignity?' He thought a moment and replied 'Placing'. I was surprised in early days by his indifference to Holbein: he thought it strange that a contemporary of Titian should remain so linear a painter. Neither he, Tonks nor Sargent could be persuaded that the *Rokeby Venus* was by Velazquez; but neither Steer nor Tonks ever saw the Prado, and their objection rested on a false theory about reflection in a mirror. Claude was of course one of his masters, as he had been of Turner. Mr. Vernon Wethered writes on this head:

Someone from North Wales wrote to ask Steer for the loan of one of his water-colours as he wanted to know how to paint trees. Steer, instead, sent him a little book of reproductions from Claude's drawings, saying that was how he had learned himself. It was always a surprise to me how, living in London for nine months of the year he had produced the landscapes he did. I have concluded that, regularly frequenting Christies' sale-room he supplemented nature by study of masters, old and new.

To Alfred Stevens, Connard reports, he gave top place among English artists. This surprises me, for it was almost a grievance in the

Moore circle that my devotion was so great. Christopher Wren, as an architect, did not occur to him. Steer is joined in Orpen's group with the admirers of Manet, and rightly, but his 'homage to Manet' was mingled with some reserves, and he was critical of that particular picture, the *Eva Gonzalez,* thinking that values were wanting in the flesh. He told Collins Baker that he was put off at first from Manet's painting by a swollen, pneumatic-tyre look of the muscles. I remember how misleading the sharp first impact of Manet's painting could be. I was carried away by the *Olympia,* but remembered it from a first visit as defined by strong dark outlines like *cloisons.* There is nothing of the sort. Manet himself was not aware of the unmistakable family resemblance of his works. He told Mallarmé that with each picture he tried to begin anew.

Classic formality did not appeal to Steer. He reckoned it a fault in Whistler's *Mother* that no one would sit like that, parallel to the wall. Here came in the baroque quirk that has set all painted interiors ajee from Hogarth onwards, for fear of shallowness, a habit that raises more difficulties in composition than it helps recession. Whistler, like Emmanuel de Witte, painter of *Bedroom with a Woman at the Harpsichord,* was a classic in square-set disposition. Cézanne Steer had summed up soberly, as have noted, in 1907, five years before the explosion about him in London. He told me then of the *Black Clock,* an early work of exquisite colour and no oddity of form which reappeared in the Burlington House Exhibition of 1932 over against some ridiculously malformed apples, proclaimed by the mystagogues to achieve rotundity by being irregular polygons, shabby in colour as well. The loud or hushed re-echoing of Cézanne's name by the literary purblind over the distortions of a failing eyesight wearied Tonks and Steer so much that they came to call him 'Mr. Harris'. Of others among so-called 'Post-Impressionists' Steer said gently, 'I suppose they have private incomes,' but the dealers and the 'Art Boys' (an American term that delighted Tonks), saw to it that the incomes swelled to fantastic heights. To Dermod O'Brien he said that Tonks did all the foaming at the mouth necessary about contemporary foreign painters, and that Matisse had nice colour. But for the so-called Sur-realists, whose 'sub-conscious' is a highly conscious portrayal of the sub-visceral, a plumber's view of humanity, he must have had a lively distaste. To console his niece for rejection at a picture-show he wrote, 'evidently you, unlike some of the ultra-modern school, had nothing in your system to get rid of.'

Of the older French, Watteau was near his heart, and he delighted in engravings of eighteenth century *scènes galantes* not only for that vein but for their equable grey tone upon a wall, as opposed to the scratchy black-

and-white of etchings. He prized also English wood-engravers of the sixty-seventies, Boyd Houghton for one. 'Charles Keene', he said to Behrend, 'is a great man, a genius. Look at the light and colour in his landscapes, a field of turnips, for instance.'

He was no snob in his judgments. In Thomas Couture, whose more ambitious work has cast a chill on his reputation, Steer admired a notable painter, more particularly impressed by his portrait, *Une Patricienne*, in the Scottish National Gallery.

Among older English contemporaries out of fashion he had a respect for J. W. North; among the Scottish of his generation for Roche, Peploe and McTaggart, thinking the smaller pictures of the last the better. He was asked, Gray tells, whether he agreed with a newspaper statement that Sickert was England's greatest artist. He replied:

'Greatest artist' is a formula people rattle off without thinking. It may be true one day and not another. Somebody said that Tintoretto was beyond criticism and beyond praise, and that, I think, is a very just estimate.

A rare instance of a critical note after visiting an exhibition relates to the group of paintings acquired by Holmes at the Degas Sale in Paris. Amiens was under fire at the crucial moment of the German advance when he brought them away rolled up in his hand-baggage:

8.12.1918
I went yesterday to see the recent acquisitions at the N.G. but it was crowded and did not see them well. I was disappointed in one of the Manets, his wife nursing a cat, which looked to me like a picture he began and not caring about never went on with it. The other for some reason I missed. I liked the look of a full-length portrait by Delacroix, and there is an Ingres portrait of a man highly wrought but not intensely interesting, to me, at any rate.

Measured in his praise of others, he was more than modest about himself. I heard him, when one shaky draughtsman had been severe about another, mutter: 'I know that *I* can't draw, and that's a comfort.' He knew at least how infinite the degrees, but perhaps did not realise how much drawing is a faculty that goes and comes, with use and disuse and occupation with linear or other aspects. Wethered recounts that:

Looking at a collection of drawings by Muirhead Bone Steer observed, 'I couldn't draw like that.' I replied, 'If you could you couldn't paint as you do.' He didn't agree to that. Also he once said 'I can't draw features. I should like to be able to draw like Orpen.'

At times he did apply himself to precise line. Behrend writes:

At Greenhithe during a heat wave of brassy sunlight, cloudless skies and no effect, we sat in the shade on the river bank. He spent three successive mornings there, with pencil, pen and colour, on the same drawing (of H.M.S. Worcester), putting it all in, including river, craft and figures. I do not know that he actually counted the portholes, though he told me, with a twinkle in his eye, that he had. He produced a highly interesting drawing, though not a typical Steer. Eventually he gave it away to a friend. He felt that kind of thing was not in his line.

When called on for a judgment or opinion, he spoke briefly to the purpose, but he could also relieve a strained situation with a comically interjected word. Thus at a 'New English' jury meeting, as Randolph Schwabe recalls, when the untrimmed nude of a woman came up for decision and there was some embarrassment because ladies were present, he interjected the word 'Beaver!' Everyone laughed and tension was relaxed. Such interventions were accompanied by an abdominal heave and chuckle or were ejaculated in a plaintively high head-voice.

At an evening party he was sitting beside a lady when, leaning on a stick, an artist entered who had lately been in court charged with assailing the virtue of a domestic. 'What's wrong with Mr. X?' Steer was asked. 'O, housemaid's knee, I suppose', was his reply.

Another instance of Steer's wit, but operating as a solvent and a kindness, is told by one of a group of artists, near neighbours of Steer, including Ethel Walker, Beatrice Bland and Louise Pickard, whom he called 'The Cheyne Walkers'. A fourth was the accomplished painter who could no longer be 'Miss' but scrupled to be addressed as 'The Lady Harberton', and therefore insisted on being 'Fairlie Harmar' without prefix. She writes:

Several of us went to a tea party at Beatrice Bland's, including Mr. Steer. B.B. said she was feeling rather upset as So-and-so had come in that morning and blasted her work, saying her flower-paintings were 'just like tin'. Most of us tried to comfort her, and said it was useless to take any notice of that painter in one of her devastating moods, but Steer said nothing, till about twenty minutes later, when he got up to go. He walked across to a vase of beautifully arranged tulips in the window, and said, 'How lovely . . . just like tin.' For a moment B.B. did not realise the subtle compliment he had paid her.

She goes on:

When I was first up for election at the New English Art Club, hardly any of the members knew me, and Steer, who had proposed me, was asked if I were a man or a woman? In his slow drawl he replied 'She dresses in female attire'. I told him that when I filled-in Exhibition forms, and was asked to state whether 'Mr., Mrs., or Miss', I generally wrote 'Neither'. Steer said, 'They will think you are a hermaphrodite.'

Steer seldom let his wit run away with him when it touched fellow-artists and might be reported to them. Once he was indiscreet at a 'New English' varnishing day over Charles Shannon's *Wounded Amazon*, calling it the 'Wounded Watts'. Winter, the sales-secretary, repeated this gaily to the painter, 'We call it', he said, 'the Wounded Watts.' Shannon was deeply offended and walked no more with us.

Steer would himself have taken such a joke or more serious rebuffs in good part. Thus:

I introduced him to a young niece who complained that her picture at the Academy was 'skied up'. He asked her what she meant by 'skied up', and when she replied 'On the second row', he remarked, 'When I sent I was five up.'

He had the Englishman's exaggerated dislike for demonstrations of feeling. One summer, with Gray and another friend, he found an old barn for studio. The last 'ran backwards and forwards in a sort of fine frenzy!' Steer turned to Gray and said 'He's very artistic, isn't he?'

Augustus John, as a stickler for propriety, writes in the P.S. to a warm letter of appreciation:

What used sometimes to get my solemn goat with Steer was his frivolity.

XIV

PAINS OF CELEBRITY

He who is aflutter for fame perceives not that of those who remember him every man will soon be dead: so too in due course will each of their successors, till the last flicker of memory, through flutterings and failings, dies altogether out. Nay, assume that those who remember you are immortal, and memory immortal, what is that to you? To you dead, absolutely nothing. Well, but to you living, what good is praise, except indeed for some secondary end? Why then neglect unseasonably nature's present gift, and cling to what one or another says hereafter?

Anything in any wise beautiful or noble owes the beauty to itself, and with itself its beauty ends; praise forms no part of it; for praise does not make its object worse or better. This is true of the commoner forms of beauty—material objects for instance and works of art—no less than of the ideal; true beauty needs no addition, any more than law, or truth, or kindness, or selfrespect. For which of these can praise beautify, or censure mar? Is the emerald less perfect for lacking praise, or is gold, or ivory, or purple, a lyre or a poignard, a floweret or a shrub?—Passages marked in Steer's 'Marcus Aurelius Antonius to Himself', a favourite book.

To Steer celebrations and honours were trials like a very hot day: he endured rather than enjoyed them. There was a private recognition of his quality as far back as 21 December 1901 in a dinner at the Café Royal organised by Rothenstein, ever active in such 'friendly leads'. Brabazon, as senior of the 'New English', was in the chair: I thought it was the turn of someone else to bear witness and put up Fry. T. B. Kennington, York Powell, and Croal Thomson also spoke.[1] Unaware that Sargent had come under promise not to be called on, I suggested he should say a word. Ever generously ready at the call of duty or kindness, he rose, clung to the table, puffed and blowed with starting eyes, made beginnings of words that never reached syntax as a sentence and were drowned in admiring applause as he sat down and mopped his brow. Steer had strictly bargained to be silent.

[1] Scribbled on a menu card for Steer are the signatures of those present: Fredk. Brown, Cyril Butler, J. G. Legge, John S. Sargent, H. B. Brabazon, L. A. Harrison, W. G. v. Glehn, Fred Pegram, W. A. Russell, Philip Treherne, F. H. Townsend, J. Derwent Wood, J. H. M. Furse, Max Beerbohm, Oswald Sickert, C. J. Holmes, Robert Ross, David Croal Thomson, H. Harris Brown, Walter Sickert, T. Cyprian Williams, Francis Bate, Francis E. James, Henry Tonks, G. W. Prothero, Herbert Trench, Roger Fry, Wm. C. Coles, Maxwell Balfour, D. S. MacColl, W. Rothenstein, Fredk. York Powell.

The Royal Academy, which in course of time has recruited so many members from the New English Art Club, would fain, no doubt, have included Steer; but secure in the rivalry of collectors for his work, and by nature loyal to old ties and indisposed to change, he was content to exhibit at the Club or with the Thomsons at the Goupil Gallery and Barbizon House. He took, however, some pride in the fact that no direct overtures had come from any Academician. Muirhead Bone testifies amusingly:

I remember a time shortly after the last war when Steer, Tonks, Orpen and myself dined together to discuss the affairs of the New English; the idea being to make it easier for the younger artists, who had come forward with their war pictures, to join the Club. We were talking afterwards in Tonks's studio and the Royal Academy came up. Steer said no Academician had ever asked him to join the R.A., whereupon Orpen with his quick Irish way said 'Well here's one asking you *now*, Steer'. Steer had forgotten, I think, that Orpen was an Academician. He was rather taken aback, indeed nettled, and protested that it wasn't fair taking a man up in a private house like that. He refused to think he could be robbed of his distinction in a moment.

Mr. Collins Baker took a hand in persuading him to yield at the Chantrey Fund's second approach:

I recall his intense reluctance to agree to sell a picture to the Chantrey people. At first (I *think* I'm right) there was a question of their buying a nude of his called *Bathsheba*: Steer practically refused to entertain the idea, which in any case fell through. Then *Mrs. Raynes* came up, and he was just as shy of letting them have that. We argued all through lunch, and finally after the table was cleared he sat down to write that he would agree. He had a lot of difficulty with the letter. But I am sure he was really pleased, once he'd got over the hedge.

He exhibited with 'Les XX' at Brussels in 1891, but, as we have seen, he chilled off about America, after sending, without result, to Pittsburgh. In 1926 I endeavoured to enlist the enthusiastic but erratic Duveen in English artists. He had proposed to me to buy up the whole annual 'output' of Sargent in watercolours; I cut that down to half-a-dozen, which I selected and induced Steer, not warm about it, to hold some pictures for him to sell. Here are letters we exchanged:

Steer wrote:

13.6.26

I'm afraid some of the pictures that were knocking about when you were here have gone, but I will be pleased to see you and Duveen on Thursday or Friday. Perhaps you would know if this is convenient when we may meet at the Committee meeting of the New English on Wednesday.

Something must have blocked this arrangement, but I wrote again later:

7.7.26

I saw Duveen yesterday, but he had various engagements, and as you had sold two of the pictures and I was not sure whether you were still in town I did not attempt to bring him on. But I talked to him about a possible exhibition in New York and Paris of pictures by a group of 'New English' artists. He said at once, 'Let's do it!' and he is coming to lunch next week to talk again. He is bent now on buying up all good English pictures or making others do so. Don't speak of this at present to anyone else, but let me know if you could reserve some work in the autumn for this purpose; and you might keep *The Reverie* in hand. I think he would certainly buy it himself if I told him. I should propose to select the works and write an introductory notice.

Steer replied:

9.7.26

I think what you tell me may lead to good results although I have little faith with regard to New York or Paris when it comes to English pictures and personally I am afraid I cannot reserve any pictures I may do this summer as I am already several deep in people I have promised to show them to, and at the moment being laid low with a bad cold I don't feel that there will be any pictures at all, but I do appreciate Duveen's attitude and what you have done to bring this about, which will be of inestimable value to many artists. I will reserve *Reverie* [of the 'Anonymous' Exhibition] in case he cares about it.

I forget what happened thereafter, but the two elusives did not meet and a promising iron must have in consequence cooled.

The prospect of having to make a speech was an excuse for not accepting the presidency of a West of England exhibiting society. He did send a *Walberswick Pier* to a 'Twentieth Century British Art Empire Loan Exhibition' in the National Gallery of Victoria in 1939, or it was sent for him.

His beloved Chelsea Arts Club itself was an occasion of dread more than once because of possible speeches. In April 1931 he wrote:

Tomorrow I have to face the Chelsea Arts Club annual dinner which fills me with horror as I shall have to get up and say a word of thanks. •

In July 1937 he was elected an honorary member of the Club, a distinction that did give him pleasure, and the Tate Gallery exhibition of 1929 brought a new rally at the Club, in which a younger generation joined. Orpen presided; Augustus John, for the young, spoke tersely but fervidly of his master, and Francis Bate was eloquent for the elders. On the same occasion Ramsay MacDonald, then Prime Minister and pleased to 'encourage art' when no expenditure or troublesome political action, as in the matter of Waterloo Bridge, was involved, proposed to put forward Steer's name for a Knighthood. He declined the well-meant offer. A characteristic letter of Tonks to Daniel may be inserted here: it deals with that offer of knighthood (made to Tonks also) and with other matters:

44 STEER IN LATER YEARS

45 (a) 'FLO'

45 (b) STEER AT BOSHAM

27.12.30

If I know my man I feel sure Steer would far rather remain as he was, *and* I will back him up by saying, so would I. Honours, if they must come, should go to young men, who would enjoy the swagger, and if you don't swagger what is the fun? . . . but old people, unless they still remained babes would feel shy and ashamed.

I have always felt Peers should only drive with four horses; otherwise what is the pleasure of being a Peer? Steer is the simplest man I have ever met. He must be pleased he has been a success. I think everyone can enjoy that pleasure, but anyone with a mind at all is able, by that very mind, to see into the far country he has not reached. His influence, by his simplicity, has been very great, beyond his outstanding gifts as an artist. He has always looked for the good qualities in works quite remote from his own. He went to the Tate the other day and was *overcome* by the fineness of Millais' *Order of Release*, thus supporting Delacroix (you know). Just because [of] it being a modern picture *not* painted under the influence of French masters, Fry would, I am sure, laugh at it. Again, he admired and analysed Windus's *Too Late*, a most remarkable work, utterly unlike his own. Men of his kind are naturally very rare; in fact the mould is only used once, yet there is a family likeness in certain great men (I fancy Faraday was of this really modest, simple kind) and it naturally makes them delightful to caricature [?] When he first told me I quite honestly condoled with him, being conversant with his feelings. Still I felt it had to be, so I suppose I was right. I hope so.

P.S. The effect of French painting on English has been Fatal. Fancy Shakespeare, supposing the dates reversed, trying to write like Racine. Shakespeare is absolutely English, so was Constable and the Preraphaelites. But this is a long subject.

In 1931 the Premier returned to the charge, offering the Order of Merit in succession to Alma Tadema, deceased. Steer's impulse was to avoid this also. Mr. Baker tells something of the negotiations:

He was *very* difficult over the O.M. That was offered him (to the best of my memory) in this way. Owen Morshead said to me there was a vacancy in the O.M. honours, and would it not be a fine thing to have Steer to fill it. If I thought so Morshead suggested I should speak to Cromer and I did. Cromer was sympathetic and asked me to sound P.W.S. because it would never do to offer and be refused. When I sounded S. he was very disinclined. He didn't care a damn about that sort of stuff. But with great reluctance he listened to my arguments—you know the sort of thing one would argue—that in honouring him art would be honoured: and he must be a sort of scapegoat etc. etc., and finally consented. And he really was pleased. Then we all, you and Northbourne, Daniel, Orpen, Gleadowe, Aitken, Russell, Rothenstein, got up a memorandum, saying that S. had served art well, and you all signed it.

I have no recollection of signing a memorial and Steer cannot have realised he was committed, for on receiving the royal offer he went round to Tonks, greatly bothered, to ask for help in draft of a letter declining the honour. Tonks, however, now rebelled, and persuaded him that here was a distinction that even he must accept. The announcement brought a spate of congratulations to which he dutifully replied, but to Blackwell he said: 'How odd it is, most men get honours for what they don't particularly want to do and I get one for doing indifferently the only thing I do like—playing about with paints.' To vary the monotony of the chorus I wrote:

31.12.30
My dear O.M.

It takes them some time to catch up. You had the D.S.M. a generation ago only, so this is almost precipitate.

Long may you adorn it!

He replied:

1.1.31
My dear MacColl

Thank you very much for your kind wishes and I am sure the O.M. will not give me anything like the thrill that the D.S.M. did years ago when a raw youth.

With affectionate greetings

Yours ever

P. Wilson Steer

My wife also took the frivolous line:

2.1.31
My dear Pussy Steer

This O.M. business delights me and you have my heartiest congratulations! I wonder if they give it to you for having painted your adorable friend?

Remember that I am coming to tea with you a day soon, and don't call me a snob, because I arranged it before the O.M. business.

A bientôt,

Andrée MacColl

Here is Gray's note about the investiture:

The morning he went to Buckingham Palace to receive the order there was much excitement at 109. Flo and Cicely were thrilled. I went to breakfast with him to look him over before he left. He had a court suit made for him and really cut a good figure: he has fine legs for silk stockings and his feet are well arched. Walter Russell, who was going to the Levée, called for him in a car. He told me after that he had enjoyed seeing the pictures in the room where they were all penned in various degrees of importance. There was an Admiral with him, [Sir Charles Madden] who also got an O.M.

He was unrepresented in the Louvre Collection of English paintings presented by Sir Edmund Davis with advice from Ricketts, but in March, 1938, an exhibition of British Painting was held in the Louvre which embraced our dead painters from Hilliard to Millais, and four living, of whom Steer was one. Paris had its first view of him side by side with Gainsborough and Crome, Turner and Constable. In the following month the Queen broke what seemed to have become a royal taboo by going outside the circle of official portrait-painters to buy a good picture, one of Steer's Chepstow Castle compositions. He was pleased when he heard from Llewellyn, a colleague of early 'New English' days become P.R.A., who had gone to Windsor on Academy business, of the anxious care that had been given to the hanging of his picture, and pleased also because he thought not every artist would have troubled to let him know.

Gray has preserved the draft of a speech Steer had anxiously prepared to read at one of the Club celebrations, and it may fitly close these notes about the shy recalcitrant:

I feel very much overcome by the honour the Club has done me by asking me to this distinguished gathering, in which I find myself surrounded by so many old friends, any of whom I enjoy talking to singly or in twos or threes, but collectively it is quite beyond me and I would that I could, like Alice in Wonderland, become suddenly very tiny and be removed from the room on a clean plate.

Even from this valorous intention he somehow escaped: the speech remained in his pocket.

XV
LAST DAYS

Steer said it was better to look ill and be well like Tonks, than to feel ill and look well like himself. You got more sympathy. (Wethered).

From his childhood Steer had been subject to bronchial attacks, and each winter in Chelsea brought on more or less severe 'colds', sometimes as many as three in a year. It was dread of such disabling times that led to the extreme precautions against draughts and changes from lighter to heavier covering that gave matter for chaff and legend. A true story is that his hostess at a Liverpool dinner-party missed him from his seat and discovered him behind a window-curtain making sure that sashes behind it were shut. Whether he was wise to live in the river mists and to huddle himself so thickly no one can say, but a man with delicate breathing apparatus whose calling took him out into the traps of English 'summer' weather at its most changeable had to take what precautions he could.

Otherwise he seemed hale and vigorous, though he declared to Vernon Wethered, 'I never had much energy,' but having no love of exercise for its own sake, he became torpid in constitution. With advancing years and a sedentary habit he suffered from disabilities which obliged him, in 1927, to get relief from the risky prostate operation. He faced it with his usual calm decision, but his friends were in suspense till his recovery was assured. There was a blank in his landscape painting that year, while he was a convalescent at Brighton.

In 1935 a worse crisis arrested his career as a painter. The threat had become serious in the previous year. Tonks, who kept me posted when I was unable to get over to Chelsea, sent this warning:—

18.3.1934

His eyes are troubling him, think of that! You might perhaps go and see him if you can spare the time (I know too well how badly *I* have treated some of my friends) but if you do perhaps it would be wiser not to know much till he begins to speak about it. Be as cheeerful as possible and above all encourage him. He means so much to his faithful friends.

The trouble grew worse and spread. For a full account of it I am indebted to Dr. Mary Nelson, who attended Steer in his last years. He had first consulted an oculist in 1928, on Tonks's advice, and had then already a serious 'macula choroiditis' of the left eye. This meant that he had no central vision in that eye, but by looking out of the side could see a certain amount. He was unconscious of this condition because he had perfect vision in the right eye. By 1935 the right eye began to shew the same symptoms, and a second eminent specialist was consulted on 27th June. He decided that an operation was ruled out, and as Steer left the room put a hand on his shoulder, saying 'God help you!' Steer grumbled, in telling the story, 'If God could not help me he would not charge me three guineas', but he was relieved that a visit to a Swiss surgeon, urged by some of his friends, was ruled out along with the desirability of an operation.

Dr Nelson's letter continues:

Thanks to the fact that Steer was a marvellous patient he retained a certain amount of vision right up to the time of his death. He was able to walk out alone up to the last, to read headlines in the paper and even as late as the summer of 1938 to attempt to paint a few seascapes at Bosham. It was tragic to see him making these last efforts, but characteristically he made light of his affliction and often said to me that it was just as well that he could not paint any more; that he had painted enough and that many people painted far too many pictures! I often wondered whether he could possibly be as modest as he appeared. Once he was discussing with me whether he should give a certain young woman a wedding present. She had called on him, announcing her marriage. He said 'I don't know what to give her, but of course I can send Flo to Harrods to find something. . . . I *could* give her a picture but how am I to know whether she *cares* for pictures?' At one period such visits from young ladies about to be married were so frequent that he got rather bored with them, so I suggested he should send a gift of 'shells', of which, as you know, he had a fine collection. It amused him to pick them out and pack them in newspaper. I do not know how acceptable they were, but he was less troubled about wedding presents after that!

When he was confined to bed for any reason I suggested a nurse and although he preferred Flo at all times to wait on him, he liked having a nurse to save her trouble, particularly at night. He only once dismissed a nurse and it was for this reason. They were sitting together listening to the wireless. The National Anthem was played. Steer although sitting up for the first time, stood to attention in the King's honour. The nurse remained seated!

Steer took his discharge stoically. His sense of colour revived, and gave him sensations the more exquisite from a vagueness of definition. He even attempted watercolour at Bosham and Chelsea, but the effort to dodge the blind spots and put objects in their places was a painful one. He could find his way about, and entered into shopping like a new game, finding vegetables where they were best for the day and cheapest. For reading the daily paper and dealing with letters, he was fortunate in the engagement successively of two ladies as secretaries. From a letter by the second of these,

Miss Winifred Alexander, I take the following notes. Steer had referred to the oculist's parting words:

He little knew, Mr. Steer said, how from that moment God had blessed him! He had become quite resigned and even found that many things looked better through a slight haze then when he could see them clearly. Though he could not see to paint, he could see quite a lot out of the corner of his eye. He held things at the side of his face.

The last watercolour he painted was about two years before he died. He told me he had not been pleased with it and had done a thing he had never done before; plunged it into a basin of water and scrubbed it gently, then brought it up to dry. The result was a lovely ethereal picture. He sold it almost at once for £45.

I feel you know so much more than I of all his quaint ways: how he used to sit with his hat on for fear of draughts, or pick it up from his side to wear when he went from room to room. He always said the English climate was eight months winter and four months bad weather!

You will know too how much he disliked having more than one visitor at a time, and how the pleasure of receiving letters was spoiled by the thought of having to answer them. When he did so he was as brief as possible, avoiding anything personal, saying one could not be too careful what one wrote; it could be so easily misinterpreted!

Of biographies, he told me, the one he had most enjoyed was of Hugh Lane by his Aunt, because it was simple and truthful, giving an exact picture of the only real Saint he had known.

Latterly he used to do most of the local shopping. He would go out with his red string-bag, and very often was accompanied by his cat and dog, one on either side of him. Both cat and dog died almost a year before him and he missed them very much.

The few things that broke the peace and caused a temporary upheaval were threatened visits from strangers, which were usually refused.

I remember hurrying to see him the morning after Chelsea Old Church had been demolished and when Riley Street was destroyed, expecting to find him in a nervous state; but both he and 'Flo' were unperturbed: in fact he did not seem to realize until several weeks after how bad it had been. He always slept in his basement shelter after the night when a small bomb exploded in the garage behind his house, smashing most of the windows. Even this he took calmly, telling me that thunder-storms upset him far more than any raid.

I remember too being surprised by his self control when 'Flo' one day discovered a young window-cleaner, who must have been slightly mad, 'touching up' a number of his nudes, entirely spoiling at least one. The window-cleaner was dismissed and he and 'Flo' set to work to undo the damage.[1]

From the former helper, Miss M. W. Glenn Huggins, previously secretary to Croal Thomson, come the following memories:

In early days Mr. Steer's family made him a small allowance which at times ran short towards the end of the month. He did not want to write home for more, since the allowance, with care, was really enough. He fended for himself and used to go to one of the cold-meat cook-shops and buy for twopence a ham bone which was nearly

[1] The scrubbing was ineffective: the studies had to be destroyed.

finished. This he boiled and, together with bread, finished the week out till the next allowance came.

(Sir) William Burrell bought his first picture of any account, and gave him £30 for it, which he considered a very good price. With that amount and some others he had £80 in hand and thought he would like to open a banking account, so he called at the Hammersmith Road branch of a Bank and saw the Manager, diffidently asking if he had enough to open an account? He remained with that Branch for the rest of his life.

He always spoke gratefully of D. Croal Thomson, saying he was most kind and encouraging in his early days.

He loved going round the many little 'junk' shops in Chelsea, picking up oddments that were either useful or pleasing to his eye and, like most people, he loved a 'bargain'. One day, after he had been making a 'round' and was telling me about it, I said 'You do love buying things don't you?', to which he replied, with a twinkle 'Yes, even if it's only a bootlace!' He was often to be seen with his string bag at the fruit and vegetable shop of World's End with 'Peter' his dog.

For a short time after his eyesight failed he could not distinguish colour and this gave him much distress. There was a Chinese painting in the drawing-room which had very strong colour, but even in this painting he was unable to pick out the colours. The red, for instance, appeared orange. Fortunately this phase was of very short duration.

One day, when looking out a certain watercolour for him, I noticed that very few were signed, and suggested he should sign them, but he said he could not see to sign them. I said I was sure, with a little help, he could sign them and he practised on a rough piece of paper. The method was to put a white piece of paper immediately under the place where he was to sign, with a ruler on the paper to guide him. He then signed in ink, I immediately blotting the signature so that the ink should not be too strong for the drawing. At first he found it very difficult, and he could sign only two or three in the morning, but it became easier and he was able to sign the drawings quickly. In this way all were ultimately signed without one being spoilt in the process. He told me he rarely signed his watercolours before he wanted them, which accounted for so many being unsigned.

Occasionally he would put either a painting or watercolour from the studio on his easel in the drawing room. One day he had put a Nude (standing) and he asked me how I liked it. I said I thought the colouring was very lovely, but I could not recollect ever having seen a Nude wearing a hat and wondered why he had painted her with the hat on.[1] He said that as she slipped off her clothes and they fell at her feet they picked up the colour in her hat and he had been struck by it and so had asked her to stay as she was while he painted. There was another painting of the same model but in a different position.

He was fond of handbells and had several. When he wanted 'Flo' he would not ring the bell in the dining room but go into the hall and call her. If she did not hear

---

[1] This must have been a variant on the lovely seated figure in the Tate Gallery, obtained by Mr. Rothenstein from the back-room of No. 109. Steer had probably held it back from exhibition in fear of the prudish, or of ribalds like the lorry-driver who, unloading Leighton's *Bath of Psyche,* addressed Charles Aitken with a broad grin and the words, 'A saucy piece!' Steer had an unpleasant encounter in early Dudley Gallery days over a nude which Mr. Walter Severn, the landlord, threatened to take down.

he would then ring the handbell which was kept on the table there. 'He liked the tone of the bell.'

He began to tidy up the studio and to scrap some of his work that he considered bad, as he was most anxious for nothing to be left that would be detrimental to his art. He would cut the canvases into small pieces and burn them on his fire in the evenings and said it was surprising what a long time they took to burn. Most of the sketch-books were scrapped: some of those he kept he asked me to make a few notes in.

When writing to me after some of the raids in London he said, 'I have not had the heart to view what remains of the Old Church. I also feel sad about the disappearance of Christie's, where I have spent so many happy hours.'

He had not liked school. Most of what he had learned was from an old tutor to whom he went for a short time.

There were drawers full of old letters, etc., when I first went to him, that had lain there for many years—so long that they were covered with dust and many of them very faded. They had not been kept for any special reason, but just stuffed into the drawers. He began to tidy these and that took a considerable time, for I had to read each one. Finally they were finished and most destroyed, the rest being put very roughly into a few folders. These I was never able to sort properly, for he talked to me and expected answers, while I tried to: so bored was he in sorting them. He felt however that such a bulk of letters would give his executors a vast amount of unnecessary trouble, so made the effort to clear up most of them.

Miss Margaret Legge, whose recollections as a Slade student have already been drawn upon, gives the following account of the semi-blind period:

Having been abroad a great deal for some years, I lost sight of Mr. Steer, but after he went blind I heard he had enquired about me from friends, so I wrote and asked if he would like to see me. His secretary rang up and fixed a date for tea, and so began a habit of running round every few weeks, whenever I felt I could amuse him and had one or two good stories that would make him laugh. After war began he had few friends left in London, so I went fairly often. If ever I should feel the burden of growing old, depressed because my faculties were not so good as they had been, or sad for the loss of old friends, I shall remind myself of Mr. Steer. In all those years I only once found him at all defeated and that was the day after Chelsea Church had been bombed. There he lived on, half blind, the man so truly described in 'The Times' obituary, 'When Steer was not painting he was waiting to paint.' He was always cheerful, ready to laugh at a naughty story, talkative—it was curious that when he could no longer express himself in paint he became a vigorous talker—and so grateful for a visit.

The day when Chelsea had been so badly smashed up, I went round to see if he was all right, and found him utterly miserable. The electricity was out of order, so that he could not use the wireless; there was no light except a couple of small fairy lamps. Directly I arrived he asked anxiously 'Have you seen the Church?' I replied 'Yes'. 'Is the tower gone?' Again 'Yes', and that broke him nearly. An outpouring followed about his blindness and how he had had nothing but one bit of bad luck after another ever since it happened. He would have told me the whole history, but I thought he was getting too much upset and tried to lead him off on other things. After strenuous efforts I succeeded in getting a few feeble laughs.

46 STEER IN HIS LAST YEAR

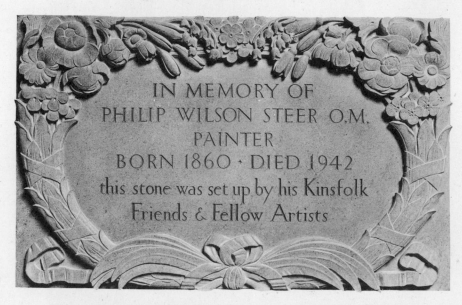

47 ST. PAUL'S MEMORIAL SLAB, *by E. R. Bevan*

Next time I saw him he was cheerful and interested as ever, but never seemed to have quite so much vitality after the bombings of Chelsea and of Christie's. 'What the Queen's Hall means to you, Christie's means to me', he said.

I was puzzled by the care he took to shelter from air raids. He told me he slept on two chairs in the basement and it seemed to me that for a man of his age, with a comfortable bedroom upstairs, to take so much trouble to preserve a life that was now emptied of nearly all that had made it worth having, was strange and unlike him. But at last I discovered the truth. He had had his room in the basement prepared as an anti-gas chamber and not a particle of air could get in. For the first time in his life he was out of a draught!

I remarked one day that though I could not possibly see many years of the strange new, future world after the war, I should like to see the beginning of it. He said 'So should I'. Some spirit after five years' semi-blindness!

Wilson Steer was a great gentleman and looked it. He had a most courteous manner, and even after his blindness would not permit a lady to go away without escorting her to the front door, and—in spite of the draught—opening it for her.

I like to remember him standing on the steps waving his hand as one went down the road.

Dr. Nelson's notes take up the tale:

For nearly two years before his death Steer never went to bed. He sat up in a chair fully dressed in hat and coat in his cellar, whether there had been a Raid Warning or not. 'Flo' sat with him in a space about 4 ft. by 10 ft. Impossible to imagine anything more uncomfortable, but neither he nor 'Flo' complained. I had put my cottage at Bosham at his disposal since the outbreak of the war, but nothing would induce him to leave London.

Steer spent some weeks each summer at Bosham for five consecutive years before the war. He liked this very much. Mr. Johnson of Bosham Garage always fetched him in a large car from Cheyne Walk and in this he and 'Flo', with a mountain of luggage and all windows tightly closed, made the sixty-mile journey. Thus he renewed his acquaintance with Bosham, which he had known and painted as far back as 1914.

Steer remained dressed because he would have had to 'fumble for his clothes and keep people waiting' if a bomb hit the house. 'Flo' completes the picture. Her master, she says, 'said his prayers night and morning.' Together they listened to the evening service, and she joined in the hymns.

Mr. Wilkie, of the Slade School, asked him whether he was affected by rationing. 'Well', he said:

I should like an egg, but I live chiefly on 'Dainty Pudding', it's called. 'Flo' makes it of flour and water and bicarbonate but it must be boiled for two hours, and if you have a little jam or syrup, it's delicious.

A memorable trait of frugality and contentment with 'small mercies' during Total War.

Steer's niece, Miss Hamilton, again puts in a more intimate picture of the man, so obstinately ordinary to slight acquaintances, and deeply reserved even with friends:

Mother and I generally stayed with him once a year when we came South. He was beginning to feel the loneliness of failing sight and death was breaking up his Circle, but his patience under the trial of blindness was the final seal upon his nobility of character. Only four times did I hear him refer to it. He told me he was fortunate in being able to meditate, 'but I have meditated all my life, so I am never bored.' He once quoted from the blind Milton, 'They also serve, who only stand and wait.'

The last time I saw him he again referred to it. 'You have had your trial, and I have had mine, but remember this, no trial is ever sent us we are not strong enough to bear.'

He was at bottom 'sentimental'. He had a hair trunk, bought for the honeymoon trip of his grandmother, Mrs. Harrison, kept in his dressing-room. In it were little parcels carefully wrapped in paper—the blue ribbon shoulder-knots he wore as a baby, a child's handkerchief printed with the head of a pussy, his grandmother's Empire wedding dress of white sarsnet silk, little toys that had belonged to his child-hood, a piece of petit-point needlework by his mother before her marriage, with the names of Philip Steer and Emma Harrison spelt with the initial letters of the flowers. These he asked me to unpack and describe to him, as he sat by my side one sweltering summer day in 1938. Some he discarded, but most we repacked and locked away. There they were, part of his life and tangible fragments of the past, not to be parted with.

Among these souvenirs was a leather note-book which had belonged to his father and in Philip Steer's beautiful Italian hand was written 'Existence is the Aim of Matrimony, Matrimony is not the Aim of Existence', and I think that was Steer's view also. Though he was a wise and delightful confidant over love affairs, he became melancholy when he had news of any friend becoming engaged. 'I have always been sorry for So-and-so, now I am *very* sorry for him.' Someone told him he ought to marry a lady artist. 'Whatever for?' asked Steer. 'Well, you would have a constant companion to talk art to.' 'That is just what I do not want to talk about.' How tickled he was at a lady who could not marry a man because he was too dull to discuss Cézanne. 'Surely enough has already been said about Cézanne,' said Steer.

Deep down in him was a strong fibre of religious feeling, and he was interested in the history of Church Councils, heretics and martyrs. A staunch Protestant, he dis-liked attitudinarians as much as platitudinarians and had a way all his own of fading out when there was so much as a hint of religious propaganda from well-meaning people, though he would speak of them afterwards with kindly tolerance. The clergy disappointed him. 'If ever I ask a parson a direct question there is always an uncom-fortable silence.'

From those graver moods he would recoil. Once when we were sitting by his open window and talking of the radiance of light shining through the young foliage of trees, he suddenly looked very droll, up went his eyebrows, and with mock severity he exclaimed, 'You must not talk about things like *that*! Don't you know it is not done?' and then *how* he laughed!

In August, 1939, Mother and I stayed at Cheyne Walk for the last time. Steer wanted a catalogue made of the pictures in his studio for the British Museum; so we set to work measuring, referring to old catalogues and describing them. It took us several days and we got very dusty and hot over the work, but he enjoyed himself. In the evenings we sat with him as we had done on previous visits, after dinner with the lights dimmed down, listening to Beethoven on the wireless. How he looked forward to a good Concert!

I can see him now, beating time with his hand and nodding his head to the magic of Beethoven, the man he considered one of the Seven Giants of the world. He was funny when he related once that he had specially asked Tonks to an early dinner so that he could share with him Beethoven's Seventh Symphony. 'I looked up and found Tonks fast asleep! You know why, of course, it was because he could not talk.'

Much to Steer's distress an urgent recall to Edinburgh because of my brother's serious illness cut short that happy time we were spending together. The evening before our hurried return to Edinburgh, I read him some passages from John Fothergill's 'An Innkeeper's Diary'. He was highly tickled with the chapter describing his stay at Thame with George Behrend and Monty Pollock in 1923. Then War broke. Mother and I went to live in Worcestershire the following year. This gave an opportunity of seeing him more often. We were anxious for his safety during those years of 1940 and 41, but he would not leave his home. He had the builders in to make a very secure shelter in the basement at Cheyne Walk, the main wall of which was discovered to be of great strength and age, being part of one that had run down to the River since Tudor times.

How sad he was over the old Church; he took me one day to look at the ruin of it which he could just discern.

When I was in London we used to go out for strolls through the quiet side streets of his beloved Chelsea. It was on such a walk, years before, while Tonks was away in the Highlands, that he quoted

> Somewhere in the Isle of Mull,
> Tonks is talking to a gull,
> Talking on the laws of art
> But that bird would fain depart.

It used to cheer him to have the honey from my bees and the asparagus and other country produce from the Vale of Evesham. He was greatly interested in the work of the Women's Rural Institute at Fladbury and enjoyed with relish the bottled fruits from that Centre. My brother used to send him eggs from Scotland as he missed his eggs and bacon very much after rationing came in.

The last time I saw him was at a snowy week-end two months before he died. The years had not bowed him; as he sat by the fire the elegance of his foot with its arched instep in a morocco mule was the foot of a young man as I had known it since childhood and there was the same characteristic droop of that beautiful hand as it hung over the arm of his chair. He was deeply disturbed by the direction the War was taking just then. I am so happy that on that Sunday night I sat up till 2 a.m. to finish off another wool Naval sleeping cap for him and flew round with it to him in a blizzard. I put it on his head and told him how I wished someone would paint him like that. He laughed and looked as pleased as a vain girl, and then I never saw him alive again.

He was being safely cared for by Florence Hood who was now his housekeeper, known to his circle and all of us, as 'Flo'.

Tonks once said, 'How I should love to draw 'Flo'; her face is *entrancing*,' it certainly was alight and full of humorous intelligence. She was not in Steer's employment during thirty-four years for nothing. She came as house-parlour-maid when she was eighteen; was trained by Mrs. Raynes (a hard training too) and was with him until his death thirty-four years later. Steer could not suffer fools gladly nor any laxness of conduct, so the young girl was approved of and moulded into his mode of life easily, becoming a good and faithful servant; she was a remarkable judge of painting and of men. Later she developed an appreciation for music which was as unexpected as remarkable. Like her master, she loved to listen to the B.B.C. Beethoven and Brahms Concerts; she loved too, to join in the hymns on the Sunday evening wireless services, with a fervour learnt in her childhood at chapel. She understood Steer's painting tackle as well as she did his daily needs.

Her devotion during the air raids toward the end of his life was heroic, for he was gradually becoming more and more dependent; he latterly became worried and unhappy if she were away from the house and to her everlasting credit she never once took even an hour 'off' for herself during the year previous to his death; before that he would not move away from home without her after his eyesight failed. She was heartbroken when death took her 'dear master'.

She had a way all her own of addressing him as 'Father'. This began by calling him 'Father' to his cat, but later on any to whom she was deeply attached were either 'Father' or 'Mother'. 'Flo' always abounded in a heartfelt hospitality to anyone Steer liked, and nothing that she could do for them was too much trouble. Wherever or whenever she moved a clatter of noise followed; she was so quick in her movements; but for all her noise she was exactly the right servant for Steer with her tact, her lovable heart and Cockney 'back-chat'. Steer, who was an astute judge of character, thought the world of her and summed her up, 'a big human being.'

Steer put off any too effusive sympathy by affecting satisfaction at having at last leave to be lazy. But in the 'World of Art' interview of 1939, already quoted, he struck another note, recalling what is told of the old Hokusai:

'If you had another eighty years to paint would your painting change again?' 'If I had another eighty years I would start where I left off. I should not have to make all my mistakes again. In fact, when my eyes failed, I had only just got going. It seems as though one has only begun to feel the way when one has to stop.'

He had the resource, however, of an aged and very dignified Scottish lady who was condoled with by her minister on being no longer able to read. 'You forget', she said, 'I have my mind.' Steer had his secret mind and, as he said to Ronald Gray, 'I sit now and put two and two together.' The 'two's' included rumination on the country's political and military affairs, but also matters in which he had been personally concerned. Occasionally he brooded over a past grievance. One of these was 'a knock' he had suffered at the Slade when Brown put Ambrose McEvoy in as a supplementary teacher of painting; a very judicious act, since McEvoy had studied oil technique closely in his copies from the masters and could expound his experience.

Gray made notes of his visits from 1938 onwards. Here are some of them:

Nov. 11th, 1939. Today Steer's nephew ... came at tea-time arrayed in uniform and medals and ribbons from the last war. He said to his uncle Phil: 'You were a special constable in the last war weren't you, and didn't you get ticked off?' and Steer told us that he was on a beat outside the electric station in Manor Street, and thinking he could get a more comprehensive view of the Station from the other side of the road he was walking up and down when a superior special came along and told him his beat was on the other side. Steer explained his reasons for walking where he was and the officer said: 'Really, we live and learn.' So Steer went back to the Station side!

March 1940. I was telling him that some of the brothers in Charterhouse seemed to me quite mad. He said that perhaps we were all mad. He had been thinking about himself lately and had come to the conclusion that he had always been mad! I said that if he was mad then we were all raving lunatics!

In March 1941 I came up for the 50th Anniversary of the Chelsea Arts Club, which was celebrated by a luncheon. The few remaining original members were invited. I took Steer, both of us original members. He went on condition he would not be asked to speak. He enjoyed himself. It was the last time he went to the Club, which he had visited constantly since its beginning.

There was a bad air raid that night. I went to see him in the morning. He was unperturbed and said that if he was to be hit by a bomb he hoped to be killed outright. He and Flo stuck out all the raids. All about his house is devastation. His back windows were blown in and roof damaged.

The following extracts are from letters of Steer to Gray.

No date.
In Chelsea we get a great deal of bombing, especially at night, and there is a time-bomb round the corner, waiting to be either salvaged, or to pop off, and Turner's house is a wreck. I and Flo are so far able to sleep in our basement shelter.

14.5.41.
My house, though battered, is still standing in spite of the two severe raids we have lately experienced, and I have not yet had the heart to view what remains of the old church, nor Christie's for that matter.

14.8.40
Chelsea has been very badly knocked about, so much so, that I cannot go into a detailed description, but no doubt other areas have been just as badly knocked about. So far Flo and I are able to get some sleep in the basement, but when one will be able to go to bed again, I haven't the least idea.

18.4.41
This is just to let you know that I and Flo have survived the very severe raid on Wednesday night, and I know you will be sorry to hear that your old house has lost the windows again, but, as I have been indoors lately with an attack of 'flu', I have not personally seen what damage has been done.

31.12.40
So far I have been fairly lucky and have nothing to report except broken glass and a damaged roof, but Riley Street is practically non-existent, and in the hands of the military, who are pulling down the houses.

Steer answered, in those years of retirement, any call made upon him to honour old comrades. On Tonks's death he was chairman of a committee

M   W.S.

which met at his house to arrange for a bust of the Professor in the Slade School and a memorial tablet on his house in The Vale. When, largely through Sir Alec Martin's activity, the money had been obtained, he attended a luncheon offered to that eager organiser, at which Brown also was present. Again, when on the initiative of Francis Dodd a large group of artists, including Academicians, joined in a tribute to Brown on his eighty-seventh birthday, Steer was again convoyed to the Greyhound Hotel at Richmond, on a rarely brilliant summer's day. Francis Bate emerged from his retreat at Bucklebury Common to take the chair at the luncheon, which brought together a big company. Brown pluckily mastered weakness and emotion to review his career, acclaimed that day by a leader in the 'Thunderer' itself, and avowed that 'having come in as a lion he was going out like a lamb—even a pet lamb'. It was the last time the three veterans of the New English were to meet. Brown was the first to go. He too, when painting had to stop, was plunged in rumination on art, public affairs and religion, and in a long correspondence broke the shy reserve he had maintained. His last letter, telling of an incendiary bomb upon his roof the night before and of his increasing weakness, reached me after his death in December, 1940.

Early in 1940 an exhibition for the Red Cross and other charities took place at Burlington House on lines I had long before advocated, namely a group of Societies, each arranging its own contribution, and Steer was an exhibitor in those rooms for the first time since 1885. When I urged that for the following Academy exhibition he and Brown should join me in leaving a card, so to speak, on our old opponents, he came up to the scratch. The eleventh hour had already struck and his Secretary was called away, but he had looked out a watercolour, contrived himself to affix a label and rang up Messrs. Chapman to convey it. Their last van had gone, but a taxi was called and I slipped in his tribute just on time. The Chantrey acquisitions of his *Mrs. Raynes* and a landscape had already, by the routine of the Bequest, been shown after purchase. The 'end', this, or suspense, 'of an old song', with the watercolour of *Easeby*.

During Steer's last year I was myself disabled, could not visit him, and had to be content with an occasional word on the telephone. In March of 1942 his old enemy, bronchitis, assailed him and this time he did not respond to treatment and rally. On the 18th the faithful 'Flo' sent out danger signals, and Gray hastened from the country to be with his friend, but was too late to see him alive. He had been spared the pains of breathlessness by use of oxygen, but in the dark morning of the 21st he roused himself, making an effort to sit up, and called for 'Flo'. She was at hand and held him when he died at 4 a.m. For the last illness he had been put to bed in the downstairs sitting-room, where was the telephone, and messages had to be sent through a friendly garage next door, an addition to 'Flo's' distractions.

That house of Steer had foretasted trouble between the Wars in the high-tide flood that swamped Chelsea and Millbank, damaging pictures and drenching Turner watercolours at the Tate Gallery, half drowning and poisoning Charles Aitken in gallant efforts at salvage. Here is Steer's description in a letter to Mrs. Hamilton, of what happened at No. 109.

10.1.28

We certainly have had a strenuous time, as the flood came into the basement on Saturday morning and at the height of the tide was 6 ft. 6 in. high. Now we have got rid of all the water but it made a dreadful mess of the kitchen and scullery, which probably will take weeks to dry out. Flo very pluckily rescued the dog, who was swimming about down stairs, and if she had been a bit later the water would have been over her head; it is a great mercy she was not drowned, as she said she lost her feet once or twice. We are now barricaded in the front with planks to height of about 18 in. in case of recurrence, but I don't think this will happen, as the cause was the wind on Friday which heaped up the tide. Luckily Jane slept through it and I don't think quite realises what happened. Compared with many people we are quite lucky and really have very little to complain of.

The house, which served Steer to the end, with some battering, has since suffered heavy damage from the 'Doodlebugs' of Hitler's desperate spite. It is being restored to use by an admirer of Steer's painting.

★

I am indebted to Charles Cheston, Steer's 'New English' Colleague, for the exquisite photograph, reproduced in the above chapter, of Steer in his latter days. Spirit in it shines through the aging flesh, as of a worn painter—visionary.

XVI
POSTHUMOUS

Thunder of traffic will not vex their sleep;
The Dome climbs in a vaster, overhead;
May light perpetual and honour keep
That dormitory of the never dead.

Cremation took place at Golder's Green on a spring day when the flame of crocuses beyond the chapel lit up and died in changes of the light. Only one or two friends were present beside members of Steer's family and attendants. It was decided, however, that his testamentary ban, 'I wish for no tombstone', need not rule out the setting-up of a memorial tablet, if possible, in St. Paul's.[1]

The extent of Steer's fortune was a surprise to his friends, none of whom was in his confidence about money-matters: Tonks at one time even feared he might be hard up. He subscribed handsomely when appealed to, and was generous to any who had claims on him whether from kinship or service, but he never appeared to go out of his way to spend for others any more than for himself: I think, indeed, he was inclined to consider poverty the fault of people rather than their misfortune, and that it was an act of piety to preserve and extend a family inheritance. On the other hand the accumulation of money must have become a pastime and game of skill, like chess, and fallen in with his collector's habit. Chancellors of the Exchequer appeared to him as raging beasts of prey seeking what they might devour of honest men's savings for the benefit of the unthrifty. A sum of £300 for the Artists' General Benevolent Fund and £50 to the Cheyne Hospital for Sick and Incurable Children were his sole bequests of money for a public purpose. He had lent £1,000 to the Treasury without interest on the collapse of France. Other dispositions in his Will, executed 19 December 1939, with a codicil of 16 August 1940, were as follows.

He directed that his portrait by Sickert should be offered to the National Portrait Gallery, his bust in bronze by Thomas Stirling Lee to the Tate Gallery and his Chinese picture, *The Drunken Sage,* to the British Museum. The bequest to the Tate Gallery was inexplicably not accepted. An early portrait of the sculptor by Steer belongs to the Chelsea Arts Club.

[1] It appears that Steer had discussed, in reply to a question from his nephew, the possibility of a tablet in 'Westminster Abbey or elsewhere', not ruling it out.

Ronald Gray was joined to members of Steer's family as an executor and to him and Sir Alec Martin was left the invidious task of deciding which of 'the unfinished pictures, sketches, watercolours and drawings' by the testator should be kept, sold or destroyed. To the second of these was bequeathed a landscape by Richard Wilson and to Geoffrey Blackwell 'my Chinese Gold Splash Incense Burner with cover and cornelian top standing on the wooden chair on the right of the tallboy in my Dining Room': to Nelson Ward (his solicitor and friend) 'the drawing by L. A. Harrison of a Bow Figure in my Drawing Room and two watercolours by me'; two others to Dr. Mary Nelson (who had attended him), the selection to be by Gray.

Money and land property were divided among members of the family; special legacies assigned to executors and to nine friends, including Miss Gough, the highly qualified and faithful housekeeper of Tonks. Those in Steer's own service, past or present, were duly provided for.

A special clause, which has its relevance for this book, was the following:

To the said Dorothea Emma Hamilton [his niece] all letters from other people found among my papers so that she can keep or destroy same as she may think fit she bearing in mind that the copyright in such letters for the purpose of publication belongs to the writers thereof.

Expert care was to be taken for security against any risk of his body being buried alive; it was then 'to be cremated and the ashes scattered to the winds'.

These instructions were scrupulously carried out. Gray and Martin gave their best judgment to the selection of paintings and drawings for survival and sale. Much was destroyed; of salvage from a great accumulation of watercolours some part was bound to be debatable or reprieved under benefit of doubt, but anxious discrimination was exercised. Miss Hamilton had a laborious task, involving much beyond letters from friends. Steer, with his careful business habit reinforced by hoarding instinct, had preserved accounts, professional correspondence and much else. All this was carefully sorted and much of it preserved and filed for the use of a biographer and will be consigned to the British Museum for future reference by any student.

A sale of pictures, drawings, prints, books, etc., was held at Messrs. Christie's on July 16–17, 1942; a second of furniture, another of porcelain and objects of art had taken place on July 15, and a sale of coins and medals at Messrs. Glendinnings followed on October 22. The amount realised at the three sales added to the sum previously declared for probate brought the total to close on £114,000.

The project, briefly discussed after the Cremation ceremony, was taken up by a group of Steer's fellow-members in the Chelsea Arts Club. A committee was formed with Henry Rushbury as chairman and A. S. G. Butler secretary. Consent of the authorities for placing a tablet in 'Painters' Corner' of the Crypt at St. Paul's was obtained. An appeal for subscriptions appeared in 'The Times': Sir Alec Martin undertook the task of Treasurer and added greatly to the range of subscribers by personal appeals, the whole cost of which, with other incidental expenses, he defrayed. In the end a sum of over £1,500 was obtained, a great part of which was contributed by members of Steer's family. The declared objects of subscription, after defraying costs of the tablet, were a silver 'Steer' medal, bearing his effigy, by way of award at the Slade School for outstanding exercises in painting, along with a small money prize; the balance to form a bursary fund for needy students. The total obtained sufficed for all those purposes. The slab, with its sculptured border of flowers, was designed and executed by Mr. E. R. Bevan. The inscription runs:

IN MEMORY OF PHILIP WILSON STEER, O.M., PAINTER, BORN 1860, DIED 1942, THIS STONE WAS SET UP BY HIS KINSFOLK, FRIENDS AND FELLOW-ARTISTS

The medal, designed by Mr. C. W. Dyson-Smith, as a light silver circle, pierced for suspension by ribbon like a miniature, shows, on its face, a profile effigy of the artist in his later years, surrounded by an inscription. The reverse, also inscribed, has a blank centre for the recipient's name and date of the award. It may perhaps escape the fate of most medals, stowed in a drawer which the winner is too shy to open for display. The inscription runs:

Face: WILSON STEER MEMORIAL MEDAL FOR PAINTING
Back: THE SLADE SCHOOL UNIVERSITY COLLEGE, LONDON

The unveiling took place on 27th October, in the presence of many friends and admirers. The Dean and Canon Alexander conducted a dedicatory service, and a short address was given by the writer. The tablet is fittingly placed just below one in honour of John Constable, and Steer takes his place in a chain of commemoration that includes Reynolds, Turner, Millais and other painters.

Before this Memorial was completed an exhibition of Steer's work had been held at the National Gallery during the months of July and August, and part of it, with some fresh accretions, was circulated in Edinburgh and in various provincial centres by C.E.M.A. organisers. The National and Tate Gallery authorities had been handicapped by War conditions, being unable, for example, to draw upon Augustus Daniel's rich collection; they also cast their net too wide by admitting secondary pictures which crowded the cramped and ill-lit quarters, and too many respectable rather than exquisite watercolours. Here, however, for the discerning eye, was 'enough for immortality'. A volume of reproductions sponsored by the Director at Millbank, Dr. John Rothenstein, and arranged by his assistant, Mr. Robin Ironside, was published by the 'Phaidon Press' in May, 1944, a useful, if not a final anthology. The scale of the present work has forbidden any large supplement to that repertory, which it would be difficult in War-time to attempt, as well as premature, but Mr. Yockney's full and careful Catalogue will render the task easier for future taste and scholarship.

ULTIMATE

Turner, Whistler, Steer; each had his place in riverside Chelsea. Steer's end of that village and of its 'Cheyne Walk' abutted on a slummy quarter threaded by 'Lot's Road' and 'World's End Passage', names that a curious fancy might count symbolical. The first of them calls up the scene of a city ablaze with fire from heaven such as visited London in the 'forties, wiped out Chelsea Old Church with its nine centuries of history, struck Turner's old lodging and made a desert round No. 109. The other name might be thought to threaten an end to the world that Steer loved and painted. Already some part of it had gone. At Thame in 1923 Behrend recalls:

. . . he did some work in a broad part of the street where there was a pleasant horse pond, which he put in the foreground of his sketches. Very soon afterwards this pond was filled up and the street levelled, for the convenience of motorists. A year after this we were painting at Long Crendon. He did some watercolours of a group of pine trees from which he painted an oil-picture. But returning to look at them a few days afterwards he found they had all been cut down and sold. At Harwich, where I was with him during a summer and David Muirhead joined us, we frequented a ship-yard, dating from Stuart times, where some of Nelson's craft had been repaired (the 'Three Cups' inn where we stayed has Nelson's name associated with it, and in its courtyard is a wooden medallion in high, coloured relief, of Lady Hamilton). Towards the end of our stay, workmen arrived and began to pull down the deserted buildings, and very difficult they seemed to find it, for those buildings appeared to be bolted and constructed as solidly as one of Nelson's battleships. Everything was levelled, and I was told the corporation intended making a car park there.

John Fothergill has a water colour in his inn of the *Blue Pool* by Steer. This was once a lovely spot off the beaten track, between Wareham and Corfe, and, when I was there in 1921, not very easily approached. Its colour was greenish blue to cerulean, owing to the colour of its bed and the white and cream and pale tints of ochres and burnt siennas of its deep shelving sides. Some years afterwards John Fothergill chanced to visit the pool and he wrote to Steer that he had been there, and had recognized it, 'as it was so unlike your water colour.' A friend of mine tells me that it is now an advertised afternoon's run for Bournemouth visitors and that there is a road to it, with dozens of charabancs and a car park, and a café and tea rooms, but whether it had been tiled and made into a bathing pool was not stated.

These no doubt were the reasons for Steer's remark that 'one half of the world seems to be constantly occupied in mucking up the other.'

Already the 'beauty-spots' of the country were thick-clustered with teashops and cars, walkers were driven from the crowded roads; ribbons of houses blotted out elm rows and pasture; cornfields were derelict; fishing-fleets and sailing barges laid up; coasts given over to asphalt, bathing-boxes or pools, 'fun fairs' and bungalows. Whether, in the new world, there will again be unloaded at such scenes as Corfe Castle coach-loads of grossly fed and apathetic tourists for the regulation round before their meal must be uncertain, and whether the skies themselves will be as crowded and stridulous with traffic as the land. There will still be 'corners' of quiet, no doubt, mountains too and mountain streams, if dams and grids have let them be, and in the museums painted images will satisfy or tease the taste for ancient peace and beauty, if that taste persist. As I write, an anony-mous correspondent, annoyed by the defence of the great view of Durham's Cathedral Castle against its stultification by a gigantic Power House, sends me this admonition with which most of our 'Local Authorities' would sympathise:

Most people, looking out of their carriage windows, would rather see a fine, modern power station (the symbol of a full and glowing life for everyone) than an old cathedral (the symbol of an evil past).

A remnant may think otherwise, and among recorders of sacred shining places, and tumultuous English skies over the scarred history of her wars Steer will not be the least of great witnesses.

'Stainless steel', said Steer, 'is a sign of "progress". In the old days a carving knife carved. A stainless steel knife won't, for you can't put an edge on it.' Painting itself, eviscerated and evacuated as it has been by theoretic gangsters, is an ancient fashion that may lapse, like others before it, but if anywhere a civilised order revive, that art will, like morning, be reborn. The battles of Beauty are never finally won; in each generation they must be fought afresh: It depends on a few voices in each of them whether Titian counts as a master. Let us not be missing among 'Knights of the Holy Ghost'.

APPENDIX

A

A Note on the Family History of Philip Wilson Steer, O.M.

BY LT. COL. W. R. HORNBY STEER

The name *Steer* is not uncommon in Devon and before the middle of the eighteenth century it was commonly spelt *Sture*; it is believed to be of Danish origin and with variations in spelling appeared in the County from the thirteenth century; in the Heralds' Visitations of Devon of 1564 and 1620 are recorded pedigrees of the family of Sture of Huish (a hamlet near Kingsbridge), one of some standing in the County and related to the famous Elizabethan naval commanders, Sir John Hawkins and Sir Francis Drake.

Steer was a direct descendant of George Sture of Hendham, whose tombstone in the Churchyard at Woodleigh records that he died on 2 May 1760 aged 76 years. George Sture was the owner of considerable property in the neighbourhood, in which he was succeeded by his son Henry, and the family have continued to own farmland in this area. Philip, a younger son of George Sture, leased the property of Borough in the parishes of Woodleigh and Charlton. This was later purchased by the family and in due course passed by inheritance to Steer and his brother Henry, the Rev. William Henry Hornby Steer. The latter's son, Steer's nephew, William Reed Hornby Steer, has now succeeded to this property.

Henry Sture's second son, Philip Steer (1751–1827) owned and farmed the property of Bickley in the parish of Halwell, where he is buried. He married Mary, a daughter of Richard Paige of Harleston. This lady, who died in 1837 aged 82, is the subject of a portrait painted by her grandson, Steer's father. It is worthy of note that a nephew of this Philip Steer crossed the Atlantic in 1824 and founded the family of *Steers* of New York, of whom George Steers was designer and builder of the celebrated yacht 'America', first winner (1851) of the trophy now known as 'The America's Cup'. The descendants of the American branch of the family have frequently visited this country. Although his brother Harry always welcomed such reunions, P. W. Steer was not much interested in his American cousins.

The eldest son of Philip Steer of Bickley, another Philip Steer (1779–1860), was Steer's grandfather. He farmed the property of Yetson in the parish of Ashprington and later that of Highhouse in the parish of Dodbrooke, in whose churchyard he is buried. He married Mary (1786–1881) daughter of Thomas Cutmore of Ashwell in the parish of Diptford by his wife Mary, daughter of Robert Pryn of Morleigh. Thus this daughter of Thomas Cutmore of Ashwell was Steer's grandmother. After her husband's death she resided at Borough, then occupied by her second son, Thomas Steer (1812–1884), Steer's 'Uncle Tom', whom he and his brother, Harry, often visited in their early years. Steer's grandmother died at the age of 95 and was interred with her husband at Dodbrooke. .

The eldest son of Philip Steer of Yetson and Highhouse, another Philip Steer (1810–1871), born at Yetson, was Steer's father. All the hamlets to which reference has here been made lie close together in the neighbourhood of Kingsbridge, and it is clear that Steer's father was born of stock which had its roots very firmly planted in the ruddy and fertile soil of that corner in Devon. Steer's father, however, did not follow the family tradition of farming, but earned his living as a painter and teacher of painting. Paintings by him now in possession of the family include the above-mentioned portrait of his grandmother, Mary Steer, and also portraits of his father, his wife, and his daughter (as a child), a self-portrait, and several scenes of the Devon coast and the Wye Valley. Philip Steer married late in life (1853) at Hanwood, Shropshire, Emma (1816–1898) the elder daughter of the Rev. William Harrison, M.A. Philip Steer's work led him to live at various places away from his native County, and thus it chanced that it was at Birkenhead that Steer, their third and youngest child, was born on the Festival of the Holy Innocents, 28 December, 1860. Later, Steer's parents lived at Whitchurch in Herefordshire, where they are buried.

Steer's mother, daughter of the Rev. William Harrison, was descended from the Yeoman family of Harrison which had owned and occupied Woodhouse Farm in the Parish of Aldford (near Chester) since the seventeenth century. Their substantial tombstones may still be seen in Aldford Churchyard. Mrs. Philip Steer was in direct descent from John Harrison of Woodhouse (1700–1778) who married Margaret, daughter of William Jeffreys of Wem, a kinsman of Lord Jeffreys of Wem, the famous Lord Chancellor. Although his brother was a strong supporter of the case so ably made by H. B. Irving in 'The Life of Judge Jeffreys', 'whitewashing' the Judge, Steer was disposed to accept the more popular view of the Chancellor's conduct. John Harrison's sister, Mary, married (1729) their neighbour, Thomas Brassey, of Bulkeley, the great-great-grandfather of the first Lord Brassey of Bulkeley.

William (1742–1812) second son of John Harrison, abandoned agriculture and embarked with considerable success on various commercial activities in Chester, of which City he was elected Mayor in 1795. He married (1767) Catharine, daughter of William Tapley, a freeman of that City. This lady was reputed to be of great beauty in her youth, and there is some evidence of this in her portrait painted in later life by her daughter-in-law, Mrs. George Harrison. This gifted daughter-in-law also painted successful portraits of her husband, herself, her father-in-law, and her cousin Thomas Jeffryes of Wem, all of which are now in possession of the Steer family.

William (1781–1859), a younger son of the above-mentioned William Harrison and the maternal grandfather of Steer, graduated at Brazenose College, Oxford, where he was awarded the Hulme Exhibition (1804). He entered Holy Orders and at one time officiated at Trinity Church, Chester, the parishioners of which presented to him a handsome silver cup weighing 5 lbs. 14 oz. avoirdupois which is now in possession of the Steer family. The Rev. William Harrison married (1815) Mary (1786–1866) the only child of Joseph Hornby, a wealthy citizen of Chester who was appointed Sheriff of that City in 1808, and at his death left his fortune to his only child, then Mrs. William Harrison (Steer's grandmother). It was on this account that at his baptism Steer's elder brother was given the name of Hornby. The wife of Joseph Hornby and mother of Steer's grandmother was Mary, daughter of Thomas Dickson of Backford. This lady, through her mother, Elizabeth, daughter of John Street of Stanney Hall by his wife Mary, daughter of Thomas Wilson of Bidston Hall, was a kinsman of Thomas Wilson who was Bishop of Sodor and Man for the amazingly long period of fifty-eight years (1697–1755) during which he wrote many important theological works, and instituted a much needed translation of the Bible into the Manx language for the use of the people in his diocese. It was out of respect to this distinguished and learned prelate that at his baptism at St. John's Church, Birkenhead, Steer was christened Wilson. He also received the name Philip, this being the Christian name borne by his father, grandfather and great-grandfather on the Steer side of the family.

It is not pertinent for the present purpose to dwell more fully on the history of the Harrison family other than to record that it played an important and active part in the life of Chester, producing several mayors and a large number of clergymen and doctors.

As already recorded, Emma, elder daughter of the Rev. William Harrison, married (1853) Steer's father. Steer was the third and youngest child of the marriage, the eldest being Catharine (Kitty), who married (1875) Charles

Edward, son of Col. Alexander Duke Hamilton of Kelvedon in Essex, and has issue one son and one daughter. The second child of the marriage between Philip Steer and Emma Harrison was Steer's only brother the Rev. William Henry Hornby Steer, T.D., M.A., J.P. (1856–1938) who, like Steer, was educated at Hereford Cathedral School. He later graduated at St. John's College, Cambridge, and entered Holy Orders. For many years he was a London Vicar, first at St. Philip's Lambeth (1898–1910), and later at All Saints', St. John's Wood (1910–1921). He married (1898) the eldest daughter of William Reed of Onslow Gardens, South Kensington, and has issue one son, the present owner of the Borough property. Steer painted a striking portrait of his brother clothed in the black silk robes of his Court dress. The parochial duties of his brother and his sister's residence in the country prevented them seeing Steer as often as he and they would have liked; nevertheless they contrived to meet regularly and were united by remarkably close ties of understanding and affection, which in later years was extended to Steer's nephews and niece.

B

'The New Coinage'

BY P. WILSON STEER

('The Art Journal', March 1893)

The advent of a new coinage must always be regarded by those who have the artistic reputation of the country at heart as a moment of profound interest and curiosity.

The past record of English coinage has, until this century, been such a brilliant one, that to beat it would be almost impossible, and to approach it, difficult. The best period, from an artistic point of view, was before the introduction of machinery and the invention of the steam-engine, when the coins were hammered. This period may be said to have extended from the reign of Edward III to that of Charles II. It was in the reign of Edward III that the magnificent 'noble' was first struck, a work which, from a decorative point of view, leaves nothing to be desired.

The designers of the new coinage before us are in the very happy position that they obviously could not do worse than Sir Edgar Boehm did in the Jubilee issue; and, as most people remember little of the past coinage of their own country, they will, no doubt, be judged, not by the exacting standard of the numismatic record of the country, but simply by comparison with the Jubilee coinage. Mr. Brock's portrait of Her Majesty, which will be used on all denominations, is a head with some character, and certainly much more suitable in scale than that of the last coinage. The workmanship is also crisper, and more in keeping with the requirements of low relief. The ear-rings, necklaces, and orders, however, give a certain tawdry look to the design, and their omission would have added to the dignity of the head. We have only to look at the bust on the coins of Queen Anne to see that a far more dignified aspect is arrived at by enveloping the shoulders in drapery, largely designed. The head, neck, and shoulders should be left to tell alone. A kind of sumptuous grandeur suggestive, not only of a portrait, but of the idea of Majesty in the abstract, would be achieved by the very simplicity and magnificence of such treatment. Mr. Poynter is less happy than Mr. Brock. The florin and shilling are 'petty' in workmanship, and the design is unduly cramped. This is, no doubt, partly due to the supposed exigency of spelling out in full the denomination round the design, a practice which seems to be obtaining more and more. It is surely childish to have to write on the florin, 'One florin—two shillings.' Why not 'Twenty-four pence' also? In the shilling, the design has been sacrificed by being crowded into a small space in the centre, to allow for an entirely disproportionate and superfluous inscription —'One Shilling'—which surrounds it. Why, I would ask, is it more necessary to write in full the denomination on the shilling and the sixpence, than on the sovereign and half-sovereign?

Mr. Brock's reverse of the half-crown exhibits a much finer sense of proportion between the design and the lettering than Mr. Poynter's reverse of the florin.

The crown is the finest coin of the set. The continuous lettering, which almost surrounds the bust, has a handsome effect, and the reverse with St. George and the Dragon, by Pistrucci, is a design which has triumphantly borne the test of time. The motto, 'Decus et tutamen', with the year of issue round the edge, is a vast improvement on the graining or milling of the Jubilee issue. It would have been well if a return had been made, in the matter of milling, to the older custom of making the lines diagonal instead of straight.

That the new coinage will be the best that has been issued during the present reign is faint praise indeed; but I feel that none higher can be awarded, when it is placed in the cabinet side by side with that of Oliver Cromwell or with the Simon Petition crown of Charles II. Nor is this comparison misleading, as these also are milled coins. The present series will be found sadly wanting—not indeed in mechanical excellency—that, alas! is present in too great a degree. It fails where perfected mechanism in Art always fails, in qualities of effect and grandeur of design.

With all the mechanical resources at the disposal of the authorities at the Mint, and partly because of the very perfection of these resources, a modern coin sinks into artistic insignificance when compared with a hasty, and, from a workman's point of view, imperfect coin of Charles I, struck in haste from the family plate of His Majesty's loyal supporters. In a word, the modern coin represents the apotheosis of machinery and the almost extinction of Art.

C

Introduction to the Catalogue of the 'London Impressionists' Exhibition'

Goupil Gallery, December 1889

By Walter Sickert

Mr. William Morris has recently made with gravity an assertion on modern pictorial art, which has been as gravely recorded, and which is doubtless quoted with gravity in decorative circles. He says, in effect, that at present picture-painting is merely a playful form of industry, and not in a condition of serious vitality. In the day of Turner, of Jean François Millet, of Corot, of Degas, and of Whistler, such an assertion is interesting from those who would offer as a substitute on our walls, for an art which is the flower of centuries of European thought and experience, the endless repetition on paper of adapted patterns printed by machinery in two or three shades of subdued colour, or a carpet which must pale before its Eastern prototype. The pictorial pessimism of this school of effort is rendered still more interesting, and is perhaps explained by the fact that it has itself produced painters and a manner of painting.

The painting is commonly excused as decorative painting, and it is against the complete misuse of the term that the efforts of serious art-criticism should, among things, be directed. Absence of convincing light and shade, of modelling, of aerial perspective, of sound drawing, of animation, of expression of all that results from keen and sympathetic observation of life are not the qualities, although it is at present heresy to say so, which render proper the application to a picture of the term decorative. Stand in a room on the walls of which are hung the works commonly described as decorative pictures. You are conscious of nothing but confused colourless surfaces, which you must approach closely before you can discover that they contain numberless touches of pigments, which may be brilliant in themselves, but which go to build up a sum devoid of light. The canvases are without eloquence, or even lucidity, just where these qualities are wanted, throughout the daily life of the room in which they hang. Surely works constructed to decorate a wall should be so painted as to appeal primarily at the distance at which they are most frequently seen. And which do we see most as we live in a given room? Not the one that is nearest to us, for on almost all occasions we have our back to it.

If this be granted, the question arises—But, if we approach the picture, what must it reveal to us on close examination? To this the essential answer, and the answer which is justified by the practice of those who have developed to its highest degree the art of painting, is: 'Not new facts, certainly, about the subject of the picture.' The embroidery on the cloak of Philip IV does not on examination reveal its construction or texture, nor on approaching the portrait of Lady Archibald Campbell, do we find the hairs of the fur cape evident. An examination of the surface of Sir Frederick Leighton's *Summer Moon* would reveal no new facts about the sleeping figures that could not be seen at the distance at which the picture is visible as a whole. What is it then that these works all yield in their different ways on nearer examination? It is nothing more than a subtle attribute which painters call 'quality' the appreciation of which is a matter, not only of temperament, but of education and experience. A certain beauty and fitness of expression in paint, apparently ragged perhaps, and capricious, but revealing to the connoisseur a thoughtful analysis of the essentials in the production of the emotion induced by the complex phenomena of vision. There is, of course, as well as true quality, no lack of work which contains false 'quality'. False 'quality' arises from an effort to achieve without sufficient knowledge an execution like one of someone else, while real quality, like style in literature, is the result of complete knowledge of the subject treated, and of simplicity and directness in the treatment.

The word 'Impressionist' has certainly been for years an elastic one. A provincial critic once applied it to the works of Mr. Spencer Stanhope, and Mr. Strudwick, and some metropolitan ones to hand-coloured tracings of instantaneous photographs. Whether the group of painters whose work is here for the first time collected in one gallery have done well in adopting it, will depend largely upon the direction that they may give to its meaning by their work. To attempt anything like an exposition of the aims of painters so varied in their intentions as the present group, would be a difficult and thankless task.

It may however be possible to clear away several sources of error by endeavouring to state what Impressionism as understood by its votaries is not. Essentially and firstly it is not realism. It has no wish to record anything merely because it exists. It is not occupied in a struggle to make intensely real and solid the sordid or superficial details of the subjects it selects. It accepts, as the aim of the picture, what Edgar Allan Poe asserts to be the sole legitimate province of the poem, beauty. In its search through visible nature for the elements of this same beauty, it does not admit the narrow interpretation of the word 'Nature' which would stop short outside the four-mile radius. It is, on the contrary, strong in the belief that for those who live in the most wonderful and complex city in the world, the most fruitful course of study lies in a persistent effort to render the magic and the poetry which they daily see around them, by means which they believe are offered to the student in all their perfection, not so much on the canvases that yearly line our official and unofficial shows of competitive painting, as on the walls of the National Gallery.

D

Mr. P. Wilson Steer on Impressionism in Art

Art-Workers' Guild, 1891

As I believe there are several papers to be read tonight on the subject of Impressionism in Art, rather than endeavour to cover the same ground I have thought it advisable to confine myself to the discussion of one point about which there appears to be much misunderstanding, namely the genealogy, so to speak, of Impressionism.

I have both read and heard it stated that Impressionists ignore tradition. Now I propose to show that so far from ignoring tradition they follow the highest tradition of all time which is inspired by nature and nature only.

Impressionism is not a new thing created by this generation. The word is new, I grant, and herein lies the trouble. Everyone seems to put his own construction on the word. For the sake of simplicity, let us substitute the word Art for Impressionism—there *can* be only two things, Art or No Art. I think the definition which someone has given that Art is the expression of an impression seen through a personality sums up the question as to what Art is, very concisely.

I think it may not be out of place if I read you one or two short extracts from the 'Discourses' of Sir Joshua Reynolds that will show you that he, himself an Impressionist, held, over a hundred years ago, precisely the same views which are held by the most advanced Impressionist of today.

We are told that Impressionism is a passing craze and nothing but a fashion. Is there any fashion, I would ask, in painting grass green instead of brown; in making a sky recede and hold its right place in the picture instead of hitting one in the eye? Is it a craze that we should recognise the fact that nature is bathed in atmosphere? Is it a fashion to treat a picture so that unity of vision may be achieved by insisting on certain parts more than others? No! it is not fashion, it is a *law*.

There are pictures painted nowadays, welcomed in high places and sold for large prices which have no unity of vision. They are like worms which, if you cut them up into half-a-dozen pieces, each bit lives and wriggles; so with these tiresome exercises of misguided industry you may make six pictures out of one and each is as finished and as badly composed as the others.

The Impressionist is inspired by his own time because his art is inspired

N   W.S.

by nature; he finds his pictures in the scenes around him, and although he works on the same principles as did the ancients he is not satisfied to produce today rechauffés of past Art but rather he tries to dignify the subjects he deals with (commonplace and ordinary though they be) with the principles which have actuated the production of great Art in all time.

Impressionism in Art has always existed from the time when Phidias sculptured the Parthenon frieze and Giotto and Donatello created saints and madonnas and Tintoret and Veronese decorated Venetian palaces and Velazquez painted poems from crinolines and dwarfs and later when Reynolds and Gainsborough dignified their sitters till they became goddesses. So Impressionism is of no country and of no period; it has been from the beginning; it bears the same relation to painting that poetry does to journalism. Two men paint the same model; one creates a poem, the other is satisfied with recording facts.

Art like everything else must be progressive; it is not enough because we admire the works of the great masters that we should be content to go on producing pictures on exactly their lines. Every great painter who has ever lived has added something of his own to the already accumulated research of his predecessors. We see constantly the commercial painter simply reproducing or manufacturing pictures like some artist whose work has been acknowledged and for which there is a demand. These painters always meet with a certain amount of success because the public has become accustomed to the kind of Art that they copy so that it has always been the case in the history of Art that the men who are trying to add something to the sum of what has already been achieved meet with opprobrium and scorn at the hands of the multitude.

E

Subjoined are the two excerpts from articles referred to in Chapter VI, p. 46.

23.4.98   'The Saturday Review'
. . . So with Steer's *Vista*; there is some impatient work in the sky, and they fasten on it like flies on a sore. We hear of imitation of Monet that falls short of the original. I know Monet's work as well as most, and every one can see that both he and Constable have gone to the making of the *Vista*; but I do not know where to find in Monet's work any original for the clear, beautiful harmony of silver green, white, blue, and cold, cold rose of this landscape.   Steer alone in England, or Europe for the matter of that, can play such a chord, is the patentee of that harmony taken from trees and sky

and sunlit ground; it has never been seen in the world of pictures before, but it will
haunt our memories now and find us out when we look at trees in cold sunshine.

The other picture by Mr. Steer is a mistake, for he can be one of the stupidest of men:
he blunders magnificently towards the centre with his instinct for colour, for light and
air and vigorous life to guide him.   He has put a model on a sofa against a screaming
red in the hope of carrying off a study in which her flesh will tell as flesh against the
red. He has failed; the red conquers and the flesh retires defeated as something brown;
there is nothing in the gawky attitude to redeem the affair; least of all in the obviously
mendacious title *Sleep*. But it would be hard to find a man who could fail so far on
towards success.

7.12.01   'The Saturday Review'

Mr. Steer keeps steadily developing and assuring his art at the point proper to his
temperament. He is not dramatic at all, and his moods would not make a very poig-
nant effect translated into a verbal lyric. But the mood peculiar to painting, its sure and
common ground in happy contemplation of the look of things, what light makes of
the bodies of women, the leaves of trees, the ranges of space, he has intensely. He is
friends with light and he is friends with paint and on these simple terms becomes
friends with beauty as hardly one of his contemporaries attains to be. His nonchalance
about other things is surprising. The most ordinary illustrator would have remarked
that in the *Mirror* neither of the two girls is in the least concerned with the ostensible
motive of the piece, the mirror. No one is using the mirror or pretending to, except
Mr. Steer, who gets a third uniting figure by its reflection of one of them. I think this
disrespect for the ostensible motive of action makes things a little uncomfortable; but
in the modelling of forms by light and colour and the capturing of charm and dainti-
ness in such a subject the picture marks a real advance.

F

Tributes to Steer

I have the pleasure of reprinting here, with permission from those con-
cerned, the effective article in 'The Times' by C. J. Holmes referred to in
Chapter VI, one by Roger Fry of later date, and a passage from George
Moore's translation of painting into words of inveigling charm.

GOUPIL GALLERY EXHIBITION OF 1909

BY CHARLES HOLMES

('The Times', April 22)

For many years Mr. Wilson Steer has been a tower of strength to the
New English Art Club; year by year his works have been seen there in

friendly rivalry with such talents as those of Mr. Sargent and, more recently, of Mr. John; while only last month his portrait of *Mrs. Styan*, in the Exhibition of Fair Women at the New Gallery, showed that he could hold his own in the most distinguished company. But these scattered examples of landscape and portraiture did not give any satisfactory material for viewing Mr. Steer's work as a whole, and the present collection of his recent work has thus quite exceptional value and interest.

Yet the collection may seem at first sight rather puzzling. Unfinished studies are hung side by side with finished pictures, and the effect of the collection, though dazzling, may also be disquieting to the newcomer. We recommend the visitor to pass at once into the larger gallery and concentrate his attention upon the works which occupy the places of honour there. An artist is always most easily and most thoroughly appreciated in the light of his more important and ambitious efforts; these show us the utmost a man can do (if not the utmost that he wishes); they show us also where his powers end, where his limitations begin. Only when we have recognised what a man's aims and powers amount to are we in a position to understand his sketches and studies.

In the case of Mr. Steer, then, we may make a start with the *Corfe Castle*, the largest picture in the exhibition, and perhaps the most important landscape, in every sense of the word, which Mr. Steer has hitherto produced. In it we recognise at once the modern successor of Constable— not the Constable of the modest sketch, but the Constable of *The Leaping Horse* and the *Salisbury from the Meadows*, the painter of the heroic subject on an heroic scale. The castle from which the piece derives its title is but a minor incident in this vast design. We look along the ridge of a great range of hills retiring in successive undulations to a far-distant horizon, dappled with long, sweeping shadows from the stormy clouds above, and illuminated with a blaze of sunshine so vivid as to be almost deceptive in its realism. In comparing it with the older master we must recognise that Constable would have depended more upon the artificial disposition and forcing of the shadows and upon certain compromises with the positive greens and blues and purples of an English summer landscape. Mr. Steer has made no such compromise. His picture has the accidental quality, the vivid pitch of Nature herself; yet such is the subtle quality of his art that he has succeeded in combining the whole into a magnificent piece of decorative design—a design too powerful indeed for most private houses, but one which would give permanent distinction to a public gallery. Turning to *The Lime Kiln*, we find a scheme in which a splendid contrast of gold with cool greys and blues takes the place of the greens and purples of the *Corfe Castle*. The exquisite passage of silvery sea in the

far distance deserves special notice. From these two superb and powerful landscapes we may pass to the most important figure piece, *The
Balcony.* Here the comparison is with the great Dutch painters of interiors;
and with those who in more recent times, like Alfred Stevens, have followed in their footsteps. One may doubt at first sight whether, in this
instance, Mr. Steer has been as prudent as his forerunners. The choice of
so large a scale for so slight a subject involves a certain risk of emptiness.
The scale undoubtedly suits Mr. Steer's handling, for his strong and summary brushwork would look coarse were the picture half its present size.
Yet so admirable is the design, so sincere the feeling which inspired it,
that he may fairly claim to have done for the London of today what De
Hoogh and Vermeer did for Holland in the 17th century.

When these three capital pictures have been examined we can more
comfortably take the remaining works in their order. In the extremely
interesting study, *The Broken Bough,* we have a woodland scene sketched as
perfectly in a few selected tones of oil paint as Rembrandt might have
sketched it in pen and bistre. A similar suggestion of Rembrandt or of
Claude's sketches will be noticed in *The Bend of the River* and elsewhere.
It may seem fantastic to find analogies between achievements in their outward appearance so wholly separate as those of Mr. Steer and Rembrandt,
but the longer Mr. Steer's work is studied the more clearly does the conviction force itself upon the mind that among modern artists no one, not
even Mr. Strang, Mr. Cameron, or Mr. Muirhead Bone, has studied the
greatest of all Dutch masters more profoundly and sympathetically. So
completely, however, has this experience become blended with other
qualities in his art that we only get a hint of it here and there as a foundation upon which his dazzling structures of sunlight and gay colour are
erected. One can trace Rembrandt, for example, in the large spacing,
broad lighting, and sheer sincerity of the *Grande Place, Montreuil;* though
in *Moon rising over the Downs,* the memory is more faint and the connection
less direct. One thinks rather of Crome or of Daubigny.

In *The Conservatory* we have one of those schemes of fresh and joyous
colour which are found nowhere save in 18th century china and in modern
painting. This is perhaps the most attractive of the smaller portrait studies.
That in this lighter vein he can descend to mere prettiness is proved by *On
the Pier,* which recalls certain works by Watts which his admirers would
like to forget. *The Blue Sash* is a much more fortunate specimen of Mr.
Steer's art in this mood, for it is as delightfully sharp and vivacious as *The
Conservatory* was joyous and fresh. In only one picture does Mr. Steer
seem to challenge Turner, and that is in *The Isle of Purbeck.* The colour
and illumination of the sky are not unworthy of the older master; the vapor-

ous blue of the middle distance resembles him, but Mr. Steer has been no more successful with the foreground than Turner was apt to be when he painted on a large scale.

Mr. Steer in his larger pictures proves himself able to stand comparison with the greatest names in English landscape. In his watercolour drawings his place is hardly less high. But he still remains too fond of the oil sketch on a considerable scale. These, with all their charm, have neither the solidity and completeness of his important pictures, nor the concentrated emphasis and rhythm of his watercolour drawings. This exhibition ought to prove finally that in him England possesses a really great living master of landscape and figure painting. If we remember what was thought of Constable's technique in Constable's day, we ought not to find Mr. Steer's handling an insuperable difficulty; and those who have the patience to pass this barrier will be well rewarded.

GOUPIL GALLERY EXHIBITION OF 1924
By Roger Fry
'New Statesman', March 29

It is a great pleasure, after so long an abstinence, to be able to enjoy an exhibition of Steer's work. There is much that everyone interested in modern art should see and study in this collection. But grateful as we are for this, it is not yet all we want. It is surely high time that Mr. Marchant, who has done so much for modern English painting, should organise a really representative show of Mr. Steer's work as a whole. Much of it is hardly known to the present generation of painters. More especially are they quite ignorant of his early impressionist work, and unless my memory has transmuted them out of recognition, this period produced some of his finest creations. Mr. Steer is one of the most gifted and one of the purest artists that we have ever had in England. His natural gifts are remarkable. Few modern artists have had a more spontaneous and instinctive feeling for colour, and though one cannot call him a great designer, he has a perfectly natural sense of spacing and of the *mise en page*. Moreover, he has been all his life absolutely above any suspicion of playing to the gallery. His record is entirely single-minded and worthy of his talents.

None the less, I think Mr. Steer has not been always fortunate in his development. He has one gift which under certain circumstances, may be a source of weakness. He is very sensitive to outside artistic influences. Almost all artists are, of course, but it so happens that diverse and perhaps mutually antagonistic influences have been brought to bear on him, and the effect of these has been sometimes to lessen the energy of his drive in one central direction.

The first influence he accepted was that of Monet. He took over from him his preoccupation with atmospheric colour, and, even, his technique of colour division.[1] But he used it for his own purposes and in his own way. He had none of Monet's intense interest in the exact notation of visual fact, none of his desire for an objective record of sensations. Steer used all the new possibilities of colour harmony which Monet had revealed to express a much more personal feeling—a typically English, 'poetical' sentiment for certain moods of nature. Without any 'literary' suggestions, without any conventional emphasis, he managed to transmit through his pictures a peculiar lyrical charm, sometimes pensive, sometimes almost exuberant. The new methods enabled him to render the moods of waves a-glitter in sunlight and the stir and flutter of the breeze as they had never been given before in English landscape. The pictures of this period have a peculiar intensity of conviction and a singleness of aim which Steer has never quite recaptured. They were composed on the simplest lines, without any research for decorative arabesque or scenic presentment. They had an almost primitive *naïveté* of presentment, but always an admirable sense of interval and spacing and a certain solidity of construction and relief which later influences have counteracted. Something of that early manner still persists in a very sober study of a rocky stream overhung by trees in the present exhibition.

But, as Monet's influence waned, the English love of decorative effect and elegance of *facture* began to attract Steer more and more. From Turner he learned much of the effectiveness of a more scenic approach; from Boucher he acquired an elaborate decorative convention. There is no example here of Steer's most effective Turneresque landscapes—a large early landscape shows something of that influence, but it retains much of the more searching observation of his earlier manner. It is far less effective, but I think more intense than these. It shows at what pains he was at this period to establish the exact relief and recession of his planes, and the influence upon colour of atmospheric envelopment. It is, I think, a little spoilt by something acid in the green of the sky, but the modelling and recession of the wooded river bank is beautifully felt.

But the present exhibition is almost dominated by the large *Toilet of Venus*, which shows how far decorative aims claimed his attention at one time. It is in its way a masterly work. Its inspiration, whatever the date of its actual execution, seems to belong peculiarly to the 'nineties of the last

[1] There is no 'colour division' in Monet's painting or in Steer's.—D.S.M.

century. There is Boucher as a basis, not a little of Whistler in the extreme discretion of the colour harmonies, and, I think, a distinct reminiscence of Beardsley in the invention. That, indeed, reminds one of the peculiarly 1890 nostalgia for an imaginary eighteenth century of conventional sensuality and sophisticated depravity. Steer's temperament is as far removed as possible from Beardsley's, but his sensitiveness to artistic impulses has enabled him to take something from the younger man's invention and convert it to his own much finer artistic purpose.

In a curious and fascinating fantasia which hangs near by we see Steer influenced by Tintoretto and El Greco, employing their tumultuous rhythm for his own gayer, less convinced—more merely amused—mood. In almost all these works in which a decorative aim predominates, Steer plays a delightful game with his colour harmonies. Essentially a colourist and one who can handle the strongest and most brilliant notes with absolute certainty, in these pieces he takes a delight in playing in the most restricted scale, seeing how far he can make a few closely related tints of almost neutral colour give the suggestion of brilliance and resonance. Only a very gifted colourist could give such *éclat* to these discreet and scarcely contrasted greys.

There is yet another class of pictures in which Steer gave fuller expression to his native powers than in these decorative pieces. There are two examples of this class here, but neither seems to me to be of the very finest quality. One is the nude on a couch with a window behind,[1] the other a girl in a brilliantly coloured dress seated by a window. In these Steer is once more, as in his early work, preoccupied with a close interpretation of nature. In these it is not the atmospheric colour of his early days that gives the motive so much as the interpretation of chiaroscuro in terms of colour. He chooses strong effects of light and shade for his theme, but it is not light and shade as such that interests him so much as the modulations of colour as it passes from light to shade. And in these his work is original and personal. He carries to a further limit ideas that are already hinted at in Vermeer and Chardin, and with an exhilarating gaiety of colour and a vivacity and freedom of handling which is always delightful, even though it is sometimes got at the expense of a certain laxity in the interpretation of form.

It is perhaps to be regretted that the examples of Steer's quite recent work could not have been shown in a separate room. They suffer by comparison with the more effective design and more brilliant colouring of his earlier work. They demand for their appreciation a greater effort on the spectator's part. Their remarkable qualities are not immediately apparent.

[1] *Sleep* in Tate Gallery.—D.S.M.

In some ways they show a return to quite early work: mainly perhaps, in the extreme simplicity of the presentment, the absence of any premeditated approach or search for effective display of the motive. On the other hand, they are far more unemphatic and undemonstrative in colour. No doubt in process of years the artist's eye has got tired of all the more striking harmonies, and he seeks for ever subtler and more difficult chords. Above all, he has in course of time perfected his methods of abbreviated statement. These landscapes are reduced to the apposition of a surprisingly small number of tones. But these are chosen with such a sense of their significance that they suffice to evoke the effect. It would be very interesting to see these beside some of Matisse's landscapes in which a similar economy of statement is contrived. The comparison would be very instructive. Both, in a sense, are impressionist, but in Matisse's case there has intervened all that research for plastic construction which pure impressionism had not dreamt of. That want of a solid scaffolding of constructive design is, I suspect, just the one thing that, owing to the conditions of his environment, has obstructed the fullest exploitation of Steer's extraordinary gifts.

CHILDREN PADDLING

By George Moore

'The Speaker', March 3, 1894

This quality, which, for want of a better expression, I call the optimism of painting, is a peculiar characteristic of Mr. Steer's work. We find it again in *Children Paddling*. Around the long breakwater the sea winds, filling the estuary, or perchance recedes, for the incoming tide is noisier —a delicious, happy, opium blue, the blue of oblivion. . . . Paddling in the warm sea-water gives oblivion to those children. They forget their little worries in the sensation of sea and sand, as I forget mine in that dreamy blue which fades and deepens imperceptibly, like a flower from the intense heart to the delicate edge of the petals. The vague sea is drawn up behind the breakwater, and out of it the broad sky ascends solemnly in curves like palms. Happy sensation of daylight; a flower-like afternoon; little children paddling; the world is behind them too; they are as flowers, and are conscious only of the benedictive influences of sand and sea and sky.

G

CHRONOLOGICAL LIST OF PLACES AT WHICH STEER
PAINTED, SIGNED BY HIM

1884 Walberswick

1885 Walberswick?

1886 Walberswick?

1887 Dannes, near Etaples

1888 Boulogne (?) Walberswick

1889 Montreuil-sur-Mer, also Walberswick

1890 Swanage

1891 Boulogne—Short visits to different places, including Hayling Island

1892 Cowes

1893 Richmond, Surrey

1894 Boulogne and Rye

1895 Richmond, Yorkshire

1896 Barnard Castle

1897 Knaresborough

1898 Ludlow

1899 Ditto

1900 Knaresborough

1901 Bridgenorth

1902 Stroud

1903 Richmond, Yorkshire

1904 Hawes, Yorkshire

1905 Chepstow

1906 Ludlow. Bredon first three weeks

1907 Montreuil-sur-Mer and Paris

1908 Corfe

1909 Newnham and Littledean

1910 Ironbridge

1911 Bridgnorth

1912 Porchester

1913 Harwich

1914 Bosham

1915 Painswick

1916 Chirk Castle

1917 Ditto. Haresfoot, Berkhamsted

1918 Dover

1919 Alum Bay, Isle of Wight

1920 Maldon

1921 Hythe, Southampton Water

1922 Shirehampton, near Bristol

1923 Brill

1924 Long Crendon

1925 Bridgnorth

1926 Shoreham, Sussex

1927 — (Illness and Operation)

1928 Framlingham

1929 Dovercourt, Harwich

1930 Dover

1931 Sandwich and Whitstable

1932 Greenhithe

1933 Maldon

1934 Walmer

CATALOGUE
OF OIL PAINTINGS

Canvas, unless described as panel: Size in inches; height first

ABBREVIATIONS

apart from recognised initials of Societies

AG	Art Gallery (Public)	Coll	Collection
BC	British Council	Exh	Exhibition
BH	Barbizon House	GG	Goupil Gallery
CAS	Contemporary Art Society	LG	Leicester Galleries
Chr	Christie, Manson & Woods	NACF	National Art-Collections Fund
CAJ	Charles A. Jackson	NG	National Gallery

Special Exhibitions in London

Goupil Gallery   1894 1909 1924
Carfax Gallery   1902
Barbizon House   1927 1934 1935 1937 1939
Tate Gallery   1929
National Gallery Memorial Exhibition, 1943, from which a Selection was made by the Council for the Encouragement of Music and the Arts for circulation in the provinces; at Leeds this collection was supplemented

Illustrations in books and periodicals are recorded in italics.

1875 A DEAD BULLFINCH. 6 × 9¾ panel Steer Chr 1942 R. Gray | Lt.-
Col. W. R. Hornby Steer | NG Exh 1943 | *Phaidon 1*

Portrait of THEOPHILUS MORGAN, Cobbler, Whitchurch, Salop.
18¾ × 13 panel Major J. A. Hamilton

1878 SELF PORTRAIT when eighteen. 30 × 25 Lt.-Col. W. R. Hornby
Steer | NG Exh 1943

188– Portrait of JOHN KEMP. 18½ × 12 Gloucester Municipal School of Art

1883 WHAT OF THE WAR? (Portrait of Mr. Bick). 36 × 28 RA 1883
Mrs. Frances E. Thorne | Anon Chr 1928 Holland | Owen
Hugh Smith | Tate Exh 1929 | Anon Chr 1945 BH | Tate
Gallery | *Times* 19 April 1929

1884 FANTAISIE. 15¾ × 14 RA 1884 Ch. W. Deschamps | E. N.
Galloway | Manchester 1884 | John Galloway | NEAC Retro
Manchester 1925 as PORTRAIT STUDY

WALBERSWICK BEACH. 14 × 10 panel Major J. A. Hamilton |
RSA 1943

AT THE WELL, WALBERSWICK (Red Cap). 12 × 8 Mrs. Charles
E. Hamilton | RSA 1943

DOLLY BROWN IN FRONT OF AN APPLE TREE, Walberswick.
24 × 20 Steer Chr 1942 Sir Alec Martin

WALBERSWICK. 11¾ × 15¾ R. W. Alston | BH | Arcade Gall |
Nicholson | Derek Hill

1885 DISCOVERY. RA 1885 Destroyed by artist

LE SOIR. RBA 1885

'CELLIST. 18 × 14 James Christie

CHILDREN IN CEMETERY, PARIS. About 20 × 12 M. Perret, Paris

GIRL SEATED AGAINST A WINDOW. 20 × 24 probably Dolly
Brown, Walberswick | *Phaidon 6*

TIRED OUT. 24 × 30 Manchester 1885 E. N. Galloway | Charles
Dunderdale | Percival Duxbury

WATER! WATER! EVERYWHERE. 14½ × 23½ Grosvenor Gall 1885
| Anon Chr 1918 Healing

1886 ANDANTE. NEAC 1886

A DAME OF THE PRIMROSE LEAGUE. RBA 1886

GREY SEA. 15½ × 21½ James Charles | J. Maddocks Chr 1910 GG
| G. E. Healing | NG Exh 1940 and 1941

THE OPEN SEA, WALBERSWICK. 16 × 22 BH 1930 Mrs. Or-
mond | *BH Record* 1932

GIRL ON A PIER, WALBERSWICK. 15 × 24 James Christie | Mrs.

Christie | Vernon Wethered | Tate Exh 1929 | Empire Art
Loan Coll Soc Australia 1939 and New Zealand 1940

A SEASCAPE. 24×24 Mrs. H. R. Williams | Exrs. Sotheby's
1940 BH | Lockett Thomson | NG Exh 1943 as THE IN-
COMING TIDE

1887 GIRL LEADING A GOAT (DUNES NEAR DANNES, ETAPLES).
36×72 Richard A. Ledward | Mrs. Ledward | Owen Hugh
Smith | Tate Exh 1929 | Adams Gall Exh 1934

MILLIE & GRACIE. RBA 1887

CHILDREN PADDLING, ETAPLES. 14½×21½ James Christie |
Mrs. Lander Johnston | GG 1924 | Hon. Sir Evan Charteris |
Tate Exh 1929

THE BRIDGE, ETAPLES. 18¾×25¼ Grosvenor Gall 1888 Ellen
M. Cobden (Mrs. Walter Sickert) | Mrs. T. J. Cobden-
Sanderson | R. Cobden-Sanderson Chr 1940 LG | Tate Gal-
lery | NG Exh 1942 | Manchester Exh 1943 | NG Exh 1943 |
Studio 1941 | *Phaidon 9*

ETAPLES. 13¾×10¾ panel Major J. A. Hamilton | RSA 1943

FISHER CHILDREN, ETAPLES. 17¾×24 Steer Chr 1942 Arnold |
R. W. Lloyd

CHATTERBOXES. NEAC 1887 Paris 1889

SOUTHWOLD. 19½×23½ Steer Chr 1942 Nicholson | Tate Gallery
| NG Exh 1943 | *Studio* 1944

AT SOUTHWOLD. 17×17 Moffat Lindner | BH 1935 | Mrs.
Philip Nichols | Venice 1936 | NG Exh 1940 and 1943 as ON
THE CLIFFS | *Illus. London News* 1935 | *BH Record* 1935

THE SPRIGGED FROCK. 23½×23½ pastel (Possibly SHY—First
Pastel Exh Grosvenor Gall 1888) Moffat Lindner | Les XX
Exh Brussels 1891 | BH 1935 | Sir Frank Brangwyn RA |
Given 1936 Morris Memorial Gall Walthamstow

PORTRAIT OF MISS JENNIE LEE, 'Jo'. 36×28 Grosvenor Gall
1888 Miss Lee | A. B. Clifton | Tate Exh 1929 | Mrs. Clif-
ton | LG Exh 1935 | Gerald Agnew | NEAC 1945 | *Phai-
don 10* | *Listener* 1945

PORTRAIT OF A LADY. Grosvenor Gall 1887

A LADY IN GREY (Mrs. Montgomery). 72×36 GG 1894 | Steer
Chr 1942 as PORTRAIT OF A LADY | Nicholson | John
Rothenstein | NG Exh 1943 | Leeds Exh 1944 | *Yellow Book*
1895

PORTRAIT OF T. STIRLING LEE (1853–1916). 26×20 Given by
sitter Chelsea Arts Club

THE SWISS ALPS AT EARL'S COURT EXHIBITION. 24 × 29½ Steer Chr 1942 Nicholson | Tate Gallery | NG Exh 1943

SURF. 6 × 29 panel RBA 1887 | Anon Chr 1910 Sampson | Anon Chr 1918 Mrs. Weldon | Chr 1919 Bates | F. Hindley Smith | Beq Fitzwilliam Mus Cambridge | *Phaidon* text

1888 ON THE PIERHEAD (Walberswick). 36 × 36 NEAC 1887 D. Croal Thomson | GG 1894 | BH 1926 | Tate Exh 1929 | Hugo Pitman | RSA 1930 | Amsterdam 1936 *Catalogue* | BC New York 1939 | *International Art* 1914 | *BH Record* 1931 | *Phaidon* 8

GIRL ON A PIERHEAD. René Valadon

A SUMMER'S EVENING. NEAC 1888 Probably THREE BATHERS ON THE SANDS. 60 × 90 | Munich 1891 | Steer Chr 1942 Lessore | Talbot Clifton

KNUCKLEBONES (Walberswick). 24 × 30 GG 1889 | G. Blackwell | Tate Exh 1929 | BH 1935 | H. E. West | Whitechapel 1939 | NG Exh 1940 | NG Exh 1943 | *Whirlwind* 1890 (from drawing by W. Sickert) | *Illustrated London News* 1935 | *Connoisseur* 1935 | *BH Record* 1935 | *Phaidon* 5

THE BEACH, WALBERSWICK. 8 × 9½ panel Sir George Clausen, R.A. | Lockett Thomson 1945

FIGURES ON THE BEACH, WALBERSWICK. 23½ × 23½ Steer Chr 1942 | BH | H. J. Paterson

SUMMER AT COWES. 19¾ × 23¾ J. G. Legge | Whitechapel 1903 | Mrs. Legge | NG Exh 1943 | Ashmolean Exh 1942

1889 HEAD OF A YOUNG GIRL. NEAC 1889

THE SOFA. 48 × 64 NEAC 1889 GG 1894 | C. R. Ashbee | Wolverhampton 1902 | Anon Chr 1910 Agnew | Judge Evans | CAS Exh GG 1913 | GG 1918 | Sotheby's 1920 | Anon Chr 1923 | Mrs. Evans | GG 1923 | Col. R. H. Whitwell | Given Municipal AG Pietermaritzburg | *Art Journal* 1906

SIGNORINA SOZO IN DRESDINA. 23½ × 30 NEAC 1890 | Les XX Exh Brussels 1891 | Sir A. M. Daniel | GG 1894 | GG 1921 | Amsterdam Exh 1936 *Catalogue* | *Whirlwind* 1890 | *Phaidon* 7

A GIRL SEATED AT NEEDLEWORK. 24½ × 18½ Pastel Steer Chr 1942 James | Viscount Bearsted | NG Exh 1943 | *Phaidon* 31

THE RAMPARTS, MONTREUIL. 23 × 23 Mrs. Knowles | Les XX Exh Brussels 1891 | Guy Knowles | Leeds Exh 1944

The following were included in the 'London Impressionists' Exh Goupil Gallery, December 1889:—

THE CITADEL

THE BEACH, WALBERSWICK

KNUCKLEBONES (see 1888)

PRETTY ROSIE PETTIGREW

THE OUTER WALL

THE MILL STREAM

A TIDAL POOL | Sir J. J. Shannon R.A. | Les XX Exh Brussels 1891

A TANNERY

1890 JONQUILS. 36 × 36 NEAC 1890 | Sir William Burrell | Les XX Exh Brussels 1891 | Anon Chr 1902 Holland | W. H. Wood | Whitechapel 1903 | Dusseldorf 1904 | Tate Exh 1929 | BH 1933 | CAJ | J. Pilling | *Art Journal* 1890 | *Phaidon 11*

PORTRAIT OF MR. WALTER SICKERT. 24 × 12 NEAC 1890| | GG 1924 | Manchester 1937 | NACF gave National Portrait Gallery 1940 | *Yellow Book* 1894.

THE ERMINE SEA (Swanage). 24 × 30 NEAC 1891 | Sir A. M. Daniel | Manchester 1911 | Newcastle 1912 | BH 1927 | Amsterdam 1936 | BC Paris 1938 | *Mag of Art* 1892 *Phaidon 23*

THE CLIFFS, SWANAGE. 19½ × 25½ G. Blackwell | Blackwell Family Collection

SWANAGE. 18 × 24½ A. B. Clifton | Tate Exh 1929 | Guillaume Gall 1929 | Sir Edward Marsh | Young Painters' Society Exh, New Burlington Gall 1930 as POOLE HARBOUR | Venice 1932 | BC Johannesburg 1936 | CAS Tour (Art Exhibitions Bureau) 1940–2 | NG Exh 1943 | *Phaidon 12*

THE BEACH, WALBERSWICK. 23¼ × 29½ G. E. Healing | Tate Exh 1929 as THREE FIGURES ON A PIER | LG | Tate Gallery | NG Exh 1942 | Manchester Exh 1943 | NG Exh 1943 | *Phaidon 22*

BEACH SCENE, WITH THREE CHILDREN SHRIMPING, BOULOGNE. 18¾ × 22½ Sir A. M. Daniel | Manchester Exh 1910 | *Phaidon 4*

AT MONTREUIL-SUR-MER. 30 × 20 Mrs. Hilton Price | BH | Sir George Sutton | Sir Michael Sadler | Fine Art Soc | H. Pattinson-Knight

AT THE SEASIDE. 8 × 10½ panel John P. Kinghorn | Edmistons, Glasgow 1929 as CHILDREN ON THE SHORE | Simpson | BH | M. Adda

A SUNLIT SEA. $23\frac{1}{4} \times 29\frac{1}{2}$ Steer Chr 1942 Hugo Pitman | NG Exh 1934 | *Phaidon 14*

SUNRISE ON THE SEA, WALBERSWICK. $15\frac{1}{2} \times 29\frac{1}{2}$ Steer Chr 1942 Hugo Pitman | NG Exh 1943

1891 PRIMA BALLERINA ASSOLUTA. NEAC 1891 ? Destroyed

PORTRAIT OF MRS. CYPRIAN WILLIAMS & HER TWO LITTLE GIRLS. 30×40 NEAC 1891 | BH 1928 | Tate Gallery | Tate Exh 1929 | NG Exh 1943 | *Artwork* 1929 | *Country Life* 1929 | *BH Record* 1929 | *Phaidon 18* | *Times Lit Sup* 1944

SKETCH OF MRS. CYPRIAN WILLIAMS while staying at Hayling Island. 9×11 panel Mrs. H. R. Williams | Exrs Sotheby's 1940

STUDY, Full length, MRS. CYPRIAN WILLIAMS. panel Mrs. H. R. Williams | Exrs. Sotheby's 1940

WHITE WINGS (Swanage). NEAC 1891

SCHOOL GIRL. 30×25

GIRL ON A SOFA—Miss Rose Pettigrew. $22\frac{1}{4} \times 24$ Mrs. George Burrell | Tate Exh 1929 | *Artwork* 1929

MOLLE MEUM LEVIBUS COR EST VIOLABILE TELIS ET SEMPER CAUSA EST CUR EGO SEMPER AMEM. 37×27 NEAC 1892 | F. H. Hoare | GG 1894 | BH 1937 as THE BLUE DRESS | G. J. Scaramanga | *Art Journal* 1893 | *BH Record* 1937

NEAR WALBERSWICK, Peasant on Road. $23\frac{1}{2} \times 29\frac{1}{2}$ T. Fisher Unwin | Anon Chr 1930 Lessore | Sir Gervase Beckett Bt | Sir Martyn Beckett Bt | *Beaux Arts Gall Cat* 1932 | *Studio* 1934

BOULOGNE BEACH. $8 \times 10\frac{1}{4}$ panel GG 1894 | Steer Chr 1942 Spink | Destroyed by enemy action 1944

FIGURES ON THE BEACH NEAR BOULOGNE. $8 \times 10\frac{1}{2}$ Steer Chr 1942 Spink | Destroyed by enemy action 1944

BATHING TENTS, BOULOGNE. $8 \times 10\frac{3}{4}$ GG 1894 | Steer Chr 1942 LG | Mrs. Pattinson-Knight

CHILDREN & NURSES, BOULOGNE. $8 \times 10\frac{1}{4}$ panel Steer Chr 1942 LG | Mrs. Pattinson-Knight

A BOY & THREE GIRLS IN RED, BOULOGNE. $8 \times 10\frac{1}{4}$ panel Steer Chr 1942 Leger | H. Pattinson-Knight

1892 BOULOGNE SANDS. 24×30 NEAC 1892 | Prof. F. Brown | GG 1894 | BH 1927 | Tate Exh 1929 | BC Johannesburg 1936 | Miss Ellen Brown | NG Exh 1943 | NACF gave Tate Gallery 1943 | Leeds Exh 1944 | *Artwork* 1929 | *Studio* 1943 | *Phaidon 15*

A PORTRAIT. NEAC 1892

PORTRAIT OF THE HON. MRS. ALBERT PETRE. NEAC 1892 Destroyed

CASINO, BOULOGNE. | T. Humphry Ward | GG 1894 | Mrs. Sandwith

ON THE PLAGE. 8 × 10 panel | Lady Cunard | Sotheby's 1933 Dr. Borenius | Hon. Mrs. Evelyn FitzGerald

GIRL IN A LARGE HAT. 24×19 George Moore | GG 1894 | Dublin 1899 as PORTRAIT OF A LADY | Lady Cunard | NG Exh 1940 as THE COSTER GIRL | Sir Kenneth Clark | NG Exh 1943 | Lady Cunard

A GIRL RECLINING ON A SOFA. 24×19 Sir William Eden | GG 1894 | Eden Chr 1899 Lacey | Eden Exrs Chr 1918 as REPOSE Sampson | CAJ | F. Hindley Smith | Arthur Crossland | Bradford 1937 | Leeds Exh 1944 as A GIRL RESTING

GIRL IN A WHITE BLOUSE ON SOFA. 29 × 24 Sir A. M. Daniel | *Phaidon 32*

GIRL IN A WHITE DRESS. 17½ × 14¾ GG 1894 | CAJ | G. Beatson Blair | Beq Manchester AG 1944

GIRL IN BLUE (THE SPOTTED BLOUSE). 22 × 18 Mrs. Schweder | BH | Redfern Gall 1937 | J. L. Paton

COWES REGATTA. 20×24 Probably YACHTS RACING GG 1894 | Alfred H. Coles | BH 1937 | G. J. Scaramanga | NG Exh 1943 | Odo Cross | *Phaidon 3*

YACHTS AT COWES. 25×19 BH | Dr. Eardley Holland | *BH Record* 1932

COWES HARBOUR. 8 × 10¼ panel Steer Chr 1942 BH

SOUTHSEA PIER. 8 × 10¼ panel Steer Chr 1942 LG | Mrs. Pattinson-Knight

YACHTS LYING OFF COWES—EVENING. Manchester 1893 | GG 1894

L'ENFANT ROSE. Manchester 1893 | Mrs. Alfred Thornton | Bath 1913 | LG | R. A. Peto

1893 A PROCESSION OF YACHTS (Cowes). 24×30 NEAC 1892 | Miss Jane Harrison | GG 1894 | Bt from Miss Harrison 1922 Tate Gallery | Tate Exh 1929 | RSA 1939 | Leeds Exh 1944 | *Artwork* 1929

A YACHT RACE. 24×30 NEAC 1893 | Newcastle 1893 | Sir George Clausen, R.A. 1897 for AG Western Australia Perth as YACHT RACING ON THE SOLENT | *Studio* 1916

YACHTS. 20×24 Dermod O'Brien PRHA | LG Exh 1946 | BH

Portrait of MISS ROSIE PETTIGREW. NEAC 1893 | Newcastle 1893 | *Pall Mall Pictures* 1893

Portrait of MISS DOROTHEA HAMILTON. 30×25 NEAC 1893 | Newcastle 1893 | Miss Hamilton

Portrait of MISS EMMA FROUDE. 30×25 NEAC 1893 | RGI 1894 | Mrs. Euan Stabb | *Studio* 1893

A CLASSIC LANDSCAPE (Richmond, Surrey). 24×30 GG 1894 | Judge Evans | Evans Coll GG 1918 | Asa Lingard | Arthur Crossland | Newcastle Exh 1939 | NG Exh 1943 as LANDSCAPE WITH RIVER AND BRIDGE | *Art Journal* 1906

GIRL IN RED FROCK. 21½×13¾ GG 1894 | A. H. Studd | Henry B. Harris 1921 | Beq 1929 Mrs. F. D. Fox

YOUNG GIRL IN WHITE DRESS. 10½×8 panel | BH 1922 | Henry B. Harris | Beq 1929 Miss Harris | *BH Record* 1922 | *Phaidon 16*

JEANETTE (Girl in Blue). 10½×8½ GG 1894 | J. G. Legge | Mrs. J. G. Legge | Ashmolean Exh 1942

BY THE WINDOW. 11½×13½ panel Steer Chr 1942 R. Gray | A. Henderson Bishop

VIEW FROM RICHMOND HILL. 8¼×10½ panel GG 1919 | F. Hindley Smith | Beq 1939 Fitzwilliam Mus Cambridge

RICHMOND ON THAMES. 8½×10½ panel John Lane | Sale Jackson Stops 1927

STRAND-ON-THE-GREEN. 8×10¼ panel GG 1894 | Steer Chr 1942 Leger | Leeds Exh 1944

THE THAMES AT RICHMOND. 8×10¼ panel Steer Chr 1942 LG | Mrs. McDougall | *Connoisseur* 1940

TWICKENHAM. 8¼×10½ G. T. Nicholson | Ashmolean Exh 1942

DANAE. 11½×14¼ panel Steer Chr 1942 M. V. B. Hill

RHODODENDRONS, Kew. 8×10¼ panel Steer Chr 1942 Leger | H. Pattinson-Knight

STAR AND GARTER HOTEL, RICHMOND, SURREY. 8×10¼ panel GG 1894 | Steer Chr 1942 Leger | H. Pattinson-Knight | probably *Yellow Book* 1895

THE LITTLE BARMAID, Richmond, Surrey. 10¼×8 panel GG 1894 | Steer Chr 1942 Leger | H. Pattinson-Knight

RICHMOND BRIDGE, SURREY with barges. 8×10¼ panel Steer Chr 1942 Fine Art Soc | Leger | Hon. Mrs. Sandeman

RICHMOND BRIDGE, SURREY. 8×10¼ panel Steer Chr 1942 Fine Art Soc | Mrs. Lewthwaite

A Young Girl holding some roses. $10\frac{1}{4} \times 8$ panel. Steer Chr 1942 Leger | Mrs. Bulter

Flowers in a Tumbler. $10\frac{1}{4} \times 8$ panel Steer Chr 1942 Spink

Girl in Pink Dress holding flowers. $10\frac{1}{4} \times 8$ panel Steer Chr 1942 Spink | Earl of Durham

The Starched Frock. GG 1894

1894 Children Paddling (Swanage). 25×36 GG 1894 | Sir A. M. Daniel | NEAC Retro 1925 | Tate Exh 1929 | French Gall Exh 1931 | *Studio* 1930 | *Phaidon 13*

Girls Running (Walberswick Pier). $23 \times 35\frac{1}{4}$ GG 1894 Sir A. M. Daniel | GG 1921 | BH 1927 | BC Paris 1938 | *Phaidon 24*

The Work Table (The Artist's mother, Emma Steer). $8\frac{1}{2} \times 10\frac{1}{2}$ panel NEAC 1894 | Mrs. Charles E. Hamilton

Portrait of The Artist's Mother. $11\frac{3}{4} \times 8$ Lt.-Col. W. R. Hornby Steer | RSA 1943

Marine. NEAC 1894

Portrait. NEAC 1894

Self Portrait with Model. 24×12 Dermod O'Brien PRHA | Tate Exh 1929 | LG Exh 1946 | Lord Moore | *Yellow Book* 1894 | *Times* 19 April 1929 | *Phaidon 19*

The Kimono. $24 \times 8\frac{1}{2}$ Dermod O'Brien PRHA | LG Exh 1946

Miss Ethel Dixon before a Mirror. $20\frac{1}{2} \times 16\frac{1}{2}$ Steer Chr 1942 | Birkenhead AG | *Yellow Book* 1895 as The Mantelpiece | *Phaidon 25*

A Girl at her Toilet. $29\frac{1}{2} \times 24\frac{1}{2}$ Steer Chr 1942 | Birkenhead AG

The Mirror (Model standing). 37×20 Dr. J. E. Sandilands | Pittsburg 1897 | Anon Chr 1935 Stanhope | Mrs. J. E. Sandilands Sotheby's 1938 Adams Bros | Beaux Arts Exh—France 1939 | *Yellow Book* 1894 | *Phaidon 17*

The Mirror (Model seated). Steer Chr 1942 as The Yellow Book $35\frac{1}{2} \times 19\frac{1}{4}$ Nicholson | John Rothenstein | *Yellow Book* 1895

Skirt Dancing. *Yellow Book* 1894

A Lady (seated in chair, profile). *Yellow Book* 1894

Syon House. $17\frac{1}{2} \times 23\frac{1}{2}$ GG 1894 | Dr. Owen Pritchard | GG 1923 | Sir W. P. Wheldon | as The River Agnew's Exh 1943 | Hugh Molson MP | NEAC 1945

Children on the Beach, Southwold. $8 \times 10\frac{1}{4}$ panel Steer Chr 1942 Leger | Hon. Mrs. P. Sandeman

BOATS ON SOUTHWOLD BEACH. $8 \times 10\frac{1}{4}$ panel Steer Chr 1942 Leger | Miss Woodall

THE STAR & GARTER HOTEL, RICHMOND. $19\frac{1}{2} \times 23\frac{1}{4}$ Steer Chr 1942 Fine Art Soc | Squadron Leader C. H. Grey

STILL LIFE. 8×11 Mrs. H. R. Williams | Exrs Sotheby's 1940 Dr. S. Charles Lewsen

1895 THE LOOKING GLASS. NEAC 1895 (possibly THE MIRROR, see 1894)

DISROBING. NEAC 1895

Portrait of DAVID CROAL THOMSON. 30×25 NEAC 1895 | Tate Exh 1929 | Beq by sitter 1930 Tate Gallery | *Pall Mall Pictures* 1895 | *Artwork* 1929

THE WATERFALL. NEAC 1895 | J. Staats Forbes | LG | NG Wellington, New Zealand | *Art Journal* 1906

Portrait of J. HAVARD THOMAS. 32×22 NEAC 1895 | Thomas Memorial Exh LG 1922 | Mrs. Havard Thomas | Tate Exh 1929

> 'And all that's best of dark and bright
> Meet in her aspect and her eyes:
> Thus mellowed to that tender light
> Which Heaven to gaudy day denies.'

NEAC 1895 | *Art Journal* 1896 as FIRELIGHT

MISS PETTIGREW in blue dress seated. $26\frac{1}{4} \times 31\frac{1}{2}$ Steer Chr 1942 Leger | Leeds Exh 1944

A view of EASBY ABBEY. $23\frac{1}{2} \times 35$ NEAC 1896 | Steer Chr 1942 R. Gray | Lt.-Col. W. R. Hornby Steer | NG Exh 1943 | *Phaidon 28*

RICHMOND CASTLE through the Trees. $25\frac{1}{2} \times 30\frac{1}{4}$ NEAC 1897 | Prof. F. Brown | Brussels 1929 | Miss Ellen Brown | BH | Rochdale AG 1944

A WATERFALL, RICHMOND, Yorks. 24×29 GG 1924 | Imperial Gall 1930 | Southampton Art Soc 1930 | Steer Chr 1942 Lessore | NG Exh 1943

A WATERFALL, RICHMOND, YORKS. Autumnal Evening $24\frac{1}{2} \times 29\frac{1}{2}$ Steer Chr 1942 Lessore | *Phaidon 41*

Portrait of R. W. ALLAN. Royal Society of Portrait Painters 1895

1896 MISS MOLLY DIXON. NEAC 1896 | Miss Dorothea Hamilton | *Pall Mall Pictures* 1896

A YORKSHIRE LANDSCAPE. NEAC 1896

A NUDE (Seated on bed). 37×43 NEAC 1896 Sir A. M. Daniel | BH 1927 | *Vogue* 1927

THE JAPANESE GOWN. 49½×39 NEAC 1894 | GG 1896 | Laurence W. Hodson | Wolverhampton Exh 1902 | Hodson Chr 1906 | Sir George Clausen, R.A. for NG Victoria Melbourne Felton Bequest | *Studio* 1894 | *Art Journal* 1906 | *Some of the Moderns* (Wedmore) 1909

THE RAPE OF THE SABINES. 28×36 GG 1924 | Sir C. K. Butler | Tate Exh 1929 | Amsterdam 1936 | BH 1937 | Lady Kendall Butler | NG Exh 1943 | BH | Hugh Molson MP | *Burlington Mag* 1943

ELIZABETH, LADY DE LA POLE. 60×48 Sir John Carew Pole

LADY EDEN. 20×18 Steer Executors | Rt Hon R. Anthony Eden

THE PILLOW FIGHT. 23×30 GG 1924 Sir C. K. Butler | Bradford Exh 1930 | BH 1937 as FROLIC | G. J. Scaramanga | *BH Record* 1937

Study for THE PILLOW FIGHT. 23×30 Hon. R. H. Bathurst

WINDFALLS (Barnard Castle). 18½×23½ Grosvenor Gall Nameless Exh 1921 | GG 1924 | Frank Green | Mrs. Simon Green

RECLINING NUDE. 25×30 D. S. MacColl | Tate Exh 1929 | NEAC 1945

RICHMOND CASTLE. 34×44 Grosvenor Gall 1917 | Matsukata Coll

BARNARD CASTLE. 19×24 Mrs. Charles Hunter | Chr 1910 | Grosvenor Gall 1917 as RICHMOND CASTLE | Mrs. Hunter Chr 1920

A view of BARNARD CASTLE. 20×24 RHA 1939 | Steer Chr 1942 | Ian Greenlees

A view of BARNARD CASTLE, Yorkshire, from the River. 20×24 Steer Chr 1942 Agnew

1897 Portrait of MRS. FREDERICK PEGRAM. 24×20 NEAC 1897 | Mrs. Pegram

RICHMOND CASTLE. NEAC 1897

A SPANISH LADY. NEAC 1897

THE LANDING PLACE. NEAC 1897

BY LAMPLIGHT. 25×23½ NEAC 1897 | Sir A. M. Daniel | *Phaidon 21* as BUST PORTRAIT OF A YOUNG WOMAN

KNARESBOROUGH. 24×18 NEAC 1897 | Walter Taylor | Eldar Gall 1919 | GG 1919 | E. Mitchell Crosse | Tate Exh 1929 | Knoedler Exh 1930 | BH 1935 | G. J. Scaramanga | H. C. Laurence | Empire Exh Glasgow 1938 | *BH Record* 1935 | *Artwork* 1938

AN OAK AVENUE (Knaresborough). NEAC 1897 | Chev. Albanesi | *Art Journal* 1905

KNARESBOROUGH. 20×18 Charles Conder | Frank Gibson |
   Anon Chr 1923 | Anon Chr 1924 | BH | Anon Chr 1926
   Leggatt | Owen Hugh Smith | Adams Gall Exh 1934

MISTY EVENING near Knaresborough. 25×30 Sir C. K. Butler |
   BH 1937 | H. C. Laurence

EVENING, LUDLOW (? KNARESBOROUGH). 16×19½ Mrs. Wel-
   don Beq 1937 Ashmolean Mus Oxford | *Phaidon 44*

KNARESBOROUGH, Clearing in a Coppice. 17½×19½ Mrs.
   Charles Hunter | Grosvenor Gall 1917 | Hunter Chr 1920
   Colnaghi | Moir Carnegie | Blackheath Sch of Art Exh 1932
   as THE OPENING IN A WOOD | *Colour* 1918

KNARESBOROUGH. 22×28 George Russell 1926 | Mrs. Russell

KNARESBOROUGH. ?11×9 Wyndham T. Vint | Whitechapel
   1939 | City Lit Inst 1939

A FOREST GLADE. 17×20 Sir William Eden | Chr 1899 Ryder

LUDLOW. 15½×23½ Sir A. M. Daniel | Norwich Exh 1925 |
   Studio 1930

Portrait of ELEANOR LARKIN (Miniature). 2¾×1¾ GG 1924 |
   Sir C. K. Butler | BH 1937 | Lady Kendall Butler | NG Exh
   1943 | *Phaidon* text

Portrait of ELEANOR LARKIN (in a painted oval). 19½×17 BH
   1937 | Steer Chr 1942 as A GIRL IN A WHITE DRESS | Les-
   sore

A NUDE STUDY. 23½×19½ Sir William Eden | Chr 1899 |
   Grosvenor Gall 1917 | Eden Exrs Chr 1918 Sampson | F.
   Hindley Smith gave Southport AG

GIRL WITH LARGE HAT. H. C. Laurence

NEGRO PAGE. 30×25 (Study for Toilet of Venus 1898) GG
   1924 | Sir J. Duveen | Lady Cunard | Sotheby's 1933 R. E.
   Wilson

BLACK PAGE. 19×24½ (Study for Toilet of Venus 1898) BH |
   Mrs. Frances Evans

Study for THE TOILET OF VENUS. 30×25 BH | Duchess of
   Roxburghe | *Phaidon 29*

1898 THE TOILET OF VENUS. 100×72 GG 1924 Frank Green |
   Given through NACF 1927 Tate Gallery | Tate Exh 1929 |
   NG Exh 1943 | *Phaidon 30*

SLEEP. 35×52 NEAC 1898 | GG 1924 | Lord Ivor Spencer
   Churchill | Given 1927 Tate Gallery | Tate Exh 1929 | Em-
   pire Exh Glasgow 1938 | BC New York 1939 | *Phaidon 33*

THE VISTA (KNARESBOROUGH). 35×24 NEAC 1898 | Dublin 1899 | Sir C. K. Butler | Coronation Exh Shepherd's Bush 1911 | GG 1921 | BH 1937 | NACF 1938 for NG South Australia, Adelaide

CHINCHILLA. 24×20 NEAC 1898 | Major J. A. Hamilton | *Phaidon 26*

Portrait of MRS. WALTER WINSLOW. 30×25 NEAC 1898

LUDLOW CASTLE, Stormy Sky. 19×25 NEAC 1898 Sir A. M. Daniel | Manchester Exh 1911 | Newcastle Exh 1912 | NEAC Retro 1925 | *Phaidon 27*

LUDLOW CASTLE. 20×26 GG 1925 | Alfred Jowett | Bradford Exh | Blackburn Exh 1927 | Harrogate Exh 1930

BIRDS NESTING (Ludlow). 22×36 NEAC 1898 | Sir C. K. Butler | Wolverhampton 1902 | GG 1921 | Cambridge 1922 | BH 1927 | Duveen Exh Stockholm 1929 | Bradford 1930 | Tooth's 1933 | Empire Art Loan Coll Soc Exh Australia, New Zealand and Tate 1935 | BH 1937 | Chantrey Fund purchase | RA 1938 | Tate Gallery | Liverpool Exh 1938 | BC Northern Capitals 1938 | *BH Record* 1937

THE APPROACHING STORM. 15×20 George Russell 1926 | Tate Exh 1929 | Mrs. Russell

THE POPLARS, LUDLOW. 23×18 Sir C. K. Butler | BH 1937 | Spurr

LUDLOW, GIRLS' SCHOOL. 16×19 Carfax 1902 | Sir Michael Sadler

LUDLOW CASTLE. 8¼×10½ panel GG 1919 | A. R. Howell | BH | CAJ | R. F. Goldschmidt | Exrs Chr 1941 CAJ | *BH Record* 1934

MRS. CYPRIAN WILLIAMS. (See 1891)

THE CHEMISE. 29×23¼ GG 1924 | F. Leverton Harris | GG 1928

THE BLACK HAT (Miss Geary). 23×19 GG 1924 | Henry B. Harris | Beq Mrs. Fox

SEATED NUDE (THE BLACK HAT). 20×16 CAS gave Tate Gallery | NG Exh 1942 | Manchester Exh 1943

NUDE. 10¼×8 panel Walter Osborne RHA | Dr. W. Crampton Gore RHA | On loan Municipal Gallery Dublin

MISS GEARY in White Dress on a Settee. 18¾×24½ Steer Chr 1942 R. Gray | A. Henderson Bishop

IN A BATH CHAIR (Miss Scobell). 24×20 GG 1924 | Davis Green | Murray Thomson | BH as CONVALESCENT | Adams Bros. | Vienna Exh 1927 | Southampton AG 1934 (Chipperfield Bequest)

1899 MORNING, LUDLOW. NEAC 1899

AMINTA (Lydia Burton-Lady Russell). 24×18 Sir A. M. Daniel | Tate Exh 1929 | Colnaghi's Exh 1934 | *Artwork* 1929 | *Studio* 1930

CARMINA. 32×16 NEAC 1899 | George Moore | GG 1914 | E. J. Hesslein Coll·

LUDLOW CASTLE. NEAC 1899

LUDLOW WALKS. 21×26 F. W. Smith | Beq 1932 Southampton AG

CHILDREN PLAYING (Ludlow Walks). 22×35 NEAC 1899 | International Exh Glasgow 1901 | G. Blackwell | Colnaghi's Exh 1934 | Tooth's 1934 | G. J. Scaramanga

UNDER THE TREES (Ludlow). 20×27 NEAC 1899 | F. Gibson | G. Blackwell | NEAC Retro 1925 and Manchester | BH 1927 | Blackwell Family Coll

A SUMMER AFTERNOON. $14\frac{3}{4}$×23 NEAC 1900 | J. Staats Forbes | Given by subscription to Municipal Gallery, Dublin | *Burlington Mag* 1908

NEAR LUDLOW. 14×$19\frac{1}{2}$ Anon Chr 1920 GG | Asa Lingard | J. Gabbitas | Mrs. Ida Machin | Sotheby's 1937 | BH 1937 as RIVER TEME, LUDLOW | G. J. Scaramanga | J. R. McGregor (Sydney).

THE EDGE OF THE WOOD, LUDLOW. $25\frac{1}{2}$×$29\frac{1}{2}$ Sir C. K. Butler | Manchester 1911 | Newcastle 1912 | Tooth's 1933 | BH 1937 as THE TOY BOAT | G. J. Scaramanga | Col. and Mrs. Harold Tetley | Leeds Exh 1944 | *BH Record* 1937 | *Phaidon* 61

CLIFFS BY THE TEME, LUDLOW. 26×32 GG 1909 | Arnold C. Taylor | E. J. Hesslein Coll | *Studio* 1909

CONVERSATION, LUDLOW. $6\frac{3}{4}$×$10\frac{1}{2}$ panel Steer Chr 1942 Leger | Mrs. Augustus John

THE RED JACKET. $18\frac{1}{2}$×16 GG 1924 | BH 1929 | H. M. Hepworth | *BH Record* 1929

1900 CASTLE WALKS, KNARESBOROUGH. 22×27 Sir A. M. Daniel | G. Blackwell | British Empire Exh Wembley 1924 as A WOODLAND GLADE | Slade School 1927 | Tate Exh 1929 | French Gall Exh 1931 | BC Johannesburg 1936 | Blackwell Family Coll | *Wembley Catalogue* 1924

THE EMBARKMENT. $21\frac{1}{2}$×27 NEAC 1900 | John S. Sargent, R.A. | Bradford 1904 | Sargent Chr 1925 Willard | CAJ | G. Beatson Blair | Tate Exh 1929 | Beq Manchester AG 1944 | *Christie's Cat* 1925

EMBARKATION. $21\frac{1}{2} \times 27$ Sir C. K. Butler | BH 1937 | G. J. Scaramanga | NEAC Canada 1939

NIDDERDALE. $33 \times 43\frac{1}{2}$ NEAC 1900 | Herbert Trench | Whitechapel 1901 | Wolverhampton 1902 | Bradford 1904 | Manchester 1910 | Whitechapel 1910 | G. Blackwell | NEAC Retro 1925 and Manchester | BH 1935 | Hamilton Bequest Purchase Glasgow Corporation AG | RSA 1936 | Liverpool Exh 1936 | Leeds Exh 1944 | *Country Life* 1925 | *BH Record* 1935 | *Illus London News* 1935

NIDDERDALE. 16×21 Sir C. K. Butler | BH | E. M. Worsley

STUDY FOR NIDDERDALE. 16×22 Sir W. Rothenstein | Tate Exh 1929 | BH | Cork AG Eire | *BH Record* 1936

GRIMBALD CRAG near Knaresborough. $19\frac{1}{2} \times 23\frac{1}{2}$ Earl of Harewood

THE BATHERS. $18\frac{1}{2} \times 13\frac{1}{2}$ NEAC 1901 | Carfax 1902 | Judge Evans | Bradford 1904 | Judge Evans Coll GG 1918 | A. A. de Pass | given South African NG Cape Town

THE TEME AT LUDLOW, Sunset. 18×24 Lady Northcliffe | Lady Hudson Chr 1923 GG | F. Leverton Harris | Marchant Chr 1927 LG | CAS for Belfast AG (Sir R. Lloyd Paterson Bequest)

KNARESBOROUGH, The Rainbow. 15×21 L. A. Harrison | BH | G. J. Scaramanga | *BH Record* 1938

KNARESBOROUGH. 14×19 L. A. Harrison | BH | NG New South Wales, Sydney

WOODLAND GLADE, KNARESBOROUGH. 22×16 Steer Chr 1942 Miss Dorothea Hamilton

MUSIDORA (Seated Nude). 24×20 BH | G. J. Scaramanga | NG Exh 1943 | *BH Record* 1938

KNARESBOROUGH, Clouds & Rainbow. $8 \times 10\frac{3}{4}$ panel CAJ | F. W. Jackson

A LANDSCAPE WITH A RAINBOW. $8 \times 10\frac{1}{4}$ panel R. F. Goldschmidt | Exrs Chr 1941 LG | Major Dent

POPLARS NEAR BUILDWAS. $10\frac{1}{2} \times 14$ panel BH | John Bain

RAINBOW NEAR BUILDWAS. $9\frac{1}{2} \times 13$ panel BH | H. J. Paterson

A WOODLAND GLADE, KNARESBOROUGH. $17\frac{1}{2} \times 23\frac{1}{2}$ Steer Chr 1942 R. Gray | A. Henderson Bishop

A WOODLAND GLADE, KNARESBOROUGH. 23×18 Steer Chr 1942 Lessore

KNARESBOROUGH, Sun breaking through the Clouds. $15\frac{1}{2} \times 19\frac{1}{2}$ Steer Chr 1942 Hugo Pitman | Miss Dorothy Palmer

HAYMAKING. 14×18½ Sir C. K. Butler | BH 1937 | Robert Mayer

TWO BRIDGES, KNARESBOROUGH. 20×24 BH | Sir Percy Sargood Trust gift NG New Zealand, Wellington 1944

THE BLUE DRESS. 20×15½ Miss Dorothea Hamilton.

NUDE. 14×10 Major J. A. Hamilton

1901 Portrait of MRS. CYRIL BUTLER & her Children. 48×60 NEAC 1900 | Sir C. K. Butler | GG 1921 | Tate Exh 1929 | Duveen Exh Stockholm 1929 | BH | RSA 1939 as THE SATIN DRESS | Lady Kendall Butler | Col. and Mrs. B. M. Edwards | *Art Journal* 1906 | *Times* 19 April 1929 | *Country Life* 1929 | *Apollo* 1939

THE HOME FARM (Knaresborough). 22×27 NEAC 1900 | Herbert Trench | G. Blackwell 1911 | Tate Exh 1929 | French Gall Exh 1931 | BC Johannesburg 1936 | NG Exh 1943 | Blackwell Family Coll | *Phaidon 38*

HYDRANGEAS. 34×44 NEAC 1901 | Sir C. K. Butler | Wolverhampton 1902 | Whitechapel 1910 | RSA 1912 | Tate Exh 1929 | Venice 1930 | BH 1937 | G. J. Scaramanga | NEAC Paris 1938 | Exh Australia 1938–1944 | *Connoisseur* 1937 | *Phaidon 35*

THE RAINBOW (Bridgnorth). 20×33½ NEAC 1901 | Sir C. K. Butler | Whitechapel 1903 | St. Louis 1904 | Dublin 1907 | Manchester 1910 | Newcastle 1912 | CAS Exh GG 1913 | GG 1921 | Newcastle 1923 | BH 1927 | Vienna 1927 | Tate Exh 1929 | French Gall 1931 | BH 1937 | G. Blackwell | NG Exh 1943 | Blackwell Family Coll | *Art Journal* 1902 | *Art Treasures of Great Britain* 1914 (C. H. Collins Baker) | *Artwork* 1929 | *Country Life* 1929 | *BH Record* 1937 | *Phaidon 39*

Portrait of MRS. MOFFAT LINDNER. 40×30 NEAC 1901 Moffat Lindner

THE MIRROR. 15×21 NEAC 1901 | Sir A. M. Daniel | Wolverhampton 1902 | St. Louis 1904 | Whitechapel 1910 | Coronation Exh Shepherd's Bush 1911 | GG 1921 | BH 1927 | Tate Exh 1929 | *Art Journal* 1906 | *Some of the Moderns* (Wedmore) 1909 | *Artwork* 1929 | *Studio* 1937 | *Phaidon 34*

THE OAK GROVE (? Bridgnorth). 22×30 Herbert Trench | Manchester 1910 | GG 1920 | G. Blackwell | RSA 1927 | Tate Exh 1929 | BC Johannesburg 1937 | Blackwell Family Coll | *Times* 1928

WOODLAND & SUN. 15½×21 GG 1924 | Sir James Murray |

Chr 1927 as THE GROVE BRIDGNORTH BH | Julian G. Lousada | Tate Exh 1929

STROUD CANAL. 16×22 L. F. Harrison | Tate Exh 1929 | NG Exh 1941

View from THE GROVE, BRIDGNORTH. 16×21½ LG | BH 1937 | G. J. Scaramanga | Col. and Mrs. Harold Tetley | *BH Record* 1937

STROUD VALLEY. 16×21½ G. Blackwell | BH 1935

NEAR NAILSWORTH. 16×21 G. Blackwell | BH 1935 | Fine Art Soc | Flying Officer C. N. Barlow

CLEARING IN A WOOD, Bridgnorth. 25×30 GG 1910 | T. W. Bacon

A VIEW ON THE RIVER, Bridgnorth. 17½×23½ Steer Chr 1942 LG | N. S. Tasker

THE GROVE, BRIDGNORTH. 18×24 GG 1909 | A. A. Hannay | Mrs. Hannay | BH | Matthews & Brooke | V. H. Shepherd as SILVERY LANDSCAPE | Adams Bros. | G. Blackwell | NG Exh 1943 as AMONG THE TREES, BRIDGNORTH | Blackwell Family Coll | *Phaidon 63*

THE MILL, BRIDGNORTH. 18½×24 | Charles L. Rothenstein 1904 | Manchester 1910 | Rutherston Coll given Manchester 1925 | Blackburn Exh 1927 | Leeds Exh 1944

LANDSCAPE WITH TREES, BRIDGNORTH. 15×21 Hugo Mallet

THE EDGE OF THE CLIFF, BRIDGNORTH. 37×39 L. A. Harrison | Tate Exh 1929 as THREE FIGURES & A DOG | BH | Fuller Exh New Zealand 1939–1944

STUDY FOR ABOVE. 13¼×13¼ BH

THE BRIDGE, BRIDGNORTH. 18×24 Charles Goy

WINDY DAY, BRIDGNORTH. 9¾×13½ panel Lockett Thomson | Agnes and Norman Lupton 1945 | *BH Record* 1936

EVENING NEAR BRIDGNORTH. 10×14 panel BH | H. C. Laurence | CAJ | O. Hughes-Jones | *BH Record* 1936

Portrait of A YOUNG GIRL. Oval 22×16 Mrs. Styan | LG | G. E. Healing

GIRL AND CAT. 22×18 Carfax 1902 | Judge Evans | Bradford 1904 | Judge Evans Coll GG 1918 | Mrs. Gandarillas

FLOWER STUDY. 10×14 W. H. Wood | Tate Exh 1929 | BH | H. M. Hepworth | Beq 1943 Leeds AG

FLOWER PIECE. 7×6 panel Carfax | Charles Moore | Sir Walter Russell RA

RICHMOND CASTLE, Yorks. 15½×21 Mrs. Cox

1902 PORTRAIT OF MRS. SPENCER BUTLER. 30×25 NEAC 1902 | Sir C. K. Butler | Tate Exh 1929 | Lady Kendall Butler

BRIDGNORTH. NEAC 1902

A NUDE (WOOD NYMPH). 26×21½ NEAC 1902 | L. A. Harrison | NEAC Retro 1925 and Manchester as SUSAN-NAH | Hugo Pitman

AN UPLAND LANDSCAPE, STROUD. 22×27 NEAC 1902 | Carfax 1913 | Henry B. Harris | Beq 1929 Tate Gallery

THE VALLEY OF THE SEVERN. 26×32 NEAC 1902 | Grafton Gall | Herbert Trench | RGI 1913 | GG 1920 | E. Mitchell Crosse | NEAC Retro 1925 and Manchester | Tate Exh 1929 as THE GOLDEN VALLEY | Knoedler's Exh 1930 | Pittsburg 1931 | BH 1935 | BC Paris 1938 | Rt. Hon. Vincent Massey 1939 | *Phaidon 36*

THE GOLDEN VALLEY, STROUD. 25×32 NEAC 1903 | Manchester 1910 | Sir A. M. Daniel | GG 1921 | *Art Journal* 1906 | *Studio* 1930 | *Phaidon 37*

DEWY MORN IN THE COTSWOLDS. 18×23 Sir C. K. Butler | NEAC Manchester 1925 | Lady Kendall Butler

STROUD, VIEW OVER THE PLAIN. 22×27 C. H. Collins Baker

THE STROUD VALLEY. 15½×21 Sir C. K. Butler | Whitechapel 1903 | BH 1937 | G. J. Scaramanga | Agnews | NACF gave Hereford AG 1943 | *Art Journal* 1906 as THE COTSWOLD HILLS | *Some of the Moderns* (F. Wedmore) 1909 | *BH Record* 1937

A MISTY SUNSET, STROUD. 28×36 NEAC 1903 | E. J. Hess-lein Coll

PANSIES—THAT'S FOR THOUGHTS. 32×26 John Maddocks | Franco British Exh 1908 | Grafton Gall 1910 | Maddocks Chr 1910 Carfax | Sir Michael Sadler | RGI 1914 | GG 1922 | Asa Lingard | BH 1927 | LG | Sir Edmund and Lady Davis gave South African NG Cape Town as ETHEL WARWICK

LIZETTE. 19×14 J. Maddocks Chr 1910 GG

1903 Portion of a Decoration for BOURTON HOUSE, SHRIVENHAM. NEAC 1903 | Sir C. K. Butler | Lady Kendall Butler (These decorations measured, one 70½×57 and four others 38¼×39½ each. See p. 108.)

Trial Piece for Decoration at BOURTON HOUSE, SHRIVENHAM. 36×27 GG | Fine Art Soc | H. Molson, MP | NEAC 1945

Sketch for Decoration, Bourton House. 10×10¾ panel Major J. A. Hamilton | RSA 1943

Sketch for Decoration, Bourton House, painted oval. 12 × 10 Sir
  C. K. Butler | Redfern Gall 1944

A TURN OF THE CARDS. 32 × 26 NEAC 1903 | E. J. Hesslein |
  Bradford 1904 | Hesslein Coll

THE SHOWER, RICHMOND, Yorks. 25½ × 31½ NEAC 1903 |
  Herbert Trench 1909 | G. Blackwell 1914 | Tate Exh 1929 |
  NG Exh 1943 | Blackwell Family Coll | *British Painting*
  (C. H. Collins Baker) | *Phaidon 42*

RICHMOND CASTLE. 14 × 18 NEAC 1904 | Dermod O'Brien
  PRHA | GG 1912 | E. J. Hesslein Coll

RICHMOND CASTLE, Yorks. 30 × 40 NEAC 1903 | White-
  chapel 1910 | Sir Michael Sadler through NACF 1917 gave
  Tate Gallery | NG Exh 1943 | *Burlington Mag* 1910 | *Phaidon 40*

RICHMOND CASTLE, Yorks. 29¼ × 34½ Lord Northcliffe | Car-
  fax Gall | Roger E. Fry for Metropolitan Museum New York
  1908

Distant view of RICHMOND, Yorks. 16½ × 22 BH 1937 | Sir Syd-
  ney Cockerell for NG Victoria Melbourne (Felton Bequest) |
  BH Record 1937

THE FALLS, RICHMOND, Yorks. 22 × 30 Sir C. K. Butler | BH
  1937 | Sir Sydney Cockerell for NG Victoria Melbourne
  (Felton Bequest)

SUNSET, RICHMOND, Yorks. 16 × 21 BH | H. C. Laurence |
  NG Exh 1943

RICHMOND, Yorks. 15½ × 21 BH 1935 | *Illus. London News* 1935

THE THREE GRACES. 26½ × 22 Sir A. M. Daniel

Portrait of MISS BENNETT in yellow dress with large blue and white
  hat. 19¼ × 19½ Steer Chr 1942 Leger | H. Pattinson-Knight

1904 Portrait of MRS. D. S. MACCOLL. 32 × 26 | D. S. MacColl |
  NEAC 1904 | NEAC Liverpool 1905 | Whitechapel 1910 |
  NEAC Retro 1925 and Manchester | Tate Exh 1929 |
  Sphere

Study for above. 30 × 25 D. S. MacColl | NEAC 1945

THE BLACK DOMINO. 40 × 30 NEAC 1904 | Manchester 1904 |
  NEAC Liverpool 1905 | George Russell 1926 | Tate Exh
  1929 | Mrs. Russell

TWILIGHT. NEAC 1904

THE STORM (Hawes). 24 × 36 NEAC 1904 | Herbert Trench |
  G. Blackwell 1914 | Tate Exh 1929 | Blackwell Family Coll |
  Studio 1914

SLEEP. 14 × 12 NEAC 1904 | E. J. Hesslein Coll

HAWES. 34×44 Herbert Trench | Blackwell Family Coll

STORMY WEATHER, HAWES. 19½×23½ Herbert Trench | GG 1920 | E. Mitchell Crosse | Chr 1925 Sampson | W. Rees Jeffreys | Tooth's Exh 1930

EVENING, HAWES. 25½×31½ Sir Hugh Lane gave Municipal Gallery, Dublin

SUNSHINE & SHADOW, HAWES. 17½×23½ Artist gave Municipal Gallery, Dublin 1904

HAWES, WENSLEYDALE. 13×17½ G. Blackwell | *BH Record* 1935 | J. Lawrence

SUNSET, HAWES. 17×21 H. C. Laurence | NG Exh 1943

PORTRAIT IN BLACK. 44×34 NEAC 1904 | Charles L. Rothenstein | Manchester 1910 | Rutherston Coll given 1925 Manchester AG | Liverpool Exh 1933 | BC Johannesburg 1936 | Empire Exh Glasgow 1938 | *Rutherston Cat* Manchester

THE POSY. 24×18 L. A. Harrison | RGI 1939 | BH

LUDLOW CASTLE with two Anglers. 24×18 R. F. Goldschmidt | Exrs Chr 1941 Adams Gall | Arthur Crossland

SPRING TIME. 40×50 Sir C. K. Butler | BH 1937 | G. J. Scaramanga | Chelsea Exh for Finland 1940 | NG Exh 1943 as SUMMER AFTERNOON, LUDLOW | BH | Birmingham AG | *BH Record* 1937 | *Apollo* 1937

HARDRAW SCAR. 27×32 NEAC 1904 | NEAC Liverpool 1905 | E. J. Hesslein Coll

THE BROKEN BOUGH. 28×36 Blackwell Family Collection | NG Exh 1943

THE BROKEN BOUGH, Study. 19½×22½ GG 1909 | Arnold C. Taylor | G. E. Healing | Tate Exh 1929

DECORATION for an OVERMANTEL. 34×39 NEAC Liverpool 1905 | L. A. Harrison | BH

1905 CHEPSTOW CASTLE. 29½×34¾ NEAC 1909 | Miss Mary Hoadley Dodge gave Tate Gallery 1909 | Tate Exh 1929 | BC Johannesburg 1936 | BC Paris 1938 | NG Exh 1943

THE WYE AT CHEPSTOW. 36×48 NEAC 1909 | Lord Justice Darling | Latin British Exh 1912 | Liverpool 1926 | Venice 1932 | Purchased with NACF from Lord Darling's Exrs Walker AG Liverpool 1936 | RGI 1937 | NG Exh 1943 | Leeds Exh 1944 | *NACF Report* 1936 | *Phaidon 43*

ON THE WYE. 15½×12 Douglas Freshfield

CHEPSTOW CASTLE. 13½×17 L. A. Harrison | BH 1927 | BH 1944 | Agnes and Norman Lupton

CHEPSTOW CASTLE. 28 × 34 Henry B. Harris | Brussels 1929 | Tate Exh 1929 | Beq 1929 Miss Harris

A VIEW OF CHEPSTOW. 13½ × 17½ Steer Chr 1942 Leger | H. P. R. Hoare

NUTTING (Chepstow). 27 × 36 L. A. Harrison | Tate Exh 1929 | Colnaghi's | Sir Hugh Walpole | French Gall Exh 1937 | Beq Tate Gallery 1941 | NG Exh 1942 | Manchester Exh 1943

RICHMOND, Yorks. 16 × 21 E. M. B. Ingram | NG Exh 1940 | Redfern Gall 1941 | Ingram beq Fitzwilliam Museum Cambridge

RICHMOND CASTLE. 26 × 17½ Mrs. Ormond

THE MAUVE DRESS. 21 × 17 John S. Sargent RA | Exrs Chr 1925 Willard | CAJ | G. F. Williams | Tate Exh 1929 | CAJ | Manchester AG 1930 | Report | NG Exh 1943 | Phaidon 20

SUMMER (Portrait of a Girl). 43¼ × 33¼ Agnew's Exh 1906 | Col Sir W. Hutcheson Poë | French Gall 1932 | Manchester AG | Report 1932

LADY IN CHEMISE. 30 × 25 L. F. Harrison

THE MANDOLINE (Study for THE MUSIC ROOM). 13¼ × 9½ panel BH 1939 | Moir Carnegie

IN THE PARK. 8½ × 10½ panel Miss E. Walker | Sam Wilson | Beq Leeds AG | Leeds Exh 1944

1906 MRS. STYAN. 45 × 33 NEAC 1906 | New Gallery 1909 | GG 1924 as IN FANCY COSTUME | Tate Exh 1929 | BH | Frank Partridge as THE GOLDEN DRESS | A. C. J. Wall | Weekly Illustrated Warsaw 1913

PORTRAIT OF THE ARTIST. 30 × 25 painted for the Uffizi Gallery Florence | NEAC 1906 | Art Journal 1906 | Studio 1906 | Weekly Illustrated Warsaw 1913

CHEPSTOW CASTLE. 35½ × 47½ NEAC 1906 | Sir C. K. Butler | Coronation Exh Shepherd's Bush 1911 | Manchester 1911 | Newcastle-on-Tyne 1912 | GG 1921 | BH 1937 | H.M. The Queen | BC New York 1939 | Phaidon 45

THE MUSIC ROOM. 40 × 51 NEAC 1906 | Sir C. K. Butler | CAS Exh Manchester 1911 and Leeds 1911 | NACF gave to Tate Gallery 1912 | RGI 1928 | Tate Exh 1929 | Liverpool Exh 1932 | BC Johannesburg 1936 | NG Exh 1943 | Art Journal 1906 | Studio 1906 | Burlington Mag 1924 | Phaidon 47

Study for THE MUSIC ROOM. 26 × 31 BH 1927 | H. M. Hepworth | BH

Miss Bennett. H. C. Laurence

The Bend of the River, Ludlow. 24½×29½ NEAC 1906 |
GG 1909 | T. W. Bacon

The Bend of the River, Ludlow. 24×29 Anon Chr 1935
BH | Herbert E. West | Whitechapel 1939 | NG Exh 1941 |
BH Record 1935

The School Girl. 31½×25½ NEAC 1906 | Nat Museum of
Wales, Cardiff 1907

The Broken Bough, Hawes. 27½×36 NEAC 1909 | Col. Sir
W. Hutcheson Poë

The Valley of the Teme. 30×40 Lord Howard de Walden
| Liverpool Exh 1933 | NG Exh 1941

The Teme at Ludlow. 30×40 George Russell 1926 | Tate Exh
1929 | Duveen Exh Stockholm 1929 | Canadian Nat Exh
Toronto 1938 | Mrs. Russell | *Country Life* 1929

The Pool, Ludlow. 20×24 CAJ 1922 GG 1923 | Sir R.
Park Lyle | Lyle sale Trollope's 1944 | LG | Ronald Tree
MP | NEAC 1945

A View of the River Teme, Evening. 30×40 Steer Chr
1942 Leger | Hon. R. H. Bathurst | Leeds Exh 1944

The Road through the Valley. 30×40 Asher Wertheimer
| Chr 1923 Knight | Anon Chr 1925 as A View at Lud-
low | Holdsworth | Anon Chr 1928 as Cliffs on Teme |
Lindo Myers

A View in North Wales. 15½×26½ NEAC 1935 | BH |
Arthur Chamberlain | Mrs. Arthur Chamberlain | *BH
Record* 1938

The Domino. 30½×22 L. F. Harrison | NG Exh 1941 | Leeds
Exh 1944

The Fur Muff. 30×20 Imperial Gall 1931 | Mrs. Frances
Evans | BH 1935 | Charles Brotherton | *BH Record* 1935 |
Apollo 1935

Richmond, Yorks. 18×24 Sir Michael Sadler | Norwich Exh
1925 | Ashmolean Exh 1942 | Given through NACF 1931
Ashmolean Museum Oxford

Richmond, Yorks. 17×13½ Sir Michael Sadler | Ashmolean
Exh 1942 | Michael Sadleir

1907 Portrait of Mrs. Hammersley. 96×60 NEAC 1907 | New
Gallery 1908 | GG 1923 | Pittsburg 1924 | Tate Exh 1929 |
BC Paris 1938 | NG Exh 1943 | Mrs. Arthur Hammersley |
Studio 1908 | *Modern Masterpieces* (Frank Rutter) | *Phaidon 48*

Study for MRS. HAMMERSLEY. 24×20 GG 1924 | Steer Chr
1942 Miss Dorothea Hamilton

THE BEAVER HAT. 50×40 NEAC 1907 | Coronation Exh
Shepherd's Bush 1911 | L. A. Harrison | BH 1927 | NACF
1937 for NG New South Wales, Sydney | *Country Life* 1927 |
BH Record 1937

A PROFILE (Miss Montgomery). 24×20 NEAC 1907 | GG
1909 | Arthur Blunt | Chenil Gall 1925 | Tate Exh 1929 |
French Gall 1931 | Mrs. Blunt | L. F. Harrison | *Studio* 1909

LA GRANDE PLACE, MONTREUIL. NEAC 1907

A COURTYARD (MONTREUIL). 36×28 NEAC 1907 | Mrs.
L. H. Myers | *Art Journal* 1908 | *Some of the Moderns* (F. Wed-
more) 1909

MONTREUIL CHURCH FROM THE SQUARE. 19×23 | GG 1909 |
Owen Fleming

LA GRANDE PLACE, MONTREUIL. 37½×47½ GG 1909 | W. S.
Marchant | RSA 1914 | Mrs. Wills | Mrs. Weldon 1918 |
Beq 1937 Ashmolean Museum Oxford

THE CHURCH AT MONTREUIL-SUR-MER. 20×24 GG 1907 |
Brighton 1907 | J. G. Lyon | Mrs. Lyon | GG 1923 | A. A.
de Pass gave 1927 South African NG Cape Town

GRANDE PLACE, MONTREUIL. 24×19 Lord Monteagle

THE DOORWAY (Quiet Occupation or Contentment, Montreuil).
24×19½ GG 1909 | Judge Bacon | Chr 1911 Sampson |
Ernest A. Knight | Manchester Exh 1916 | Huddersfield AG
1931

THE OUTSKIRTS OF A TOWN (Montreuil). 38×48 NEAC
1908 | Liverpool 1908 | GG 1909 | G. E. Healing | Cor-
onation Exh Shepherd's Bush 1911 | Tate Exh 1929 | NG
Exh 1940 | *Studio* 1909 | *Artist* 1933 | *Connoisseur* 1940 |
Phaidon 50

Study for THE OUTSKIRTS OF A TOWN. 19×24 Mrs. Fisher |
GG 1920 | F. Hindley Smith | Tate Exh 1929 | London
Artists Assoc 1930 | Wildenstein Exh 1937 | F. H. Smith
beq 1940 Ashmolean Museum Oxford | *Phaidon 57*

MONTREUIL FROM THE RAMPARTS. 20×24 BH | Montague
Shearman | Redfern Gall 1940 | E.M.B. Ingram Beq Fitz-
william Museum Cambridge

MONTREUIL-SUR-MER (Interior with a Maid carrying a Tray).
24×20 Steer Chr 1942 Lessore

ON THE PIER. 32×25¾ GG 1909 | Baron Caccamisi | Mme

Blanche Marchesi | Chr 1916 Col. Brotherton | Charles
Brotherton

LADY ROTHENSTEIN. 22 × 18 Steer Executors | John Rothen-
stein | Leeds Exh 1944

MISS MONTGOMERY. 26 × 20 Major J. A. Hamilton

MISS MONTGOMERY. 36 × 28 Mrs. Charles Ratcliffe|Leeds Exh 1930

SPENCER P. BUTLER. 29½ × 24 Sir C. K. Butler | BH 1927 |
Lady Kendall Butler

LE CHAPEAU DE PAILLE. 30 × 25 L. A. Harrison | BH | Charles
Brotherton

1908 THE MORNING ROOM (Reverie). 36 × 30 NEAC 1908 | E. J.
Hesslein Coll | *Studio* 1908

IN A CONSERVATORY (Miss Montgomery). 30 × 25 | GG 1909 |
Miss B. Davy (Mrs. Lumsden)

REVERIE (Miss Montgomery). 26 × 22 BH 1927 | RSA 1929 |
Lord Blanesburgh | *Country Life* 1927

GIRL READING (Miss Montgomery). 26 × 20 GG 1924 | L. F.
Harrison pres Red Cross Chr 1942 | bought by donor

Portrait of MISS MONTGOMERY in white dress, seated reading a
book. 47 × 36 Steer Chr 1942 Lessore | Talbot Clifton | NG New
South Wales, Sydney, 1945

THE ISLE OF PURBECK. 33½ × 44 GG 1909 G. Blackwell |
Manchester 1910 | Tate Exh 1929 | NG Exh 1943 | Black-
well Family Coll | *Phaidon 49*

POOLE HARBOUR. 30 × 40 GG 1908 | W. W. Wingate (after-
wards W. W. Pemberton) | RSA 1911 | Cambridge 1922 |
NEAC Retro 1925 | Tate Exh 1929 | BC Paris 1938 | Cap-
tain Jeremy Pemberton | NG Exh 1943 | *Art Journal* 1909 |
Burlington Mag 1925 | *Connoisseur* 1943 | *Phaidon 55*

POOLE HARBOUR, Study. 18 × 26 GG 1909 | Major Sir W.
Evans Gordon | Marchioness of Tweeddale | Chr 1920 CAJ
| Hanley Exh 1926 | J. B. Broadley | Anon Chr 1927 as RAIN
CLOUDS | BH | H. M. Hepworth gave Leeds AG 1934 |
Leeds Exh 1944 | *Some of the Moderns* (F. Wedmore) 1909 |
Artwork 1929

A WOODLAND SCENE NEAR CORFE CASTLE. 24½ × 31½ Anon
Chr 1928 BH | A. Chester Beatty

EFFECT OF RAIN (Corfe). 17½ × 23½ GG 1909 | W. Somerset
Maugham

THE LIMEKILN. 18 × 24 G. Blackwell | Tooth's Exh 1943 | Rt.
Hon. Vincent Massey

THE LIMEKILN, Sketch. 18 × 25½ G. Blackwell | Agnew's, New York 1930 | Blackwell Family Collection

MOON RISING OVER THE DOWNS. 29½ × 39½ GG 1909 | Herbert Trench | G. Blackwell | BC Johannesburg 1936 | Blackwell Family Coll | *Studio* 1914

STORMY FOREST. 24 × 31 Ernest A. Knight

GOLDEN AFTERNOON. 17½ × 23½ GG 1909 | T. Mackintosh | Anon Chr 1919 Sampson | R. Haworth | BH | Mrs. Cazalet | *BH Record* 1931

1909 THE HORSE-SHOE BEND OF THE SEVERN. 40 × 60 NEAC 1909 | Sir Michael Sadler | Manchester 1910 | Rome 1911 | Newcastle 1912 | Leeds University 1914 | GG 1919 | Aberdeen AG | Tate Exh 1929 | Liverpool Exh 1932 | NG Exh 1943 | *Artist* 1933 | *Phaidon* 53

THE BEND OF THE SEVERN, Littledean. 31½ × 47¾ Manchester 1910 | Sir Hugh Lane beq Municipal Gall Dublin | NG Exh 1943 | *Studio* 1911

THE HORSE-SHOE BEND OF THE SEVERN. 29½ × 40 GG 1909 | A. C. Hammersley | Mrs. Hammersley | GG 1923 | Manchester AG 1923 | *Report* | Liverpool Exh 1935 | *Phaidon* 51

LITTLEDEAN, BEND OF THE SEVERN. 20 × 30 C. H. Collins Baker | Tate Exh 1929

LITTLEDEAN. 20 × 30 CAJ | Ernest A. Knight † Anon Chr 1927 Knoedler | Pittsburg Exh 1931 | Adams Bros Exh 1934 | BH | J. R. McGregor (Sydney) London Artists Assoc 1930 Exh *Catalogue*

THE PICNIC (Littledean). 48 × 36 | GG 1909 | E. J. Hesslein Coll

A BEND OF THE SEVERN, LITTLEDEAN. 18 × 28 W. Somerset Maugham | French Gall Exh 1931

THE HORSE-SHOE BEND OF THE SEVERN, near LITTLEDEAN. 40 × 60 Steer Chr 1942 Leger | Leeds Exh 1944

IN A PARK, LUDLOW. 34 × 44 GG 1909 | A. C. Hammersley | Mrs. Hammersley | GG 1923 | G. Blackwell | Tate Exh 1929 | Tooth's Exh 1943 | Blackwell Family Coll | *Phaidon* 52

SEPTEMBER MORNING, LUDLOW. 19 × 24 GG 1909 | Blackwell Family Coll

THE BALCONY (A Chelsea Window). 48 × 36 GG 1909 | Sir Hugh Lane for Johannesburg AG given by Sir Lionel Phillips | Whitechapel Exh 1910 | *Art Journal* 1909 | *Burlington Mag* 1909 | *Studio* 1909

THE LIMEKILN (Corfe). 34 × 44 GG 1909 | Sir Hugh Lane for Johannesburg AG given by Lady Phillips | Whitechapel Exh 1910 | *Studio* 1909

CORFE CASTLE. 40 × 56 GG 1909 | Sir Hugh Lane for Johannesburg AG given by Lady Phillips | *Some of the Moderns* (F. Wedmore) 1909 | *Studio* 1909 | *Burlington Mag* 1909 | *Art Journal* 1910

CORFE CASTLE & THE ISLE OF PURBECK. 18 × 24 BH 1935 | Walker AG Liverpool | Leeds Exh 1944 | *BH Record* 1935

THE BLUE SASH (Miss Montgomery). 29½ × 24½ GG 1909 | G. E. Healing | *Weekly Illustrated* Warsaw 1913

NUDE. 33½ × 19½ GG 1909 | Col. Sir W. Hutcheson Poë | Exrs Chr 1936 as THE BATHER BH | BC Johannesburg 1936 | CAJ | C. J. Aron | *Studio* 1934

1910 THE MUSLIN DRESS. 39 × 56 NEAC 1910 | G. Blackwell | Rome 1911 | BH 1927 | Tate Exh 1929 | Venice 1932 | Empire Art Loan Coll Soc New Zealand, Australia and Tate Exh 1935 | BH 1935 | Viscount Leverhulme | Liverpool Exh 1936 | Port Sunlight Exh 1936 | NG Exh 1943 | *Rome Souvenir* 1911 | *Weekly Illustrated* Warsaw 1913 | *Artwork* 1929 | *BH Record* 1936 | *Phaidon* 58

GIRL IN BLUE. 30 × 24¼ NEAC 1910 | Sir Hugh Lane gave 1911 Municipal Gallery Dublin as THE BLUE GIRL | NG Exh 1943 | *Art Journal* 1911

A DESERTED QUARRY. 35½ × 53½ NEAC 1910 | GG 1912 | Liverpool 1915 | Manchester 1916 | RSA 1923 | English Speaking Union New York 1925 | Pittsburg 1926 | GG 1929 | Manchester AG 1929 | *Report* | Empire Exh Glasgow 1938 | *Modern Art* (Colour)

MISS MONTGOMERY in a blue dress resting on a settee. 15½ × 21½ Steer Chr 1942 R. Gray | A. Henderson Bishop

IRONBRIDGE, Bridgnorth. 30 × 40 CAJ | F. Whalley | Arthur Crossland | Bradford Exh 1937 | NG Exh 1943

IRONBRIDGE, Sunset. 30 × 42 Sir Hugh Lane gave 1910 Municipal Gallery Dublin | *Studio* 1915

IRONBRIDGE, Sunset. 21 × 30 CAJ | F. Hindley Smith

IRONBRIDGE, The Rainbow. 30 × 40 Grosvenor Gall 1917 | Matsukata Coll

A VIEW OF IRONBRIDGE. 20½ × 23½ Steer Chr 1942 Leggatt

VIEW OF LUDLOW, Autumn Sunset. 22 × 35½ G. Blackwell | Tooth's Exh 1943 | Blackwell Family Coll

EFFECT OF RAIN. 21 × 29 Anon Chr 1918 Morrison

VALLEY RICHLY WOODED & RIVER. 21 × 30 Lord Howard de Walden

1911 THE END OF THE CHAPTER. 45 × 57 NEAC 1911 | Liverpool 1911 | Bradford 1912 | Bought Bradford AG 1912 | Brussels Exh 1929 | Tate Exh 1929 | Liverpool Exh 1932 | NG Exh 1943 | *Studio* 1911 | *Yorkshire Observer* 1912 | *Weekly Illustrated* Warsaw 1913 | *Studio* 1930 | *Phaidon 59*

THE PATH OF THE STORM (Bridgnorth). 30 × 43½ NEAC 1911 | G. Blackwell | BH 1927 as THE PASSING STORM | Agnew's, New York 1930 | BC New York 1939 | Blackwell Family Coll | *Studio* 1914 | *Country Life* 1927

THE QUAY, BRIDGNORTH. 23½ × 35¼ Sir A. M. Daniel | BH Exh 1927

BRIDGNORTH. 24 × 36 Grafton Gall 1911 | G. E. Healing

BRIDGNORTH, Edge of a Wood. 28½ × 34 Sir C. K. Butler | Newcastle 1912 | Tate Exh 1923 | Amsterdam 1936 | BH 1937 | G. J. Scaramanga | NG Exh 1943 | *BH Record* 1937 | *Phaidon 56*

BRIDGNORTH, Sunset. 22 × 29 GG 1919 | Henry B. Harris | Beq 1929 Miss Harris

HIDE AND SEEK, BRIDGNORTH. 28½ × 33½ GG 1911 | Sir Michael Sadler | GG 1922 | Liverpool 1922 | BH | Sir George Sutton | Anon Chr 1946 BH | Royan Middleton

BRIDGNORTH. 19 × 23½ Earl of Sandwich | BC New York 1939

BRIDGNORTH, After a Storm. 20 × 34 Bradford | E. J. Hesslein Collection

THE GROVE, BRIDGNORTH. 24 × 36 A. W. Wilmer gave 1912 Birkenhead AG | Bury Exh 1926 | Rochdale Exh 1926 | *W. J. Stacey* Colour collotype

THE STORM. 22½ × 29½ L. F. Harrison | NG Exh 1941 | *Connoisseur* 1941

TREES. 15 × 20 Mrs. Hugh Hammersley

MRS. GEOFFREY BLACKWELL. 48 × 38 National Portrait Society Grafton Gall 1911 | Blackwell Family Coll

HEAD OF A YOUNG GIRL. NEAC 1911 | Bath Exh 1912 | *Studio* 1912

THE BLUE GIRL. 24 × 20 E. J. Hesslein Coll

THREE GIRLS BATHING, THAME. 28 × 36 Miss Dorothea Hamilton

1912 A WOODLAND SCENE. 14×18 NEAC 1912 | Bath 1912 | George Russell 1926 | Mrs. Russell

Portrait of LADY CLARE ANNESLEY. 19½×16 NEAC 1912 | BH | G. J. Scaramanga | *BH Record* 1938

WITH THE TIDE. 30×44 NEAC 1912 | GG 1913 as YACHTS | J. Staudt | E. J. Hesslein Coll

THE WHITE YACHT (Porchester). 24×36 NEAC 1912 | G. E. Healing | NEAC Retro 1925 | Tate Exh 1929 | NG Exh 1943

SUNSET OVER THE SEA. 24×36 1st Countess of Cromer | Hon. Sir Evelyn Baring

PORCHESTER. 24×36 BH 1927 Duveen Exh Buenos Aires 1928 | *BH Record* 1933

SUMMER EVENING, PORCHESTER. 24×36 GG 1912 | Henry B. Harris | Tate Exh 1929 | Beq 1929 Fitzwilliam Museum Cambridge

THE ESTUARY, PORCHESTER. 23½×35½ Sir Hugh Lane | Beq Municipal Gall Dublin | *Studio* 1918

PORCHESTER. 15×23½ G. Blackwell | BH 1935 | Rev. A. S. Prior

PORCHESTER CASTLE. 30×40 Bradford | Matsukata Coll 1918

THE INNER HARBOUR. 24×36 NEAC 1913 | G. Blackwell | BH 1927 | Tate Exh 1929 | Blackwell Family Coll

SEA GULLS, THAMES EMBANKMENT. 15¼×23½ GG 1924 | Earl of Harewood

MISS MONTGOMERY in a blue dress seated. 25¼×19½ Steer Chr 1942 Leger | G. O. Kay | Leeds Exh 1944

1913 Portrait of MRS. HUGH HAMMERSLEY. 37×29 NEAC 1913 | Mrs. H. Hammersley

SUNSET (Harwich). 24×36 NEAC 1913 | Lady Esher | BH 1935 | R. S. Clark (Paris) | *Apollo* 1935 | *BH Record* 1936

THE BREAKWATER (Harwich). 24×36 NEAC 1913 | See GATHERING SEAWEED 1932

MISTY EVENING, HARWICH. 23½×35½ Manchester AG 1914

A MISTY DAY, HARWICH. 19½×25½ BH 1927 | Mrs. Frances Evans

SUNSET, HARWICH HARBOUR. 24×36 G. Blackwell | BH 1935 | Tooth's Exh 1943 | NG Exh 1943 | Blackwell Family Coll | *Illus London News* 1935

BOATS, HARWICH HARBOUR. 24×36 G. Blackwell | Tooth's Exh 1943 | Blackwell Family Coll

HARWICH, Estuary with Shipping. 26×36 Sir Gervase Beckett | Beq Mrs. Bathurst Norman

SEASCAPE. 24×36 1st Countess of Cromer | Hon. Sir Evelyn Baring

DOVERCOURT, Sunset. 20×26 CAJ | Charles Goy | Anon Chr 1928 as SUNSET, HARWICH Bucknall | Owen Hugh Smith | Adams Gall Exh 1934

YACHTS OFF HARWICH. 19¾×26 CAJ | G. Leeming | Anon Chr 1928 Oliver | Anon Chr 1930 Gooden & Fox | W. H. Woodward | Cambridge 1931 | Woodward Exrs Chr 1942 as THE GATHERING STORM, HARWICH HARBOUR Leger | Mrs. Cecil Feilden

YACHTS NEAR HARWICH. 19½×25½ GG 1923 | Edmund Walker

THE PANAMA HAT. 33×19½ Grosvenor Gall 1917 | CAJ | H. Coleman 1919 | G. Leeming 1922 | CAJ | NEAC Retro 1925 | Lord Ivor Churchill 1926 | Pittsburg 1926 | Fine Art Soc | Studio 1943

LADY IN A MUSLIN DRESS. 30×25 | George Russell 1926 | Mrs. Russell

PORTRAIT OF A GIRL. 29×24½ CAS Exh Grosvenor House 1923

1914 A SUMMER EVENING. NEAC 1914 | Grosvenor Gall 1917 as BATHERS (possibly A SUMMER'S EVENING 1888)

FISHING BOATS AT ANCHOR. NEAC 1914

GOLDEN EVENING, BOSHAM. 23×28½ H. M. Hepworth | Given 1934 Leeds AG | NG Exh 1943 | Leeds Exh 1944 | Phaidon 60

BOSHAM. 18×24 BH | Montague Shearman | Redfern Gall 1940 | W. Rees Jeffreys

BOSHAM, STORMY SKY. 24×36 G. Blackwell | Tooth's Exh 1943 | Hon. Hugh Smith

LOW TIDE, BOSHAM. 24×36 BH | H. C. Laurence | NG Exh 1943

MARINE (BOSHAM). 24×36 Grosvenor Gall 1917 | Matsukata Coll

LADY WITH A PARASOL. 36×24 Mrs. Charles Hunter | Grosvenor Gall 1917 | Hunter Chr 1920 GG | A. A. de Pass | Given South African NG Cape Town 1927

THE BLUE DRESS (Miss Montgomery). 23×19¼ GG 1924 | Herbert E. West | Whitechapel Exh 1939

A VIEW AT LUDLOW. 40 × 50 GG 1924 | Steer Chr 1942 Lessore

1915 STORMY WEATHER. NEAC 1915

SKETCHING. NEAC 1915

PAINSWICK BEACON. 24 × 36 NEAC 1915 GG 1924 | Clarke Fund Tate Gallery 1924 | Tate Exh 1929 | Sunderland Exh 1935

A QUARRY IN THE COTSWOLDS. 24 × 36 Rt. Hon. Lord Jowitt

STORMY SUNSET NEAR PAINSWICK. $20\frac{1}{4}$ × 36 G. Blackwell | BH 1935 | Dr. Gayer Morgan | *BH Record* 1935

THE VALE OF GLOUCESTER. 32 × 53 NEAC 1916 | G. Blackwell | Colnaghi's Exh 1934 | Tooth's Exh 1943 | Blackwell Family Coll

MOONRISE, PAINSWICK. 24 × 36 BH | Steer Chr 1942 | NACF and Birkenhead AG

A COTSWOLD QUARRY, PAINSWICK. 24 × 36 Mrs. Charles Hunter | Grosvenor Gall 1917

HARESFIELD BEACON. 24 × 36 BH | BC Johannesburg 1936

1916 THE RETURN OF THE FISHING FLEET. NEAC 1916

THE TERRACE WALK (CHIRK CASTLE). 18 × 27 NEAC 1916 Lord Howard de Walden | NG Exh 1943

CHIRK CASTLE. 18 × $26\frac{1}{2}$ NEAC 1916 Lord Howard de Walden | Pwllheli 1925 | NG Exh 1943 | *Vogue* 1916 | *Studio* 1917

SCENE IN A PARK (CHIRK). 16 × 27 NEAC 1916 | Lord Howard de Walden

Portrait of LADY HOWARD DE WALDEN. 30 × 24 Lord Howard de Walden

LANDSCAPE (CHIRK). 16 × 27 Lord Howard de Walden

LANDSCAPE (CHIRK). 18 × 27 Lord Howard de Walden (Lord Howard de Walden owns other landscapes painted by P. Wilson Steer in the neighbourhood of Chirk Castle)

VIEW FROM CHIRK CASTLE. 16 × 27 G. Blackwell | Tooth's Exh 1943 | R. Heathcote Amery

CHIRK CASTLE, Stormy Sunset. 18 × 27 Steer Chr 1942 | Lord Kenyon and Louis C. G. Clarke gave 1943 Nat Museum of Wales Cardiff

1917 BRIDGNORTH. 30 × 44 NEAC 1912 and 1917 Sir A. M. Daniel | Tate Exh 1929 | BC Paris 1938 | *Artwork* 1929 | *Phaidon* 54

PORTRAIT SKETCH. NEAC 1917

THE TEMPLE, CHIRK CASTLE. 19×26 NEAC 1917 Lord Howard de Walden

BETTY (ELWES). 19½×15½ NEAC 1917

VIEW IN HARESFOOT PARK. 17½×26 Possibly NEAC 1917 as LANDSCAPE, BROKEN WEATHER | G. Blackwell | Blackwell Family Coll

HARESFOOT, BERKHAMSTED. 18×27 Matsukata Coll

HARESFOOT, THE DRIVE. 16×27 Matsukata Coll

THE AVENUE. 18×24 CAJ | J. H. Hoyle

MASTER ROBIN GRANT-LAWSON (died on active service 1944). 24×20 Mrs. Charles Hunter | Grosvenor Gall 1917 | Lady Grant-Lawson

GRISELDA GRANT-LAWSON. 24×20 Mrs. Charles Hunter | Grosvenor Gall 1917 | Lady Grant-Lawson

1918 MRS. JOSEPH HOLBROOKE. NEAC 1918

DOVER HARBOUR. 42×60 Imperial War Museum | War Paintings RA Winter Exh 1919–20 | Manchester 1920 | Edinburgh 1921 | Duveen Exh Buenos Aires 1928 | Bradford 1930 | NG Exh 1943 | *Vogue* 1920 | *Plus Ultra* 1928 | *Studio* 1930 | *Phaidon 66*

DOVER HARBOUR FROM THE PARADE. 16×24 Sir Muirhead Bone gave Imperial War Museum | War Paintings RA Winter Exh 1919–20 | Tate Exh 1921 | Tate Exh 1929

DOVER HARBOUR, EVENING. 21×29 G. Blackwell | BH 1927 | Tooth's Exh 1943 | Sir Victor Mallet

DOVER HARBOUR & CASTLE. 21×30 G. Blackwell | Colnaghi's Exh 1924 | British Empire Exh Wembley 1925 | Tate Exh 1929 | Tooth's Exh 1943 | Blackwell Family Coll

DOVER HARBOUR. 21×30 J. G. Lousada | BC Johannesburg 1936 | BH 1937 | Pittsburg 1937 | LG | M. V. B. Hill | Ashmolean Exh 1942

DOVER HARBOUR LOOKING OVER ESPLANADE. 16×24 | Anon Chr 1936 BH | FAS | H. J. Paterson

DOVER WITH RAINBOW. 15½×23½ CAJ | H. Coleman

RAINBOW, DOVER. 16×24 Anon Sotheby's 1931 Beecroft

THE DOCKS, DOVER. 20½×29½ Steer Chr 1942 James

THE RIVER AT CHELSEA. 18×24 Hugo Pitman | BH 1927 | NG Exh 1940

1919 THE CLIFFS, ALUM BAY. 20×30 Sir Alexander Fleming

NEAR ALUM BAY, ISLE OF WIGHT. 17½×29½ G. Blackwell | BH 1935 | Hon. Sir Evan Charteris

FRESHWATER BAY. $17\frac{1}{2} \times 29\frac{1}{2}$ CAJ | G. Leeming | Stoke-on-Trent AG 1923

STORMY SUNSET, ISLE OF WIGHT. 18×30 | GG 1919 | Henry B. Harris | Beq 1929 Mrs. F. D. Fox

THE NEEDLES, ISLE OF WIGHT. 20×30 G. E. Healing | BH Exh 1927

MIST OVER THE NEEDLES. $17\frac{1}{4} \times 29\frac{1}{2}$ F. Hindley Smith | CAJ | Manchester AG | *Report* 1929 | Leeds Exh 1944

THE NEEDLES FROM ALUM BAY. $19\frac{1}{2} \times 29\frac{1}{2}$ CAJ | H. Coleman | CAJ | G. Leeming 1922 | Fine Art Soc | Agnes and Norman Lupton | Leeds Exh 1944 as THE NEEDLES IN MIST

EVENING, ISLE OF WIGHT. $19\frac{1}{4} \times 29\frac{1}{2}$ CAJ | G. Beatson Blair | Beq 1944 Manchester AG

PORTRAIT OF THE REV. W. H. HORNBY STEER. 36×33 National Portrait Society Grafton Gall 1921 | Lt.-Col. W. R. Hornby Steer

1920 PORTRAIT OF THE ARTIST. $28\frac{1}{2} \times 22\frac{3}{4}$ NEAC 1920 | Given by the artist to Fitzwilliam Mus Cambridge | *Modern Masterpieces* Frank Rutter

THE ARTIST (possibly Study for above). 28×23 Sir A. M. Daniel | Tate Exh 1929 | LG Exh 1935 | *Country Life* 1929 | *Phaidon 64*

(See 1906 for the Uffizi Portrait of the Artist)

YACHTS ON THE SOLENT. 20×32 LG | CAS 1929 for Belfast AG (Sir R. Lloyd Paterson Bequest)

MALDON. 18×30 Alfred Willey | Asa Lingard | J. E. Fattorini | Adams Bros. | BH

MALDON CREEK. $18 \times 29\frac{1}{2}$ G. Blackwell | Adams Bros.

MALDON HARBOUR, Still Summer Morning. $19\frac{1}{2} \times 31\frac{1}{2}$ Henry B. Harris | CAS Exh Grosvenor House 1923 | BH 1927 | Beq 1929 Mrs. F. D. Fox

RETURN OF THE FISHING FLEET, MALDON. $17\frac{1}{2} \times 29\frac{1}{2}$ CAJ | G. Beatson Blair | Beq Manchester AG 1944

FISHING BOATS RETURNING, HIGH TIDE (Maldon). $19\frac{1}{2} \times 31\frac{1}{2}$ GG 1920 | J. Q. Rowett | Sale Hampton's 1924 | GG | Lord Ivor Churchill 1925

THE QUAY, MALDON. 18×30 G. E. Healing

YACHTS, MALDON. 18×29 CAJ | C. Billington | Mrs. Myott

YACHTS, MALDON. 20×30 CAJ | R. F. Goldschmidt | Albert Mackinson | O. Hughes-Jones | Lefevre Gall

Low Tide at Maldon. 19½ × 31 BH 1927 | BC Johannesburg 1936 | Steer Chr 1942 Lessore | BH 1946 | M. Balfour

1921 Portrait. 24 × 20 NEAC 1921 | G. Blackwell | Tooth's 1943 as The Artist's Model | Rt. Hon. Vincent Massey | *Times* 21 July 1928

Bathsheba. 27 × 20 NEAC 1922 | CAS Exh Grosvenor House 1923 | Canterbury 1924 | BH 1927 | Henry B. Harris | Brussels 1929 | Tate Exh 1929 | Beq Tate Gallery 1929 | *BH Record* 1928

Southampton. 20 × 31½ GG 1921 | R. Skinner

Southampton Water. 17 × 29 Grosvenor Gall 1921 | Asa Lingard | Sotheby's 1944 BH | Lady Tennyson for Thomas J. Watson USA (Museum)

Southampton Water, Passing Storm. 17½ × 29¼ Henry B. Harris | Beq 1929 Mrs. F. D. Fox

Harbour Entrance, Southampton. 19½ × 31½ Herbert Coleman | GG 1922 | R. S. Dawson

Southampton Water. 19½ × 31 Randall Davies for NG Victoria Melbourne (Felton Bequest)

A Shipyard, Southampton Water. 18 × 30 NEAC Paris 1938 | NEAC Birkenhead, Bath, Worthing, 1938 | NEAC Canada 1939

The Battle of Jutland. 39 × 84 Admiral of the Fleet Sir Cecil Burney

1922 Mrs. Raynes. 27 × 22 NEAC 1922 | Chantrey Fund Purchase | RA Winter 1922 | Tate Gallery | Tate Exh 1929 | NG Exh 1943 | *Studio* 1942 | *Artwork* 1929 | *Phaidon 65*

The Ferry, Avonmouth. 20 × 30 GG 1922 | Charles L. Rutherston | Rutherston Coll given 1925 Manchester AG | Tate Exh 1929

Avonmouth from Pill. 16½ × 24 Sir A. M. Daniel

Pill St. George. 17¼ × 25½ NEAC 1923 | CAJ | F. S. J. Broome | Exrs. Chr 1936 as The Avon, Avonmouth | Fine Art Soc

Avonmouth. 17½ × 23½ GG 1924 | Sir Michael Sadler | LG Exh 1944 as Estuary

Low Tide, Shirehampton. 14 × 18 Steer Chr 1942 Fine Art Soc | P. M. Turner

Morning on the Medway. 20 × 31 Liverpool 1933 | Lord Howard de Walden

Professor W. P. Ker. 23½ × 19½ NEAC 1923 | University College, London

1923   GEOFFREY BLACKWELL, Esq.   23½ × 19½   NEAC 1923 | Black-
well Family Coll

LADY MARJORIE BECKETT.   15½ × 12½   Lady Marjorie Beckett

LADY MARJORIE BECKETT.   24 × 20   Steer Exrs gave Chelsea Arts
Club | NEAC 1945

THE THAMES AT CHELSEA, Sunset.   16 × 24   GG | Julian G.
Lousada | Tate Exh 1929 | J. G. Lousada Chr 1935 Nelson |
LG 1936 | Rt. Hon. Vincent Massey

DOVER HARBOUR.   15½ × 24   Sir George Sutton | Anon Chr 1943
BH | Agnes and Norman Lupton | Leeds Exh 1944

OXFORDSHIRE LANDSCAPE.   20 × 30   Sir Michael Sadler | Ash-
molean Exh 1942 | LG Exh 1944 | Major R. D. Girouard

NEAR BRILL.   18½ × 25   Sir Michael Sadler | Ashmolean Exh
1942 | LG Exh 1944

GOLDEN AFTERNOON, BRILL.   17 × 25   GG 1924 | Major Sir
Henry Aubrey-Fletcher

THE GROVE, BRILL.   17 × 25   GG 1924 | BH | T. W. Bacon

STORMY EVENING, BRILL.   17 × 25   Hon. Sir Evan Charteris

A DISTANT VIEW, BRILL.   18 × 26   GG 1924 | F. T. Simpson |
Mrs. Hamond

A VIEW AT BRILL.   17 × 25   Steer Chr 1942 Agnew

BRILL.   17 × 25   BH 1935

BRILL.   18 × 26   CAJ | Dr. A. W. Laing

1924   MRS. THOMAS LOWINSKY.   28 × 23   NEAC 1924 | T. Lowinsky
| Tate Exh 1929 | Ashmolean Exh 1942

LONG CRENDON, Clearing after Rain.   16 × 26   Lady Cunard |
Chr 1933 BH | Vancouver AG as MORNING IN BUCKING-
HAMSHIRE | *BH Record* 1933

TOWARDS THE LIGHT, LONG CRENDON.   20 × 24   Southport
1925 | NEAC 1926 | BH 1927 | Hon. Sir Evan Charteris |
Tate Exh 1929 | BH 1935 | Gerald Kelly RA | BC Johannes-
burg 1936 | BH 1945 | Mr. and Mrs. Frank Ricardo | *BH
Record* 1927 | *Country Life* 1927

COWS GRAZING, LONG CRENDON.   16 × 23   Lt.-Col. Ernest Armstrong

A COMMON, LONG CRENDON.   20 × 28   Julian G. Lousada

BUCKINGHAM LANDSCAPE (Long Crendon).   15¼ × 26   GG 1924
| Lord Ivor Churchill

THE OLD MILL, LONG CRENDON.   19 × 25   GG 1922 | Mrs.
H. G. Clegg | Lady Ismay

LONG CRENDON.   20 × 24   Miss Dorothea Hamilton

A Farmstead, Long Crendon. 16×20 Mrs. E. M. Smith |
  Exrs Chr 1938 BH | J. W. Blyth
Long Crendon, Evening, After Rain. 15½×19½ GG 1924 |
  Marchant Chr 1927 LG | Mrs. Victor Smith
Long Crendon. 17×25 BH | Charles Brotherton
The Surf. 28×36 GG 1924 | Earl of Sandwich | Vernon
  Wethered | Tate Exh 1929
1925 Bridgnorth, by the Severn. 17×25 GG 1925 | Hon. Sir Evan
  Charteris
A Misty Morning on the Severn. 18×25½ GG 1926 | Im-
  perial Gall 1927 | South African NG Cape Town
Distant View of Bridgnorth. 19½×29½ BH 1927 | A.
  Henderson Bishop
Bridgnorth, a Distant View looking towards. 19½×31½ Steer
  Chr 1942 | NACF and Birkenhead AG
The Old Sandpit, Bridgnorth. 17×25 *BH Record* 1930
The Thames at Chelsea. 29½×53 NEAC 1925 | *Country
  Life* 1925
1926 Digging for Bait (Shoreham). 20×32 NEAC 1926 | BH 1927
  | Southampton Art Soc 1930 | Southampton AG (Chipper-
  field Bequest) | NG Exh 1943 | *BH Record* 1931 | *Phaidon 68*
Facing the Light, Shoreham. 19½×31½ Hon. Sir Evan
  Charteris | Tooth's Exh 1930
Sand Barges, Shoreham. 19½×31½ BH 1927 | Liverpool 1934
  | Steer Chr 1942 R. Gray | Lt.-Col. W. R. Hornby Steer |
  NEAC 1942 | NG Exh 1943 | *Connoisseur* 1943
Boats at Shoreham. 17×25 BH 1927 | Venice 1932 | Steer Chr
  1942 R. Gray | Lt.-Col. W. R. Hornby Steer | NG Exh 1943
A Shipyard, Shoreham. 19½×31½ BH 1927 | Steer Chr 1942
  LG | Birmingham AG | *Burlington Mag* 1943 | *Phaidon 67*
The Creek, Kingston. 20×32 Sir A. M. Daniel | BC Paris
  1938 | *Phaidon 69*
1927 Mellow Evening (?Shoreham). 23¼×31 NEAC 1927
Bridgnorth. 23½×31½ BH 1929 | Mrs. Chester Beatty | *BH
  Record* 1929
Battersea Reach. 14½×26½ BH | Duveen Exh Tokio 1931 |
  Prince Chichibu | *BH Record* 1927
1928 Framlingham from the Meadows. 14½×26¾ Steer Chr 1942
  R. Gray | Lt.-Col. W. R. Hornby Steer
1929 Lady Kenneth Clark. 16×13 NEAC 1930 | Sir Kenneth
  Clark

EVENING, LONG CRENDON. 16¾×24¾ BH 1935 | Pittsburg 1935 | United Artists' Exh RA 1942 | Steer Chr 1942 Lessore

THE THAMES from 109 Cheyne Walk. 8½×10½ panel Major J. A. Hamilton

1930 PORTRAIT OF LOCKETT THOMSON Esq. 19¼×15½ Blackheath Art School 1932 | NG Exh 1943 | Lockett Thomson

A SEATED NUDE. 20×15½ Sir Kenneth Clark | NG Exh 1943

NUDE ON A BLUE SOFA. 8×14 Agnes and Norman Lupton | Leeds 1944

BATTERSEA REACH. 6×12 Agnes and Norman Lupton

1931 WHITSTABLE. 19¼×31½ Fine Art Soc | R. I. Gunn

1932 PORTRAIT (Girl in profile). 24×20 NEAC 1932 | A. Henderson Bishop

GATHERING SEAWEED, HARWICH (1913–1932). 24×36 NEAC 1913 as THE BREAKWATER | BH | Steer Chr 1942 Fine Art Soc | Rt. Hon. Vincent Massey | NG Exh 1943 | *Phaidon 62*

FRAMLINGHAM. 18×25 CAJ Dr. A. W. Laing

1933 RECUMBENT. 20×24 NEAC 1933 | A. Henderson Bishop | Empire Exh Glasgow 1938

FRAMLINGHAM CASTLE. 24×36 BH 1933 | Sir Gervase Beckett | Beq 1938 Leeds AG | NG Exh 1943 | *BH Record* 1933

MALDON. 15½×21½ BH 1935 | Steer Chr 1942 BH

THREE SAILING BARGES OFF THE COAST. 15½×21½ Steer Chr 1942 Miss Dorothea Hamilton
(The Artist's Last Painting)

1935 THE CORAL NECKLACE. 15½×12½ BH 1935 | Steer Chr 1942 Smith | Lord Blanesburgh

FRAMLINGHAM, A view with the Castle in the background. 29¼×53½ BC Johannesburg 1936 | BH 1937 | Steer Chr 1942 Leger | H. Keuman

DATES UNKNOWN

THE AMAZON. 20×20 E. J. Hesslein Coll

AUTUMN WOODS WITH CATTLE. 39½×35 Sir Michael Sadler | Ashmolean Exh 1942 | Michael Sadleir

BEACH SCENE. 8½×10½ panel Sir Walter Russell RA

BLACKBERRYING. 29¾×41¾ GG 1910 H. H. Williams

BLACK BOW, The. 32×26 GG 1924 | Herbert E. West | Tate

Exh 1929 as PORTRAIT OF A GIRL | Whitechapel 1939 | NG Exh 1941

BLUE & SILVER. 20 × 16 BH | Agnew's Exh 1939 | RGI 1940 | Steer Chr 1942 Blundell | *Burlington Mag* 1939

THE BLUE DRESS. 9½ × 7¼ | GG 1909 | Sir Hugh Walpole | French Gall Exh 1937 | Beq Tate Gallery 1941 | NG Exh 1942 | Manchester Exh 1943

BOATS BECALMED, EVENING. 23½ × 35½ GG 1913 | Rt. Hon. Sir Philip Sassoon

THE BRIDGE, BRIDGNORTH. 16 × 22 Sir Hugh Walpole | French Gall Exh 1937 | LG Exh 1945 | R. A. Peto

THE CAT. 24 × 20 E. J. Hesslein Coll

CHEVAL GLASS, The. 26½ × 14½ BH 1927 | Artist | Mrs. Hesslein

DANAE (GOLDEN RAIN). 48 × 60 E. J. Hesslein Coll

DECORATIVE PANEL. 10 × 8 Miss Dorothea Hamilton

DESIGN FOR A TAPESTRY. 35½ × 26½ Sir C. K. Butler | GG 1924

GIRL WITH RED HAIR IN BLUE DRESS. 24 × 20 L. F. Harrison | Tate Exh 1929

GIRL IN PROFILE, Head of a. 24 × 20 Harry Collison | NG Exh 1940

GIRL READING A BOOK. 24½ × 29½ Steer Chr 1942 R. Gray | Lt.-Col. W. R. Hornby Steer

GIRL IN WHITE DRESS READING. 8 × 10¼ panel Steer Chr 1942 Fine Art Soc | A. M. Piron

A GLADE. 8½ × 10½ panel Sir Walter Russell RA

HARBOUR WITH SHIPPING. Rt. Hon. Sir Philip Sassoon | BC New York 1939 | Marchioness of Cholmondeley

HILLSIDE QUARRY. 15 × 20 E. J. Hesslein Coll

LADY IN PINK DRESS & BLUE CAP. 19¼ × 15½ Steer Chr 1942 Lessore | Talbot Clifton

LANDSCAPE. Steer Executors gave Chelsea Arts Club

MATERNITY. 18¾ × 23 GG 1924 | Sir Michael Sadler | Chr 1928 as A MOTHER & CHILD LG | Sir Michael Sadler again | Liverpool 1933 as NUDE | BC New York 1939

MODEL WEARING A FUR CAP. 21½ × 17½ Steer Chr 1942 Merton | Sir Alec Martin | Dermod O'Brien PRHA | LG Exh 1946

HEAD OF GEORGE MOORE. 10½ × 8 panel Steer Chr 1942 Sinclair

NOCTURNE. 20 × 24 E. J. Hesslein Coll

NUDE FEMALE MODEL seated on a Settee. $33\frac{1}{2} \times 43\frac{1}{2}$ Steer Chr 1942 R. Gray | Lt.-Col. W. R. Hornby Steer

NUDE FEMALE MODEL reclining on a Couch. $13 \times 16\frac{1}{2}$ Steer Chr 1942 | Sir Alec Martin

PASTORAL. 29×21 | Baron de Meyer | GG 1909 | Sir R. Leicester Harmsworth

SCHOOL GIRL STANDING BY A DOOR. $29\frac{1}{2} \times 24\frac{1}{2}$ Steer Chr 1942 R. Gray | Lt.-Col. W. R. Hornby Steer

SUMMER AFTERNOON. 24×36 GG 1913 Sir R. Park Lyle

SUSANNAH. $23\frac{1}{2} \times 19\frac{1}{2}$ Steer Chr 1942 R. Gray | A. Henderson Bishop

YOUNG WOMAN SEWING. $19 \times 15\frac{1}{2}$ Chelsea Exh for Finland 1940 | Steer Chr 1942 Agnew

WATERCOLOURS AND DRAWINGS IN GALLERIES AND INSTITUTIONS

A Collection of Sketch Books and Studies for Pictures was given by Steer Executors 1943 to the Victoria and Albert Museum

1894 EMIL SAUER, with Grand Piano. $10 \times 12\frac{1}{2}$ Pencil T. Lowinsky | Given Ashmolean Museum Oxford | Ashmolean Exh 1942 | A Pencil Study Head and Shoulders was illustrated *Yellow Book* 1895 | LG Exh 1946 | T. Lowinsky

1899 LANDSCAPE NEAR LUDLOW. $9\frac{1}{2} \times 14\frac{1}{2}$ Steer Chr 1942 | Walker AG Liverpool

THE RIVER TEME AT LUDLOW. $9\frac{3}{4} \times 14\frac{1}{2}$ Steer Chr 1942 Agnew | Walker AG Liverpool | Leeds Exh 1944

1901 THE GROVE, BRIDGNORTH. $9\frac{1}{4} \times 13\frac{3}{4}$ BH | Martin Birnbaum | Grenville L. Winthrop NY | Beq Fogg Mus Harvard University Mass

1902 THE VALLEY OF THE SEVERN from Rodborough Common.
$9\frac{5}{8} \times 14\frac{1}{4}$ Given by the Artist to the British Museum

CANAL LOCK GATES, STROUD. $9\frac{3}{4} \times 14\frac{1}{2}$ Steer Chr 1942
NACF | Given British Museum

STROUD, GLOUCESTERSHIRE. $12\frac{1}{2} \times 9\frac{1}{4}$ Steer Chr 1942 Victoria
and Albert Museum

EXTENSIVE VIEW NEAR STROUD. $8\frac{1}{4} \times 14\frac{1}{2}$ Steer Chr 1942
Agnew | Walker AG Liverpool | Leeds Exh 1944

NEAR STROUD. $9\frac{1}{2} \times 14$ BH | Martin Birnbaum | Grenville L.
Winthrop N.Y. | Beq Fogg Mus Harvard University Mass.

1903 RICHMOND, A WATERFALL. $9\frac{1}{2} \times 14\frac{3}{8}$ Whitworth AG Manchester 1920

RICHMOND, YORKSHIRE. $9\frac{3}{4} \times 14\frac{1}{2}$ Steer Chr 1942 Walker AG
Liverpool

VIEW OF RICHMOND, YORKSHIRE. $9\frac{1}{2} \times 14\frac{1}{2}$ Rutherston Coll |
Given 1925 Manchester AG | Tate Exh 1929

VIEW OF RICHMOND, YORKSHIRE. $9\frac{1}{2} \times 13\frac{1}{2}$ Bradford AG
1926

RICHMOND CASTLE. $10 \times 14\frac{1}{4}$ F. Hindley Smith | Tate Exh
1929 as CASTLE AND LAKE | Beq Royal Albert Memorial
Museum, Exeter | *Phaidon 70*

1904 VIEW AT HAWES. $14\frac{1}{2} \times 9\frac{3}{4}$ Steer Chr 1942 Walker AG Liverpool

HAWES BRIDGE, WENSLEYDALE. $10 \times 14\frac{1}{2}$ BH 1939 | Lady
Lever AG Port Sunlight

HAWES WATER. $9\frac{1}{2} \times 14\frac{1}{2}$ LG | CAS 1929 for Belfast AG (Sir
R. Lloyd Paterson Bequest)

1905 THE WYE AT CHEPSTOW. $14\frac{3}{4} \times 10$ Miss Dorothea Hamilton |
Given 1942 Whitworth AG Manchester

CHEPSTOW. $9\frac{3}{4} \times 14\frac{1}{4}$ Geoffrey Blackwell | Given 1915 through
NACF Tate Gallery | Tate Exh 1929 | *NACF Report*

CHEPSTOW. $9\frac{3}{4} \times 14\frac{3}{4}$ Fine Art Soc | Nat Museum of Wales
Cardiff

NEAR CHEPSTOW. $9\frac{1}{2} \times 13\frac{1}{2}$ LG | Leicester AG 1936

CHEPSTOW. $9\frac{1}{2} \times 14\frac{1}{2}$ Huddersfield AG 1931

LANDSCAPE. $9\frac{7}{8} \times 14\frac{1}{2}$ Roger E. Fry for Metropolitan Museum
New York 1908

1906 YORKSHIRE MOORLAND. $10 \times 14\frac{1}{2}$ G. R. Halkett | Given Red
Cross Sale Chr 1918 | Sir Marcus Samuel (Viscount Bear-
sted) | Given 1918 through NACF Tate Gallery | Tate Exh
1929

1907 A STREET IN MONTREUIL. $12\frac{3}{4} \times 9\frac{1}{2}$ Sir Thomas D. Barlow | Given 1917 Whitworth AG Manchester

LANDSCAPE WITH CASTLE. $9\frac{1}{2} \times 14$ 'A Friend' gave 1920 Brooklyn Museum USA

1908 POOLE HARBOUR. $9\frac{3}{4} \times 14$ F. Hindley Smith | Given 1923 Atkinson AG Southport

1909 A BEND IN THE SEVERN, below GLOUCESTER. $9\frac{7}{8} \times 14$ Geoffrey Blackwell | Given through NACF British Museum

THE SEVERN, LITTLEDEAN. $10 \times 14\frac{1}{2}$ Sir Michael Sadler | Given through NACF 1931 City AG Leeds | Leeds Exh 1944

THE BEND OF THE SEVERN. $9\frac{1}{8} \times 13\frac{3}{4}$ Bradford AG

THE HORSESHOE BEND OF THE SEVERN. Fine Art Soc | Aberdeen AG

1910 COALPORT. $9 \times 13\frac{3}{4}$ CAJ | Alderman F. Todd | NEAC Retro Manchester 1925 | Given Manchester AG | Leeds Exh 1944

A WOODLAND SCENE, IRONBRIDGE. $9 \times 12\frac{3}{4}$ Steer Chr 1942 | CAS (Prints and Drawings Fund) | Given British Museum

TOWN IN THE MIDLANDS. $9 \times 13\frac{1}{4}$ F. Hindley Smith | Tate Exh 1929 | Beq Royal Albert Memorial Museum, Exeter

1911 BRIDGNORTH. $9\frac{1}{4} \times 14$ A. E. Anderson | Given 1924 Whitworth AG Manchester

1912 PORTSDOWN HILL. $9\frac{1}{2} \times 13\frac{3}{4}$ Sir Hugh Lane | Beq Municipal Gallery, Dublin

WITH THE TIDE. $9\frac{1}{2} \times 13\frac{1}{2}$ Sir Hugh Lane | Beq Municipal Gallery, Dublin

PORCHESTER CASTLE. $9\frac{1}{4} \times 13\frac{1}{2}$ Sir Hugh Lane | Beq Municipal Gall, Dublin

A STORMY DAY. $9\frac{3}{4} \times 13\frac{1}{2}$ Sir Hugh Lane | Beq Municipal Gall, Dublin

GREY DAY, BOSHAM. $9\frac{1}{2} \times 13\frac{1}{2}$ F. Hindley Smith | Beq 1940 Norwich AG

PORCHESTER. $9\frac{1}{4} \times 13\frac{3}{4}$ Imperial Gall Exh 1926 | South African NG Cape Town

1913 THE NORTH SEA. $9\frac{1}{4} \times 13\frac{3}{4}$ Given by the Artist to British Museum

HARWICH, SUNSET. $9\frac{1}{4} \times 13\frac{1}{4}$ F. Hindley Smith | Beq 1940 Norwich AG

1914 SUSSEX DOWNS. $9\frac{1}{2} \times 13$ G. P. Dudley Wallis | Walker AG Liverpool 1933

BOSHAM, FISHING BOATS. $9\frac{1}{2} \times 13\frac{1}{2}$ F. Hindley Smith | Beq 1940 Norwich AG

BOSHAM. $9\frac{1}{2} \times 13\frac{1}{4}$ Steer Chr 1942 | Victoria and Albert Museum

1915 A WOODED VALLEY, PAINSWICK. $9\frac{1}{2} \times 13\frac{1}{4}$ Sir Michael Sadler | Given through NACF 1931 Ashmolean Museum Oxford

A WINDY DAY. $9 \times 13\frac{1}{2}$ BH 1938 | Hereford AG

TREES IN HARESFOOT PARK. $9\frac{3}{4} \times 13\frac{3}{4}$ Steer Chr 1942 | CAS (Prints and Drawings Fund) | Given Birmingham AG

1916 WOODY LANDSCAPE. $5\frac{1}{2} \times 9\frac{1}{2}$ H. Collison Coll Winchester College

LANDSCAPE ? POOLE HARBOUR in distance. $9\frac{1}{4} \times 13\frac{1}{2}$ H. Collison Coll Winchester College

THE AVENUE, CHIRK. $9\frac{1}{2} \times 13\frac{1}{4}$ Manchester AG | Leeds Exh 1944

1917 CHIRK CASTLE. $9\frac{3}{4} \times 13\frac{1}{2}$ Steer Chr 1942 Victoria and Albert Museum

LANDSCAPE ? CHIRK. $10 \times 13\frac{1}{2}$ Imperial Gall Exh 1926 | South African NG Cape Town

EVENING LANDSCAPE. $8\frac{1}{4} \times 13\frac{5}{8}$ A. E. Anderson | Given 1927 Whitworth AG Manchester | Tate Exh 1929

IN A COUNTRY PARK. $9\frac{3}{4} \times 13\frac{1}{2}$ H. Collison Coll Winchester College

1917 THE MEADOW. $9\frac{3}{4} \times 13\frac{3}{4}$ H. Collison | NG Exh 1940 | Winchester College

VIEW IN HARESFOOT PARK. $13\frac{1}{2} \times 9\frac{1}{2}$ Steer Chr 1942 | NACF and Williamson AG Birkenhead

VIEW IN HARESFOOT PARK. $13\frac{1}{2} \times 9\frac{1}{2}$ Steer Chr 1942 | NACF and Williamson AG Birkenhead

1918 OVERLOOKING THE DOCKS, DOVER. $14\frac{1}{2} \times 10\frac{1}{2}$ Steer Chr 1942 | NACF and Williamson AG Birkenhead

DOVER FROM THE DOCKS. $14\frac{1}{2} \times 10\frac{1}{2}$ Steer Chr 1942 | NACF and Williamson AG Birkenhead

STUDIES OF MEN-OF-WAR AT DOVER. $14\frac{1}{2} \times 10\frac{1}{2}$ Steer Chr 1942 | NACF and Williamson AG Birkenhead

MINESWEEPERS AT DOVER, MORNING. $9\frac{1}{2} \times 13\frac{1}{2}$ Sir Muirhead Bone gave Imperial War Museum | War Paintings RA Winter Exh 1919–20 | Manchester 1920 | Soc Scottish Artists Edinburgh 1921 | Art Exhibitions Bureau Tour 1941–5

MINE SWEEPERS AT DOVER, EVENING. $8\frac{1}{4} \times 13$ Sir Muirhead Bone gave Imperial War Museum | War Paintings RA Winter Exh 1919–20 | Manchester 1920 | Whitechapel 1922

THE DOCKS, DOVER. $9\frac{1}{2} \times 13\frac{1}{2}$ Sir Muirhead Bone gave Im-

perial War Museum | War Paintings RA Winter Exh 1919–
20 | Tate Exh 1921 | Northampton 1933 | Art Exhibitions
Bureau Tour 1941–5

THE WESTERN HEIGHTS, DOVER. $9\frac{1}{2} \times 13\frac{1}{4}$ Given by Artist
Imperial War Museum | War Paintings RA Winter Exh
1919–20 | Tate Exh 1921 | Harrogate Exh 1932

DOVER CLIFFS & SHIPPING. $9\frac{3}{4} \times 13\frac{1}{4}$ Whitworth AG Man-
chester | Tate Exh 1929

DOVER CASTLE. $9\frac{1}{2} \times 13\frac{1}{2}$ Leeds AG 1933 (Bilbrough Bequest)
| Empire Exh Glasgow 1938 | BC Northern Capitals 1939

DOVER HARBOUR. $8\frac{7}{8} \times 11\frac{3}{4}$ H. Collison Coll Winchester College

DOVER HARBOUR. $8\frac{1}{2} \times 13$ H. Collison Coll Winchester College

DOVER CASTLE. $9\frac{1}{2} \times 13\frac{1}{2}$ H. Collison Coll Winchester College

VIEW FROM CHIRK CASTLE. $9\frac{1}{4} \times 13\frac{1}{2}$ NACF 1941 for NG
South Australia Adelaide | *Bulletin* 1944

1919 A GREY DAY or A CALM DAY, Dover Harbour. $9\frac{1}{2} \times 13\frac{1}{2}$
Charles A. Jackson | Given 1920 Victoria and Albert
Museum

FARMYARD. $9\frac{1}{2} \times 13\frac{3}{4}$ NEAC 1920 | Sir Joseph Duveen (Lord
Duveen) | Given 1920 Tate Gallery | Tate Exh 1929

ALUM BAY, ISLE OF WIGHT. $9\frac{1}{2} \times 13\frac{3}{8}$ Whitworth AG Man-
chester | Tate Exh 1929

SANDY SHORE, Isle of Wight. $9\frac{1}{4} \times 13\frac{1}{4}$ Rochdale AG

THE NEEDLES. $9\frac{1}{4} \times 13\frac{1}{4}$ W. Crossley | Given 1921 Rochdale
AG

THE NEEDLES, A CALM. $9\frac{3}{4} \times 14$ F. Hindley Smith | Given
1923 Atkinson AG Southport

TOTLAND BAY, ISLE OF WIGHT. 9×12 Graves AG Sheffield

THE NEEDLES. $9\frac{1}{2} \times 13\frac{1}{4}$ Frank L. Babbott | Given 1929 Brook-
lyn Museum USA

MOORLAND SCENE. $9\frac{3}{4} \times 13\frac{1}{2}$ Imperial Gall Exh 1926 | South
African NG Cape Town

1920 RIVER SCENE, LOW TIDE WITH YACHTS. $8\frac{1}{4} \times 13$ R. J. Dyson |
Beq 1943 Victoria and Albert Museum

RIVER SCENE (Heybridge Basin). $9\frac{1}{2} \times 13\frac{1}{2}$ A. Watson | Man-
chester AG 1938 | Leeds Exh 1944

BOATS. $9\frac{3}{4} \times 13\frac{1}{2}$ Sir Michael Sadler | Given through NACF
1933 Cooper AG Barnsley

BOATS, LOW TIDE. $9\frac{1}{2} \times 13\frac{1}{2}$ Rochdale AG

RIVERSIDE, MALDON. $9\frac{1}{2} \times 13\frac{1}{2}$ H. M. Hepworth | Given Leeds
AG 1934

MALDON, BARGES ON THE STOCKS. $9\frac{1}{2} \times 13\frac{1}{4}$ A. Watson |
Given Leicester AG 1920

MALDON, STORM PASSING. $8 \times 13\frac{1}{4}$ NEAC 1921 | Sarjeant AG
Wanganui NZ

BOATING AT MALDON. National AG Wellington NZ 1939

1921 SOLENT NEAR SOUTHAMPTON. $9\frac{1}{4} \times 12\frac{1}{2}$ Imperial Gall Exh 1926
| South African NG Cape Town

FULL TIDE (Southampton Water). $9\frac{1}{4} \times 13$ NEAC 1922 | H.
Isherwood Kay | C. H. Collins Baker | Destined for British
Museum

1922 ELM TREES. 9×13 A. E. Anderson | Given through NACF
1923 Tate Gallery | Tate Exh 1929 | BC Johannesburg 1936 |
NG Exh 1943 | *NACF Report*

PILL FROM SHIREHAMPTON. $8\frac{3}{4} \times 13$ Steer Chr 1942 | Bristol AG

RIVER SCENE. 9×12 Graves AG Sheffield

NEAR AVONMOUTH. $9\frac{1}{4} \times 13\frac{1}{2}$ NACF 1941 | NG of South
Australia, Adelaide

1923 THE HORSE POND, THAME. $9\frac{3}{8} \times 13\frac{3}{4}$ A. E. Anderson | Given
Whitworth AG Manchester

HIGH STREET, THAME. $8\frac{3}{4} \times 13\frac{1}{8}$ GG 1924 | Whitworth AG
Manchester

THE DEAD TREE. $9\frac{1}{2} \times 13\frac{5}{8}$ GG 1924 | Whitworth AG Man-
chester | Tate Exh 1929

LANDSCAPE. $9\frac{1}{4} \times 13$ Williamson AG Birkenhead | 1933

THE COMMON. $9\frac{1}{4} \times 11\frac{3}{4}$ Sir Michael Sadler | Given through
NACF Cooper AG Barnsley

UPLANDS, THAME. 9×12 GG 1924 | Frank Rinder for NG
Victoria Melbourne (Felton Bequest)

1924 A LANE. $8\frac{3}{4} \times 12$ Huddersfield AG 1928 | Harrogate Exh 1930

LANDSCAPE NEAR LONG CRENDON. $8\frac{3}{4} \times 12\frac{3}{4}$ R. H. Kitson |
Given 1926 Leeds AG | Leeds Exh 1944

1925 LANDSCAPE, with a Clump of Trees on the left. $7\frac{1}{8} \times 10\frac{3}{4}$ Henry
B. Harris | Given British Museum

THE BANKS OF THE SEVERN, BRIDGNORTH. A. E. Anderson |
Given 1925 through NACF Ashmolean Museum Oxford

BRIDGNORTH, A GLADE. A. E. Anderson | Given 1925 through
NACF Ashmolean Museum Oxford

OLD WATER MILL, BRIDGNORTH. $8\frac{1}{2} \times 12\frac{1}{4}$ Sir Michael
Sadler | Given through NACF 1931 Ashmolean Museum
Oxford

HIGH ROCK, BRIDGNORTH. $8\frac{3}{4} \times 13$ GG 1925 | A. E. Anderson | Given 1927 Fitzwilliam Museum Cambridge

THE LIBRARY STEPS, BRIDGNORTH. $8\frac{1}{4} \times 12\frac{1}{4}$ Eton College 1928

1926 A BACKWATER, SHOREHAM. $8\frac{1}{2} \times 12\frac{7}{8}$ Steer Chr 1942 | NACF | Given British Museum

THE BEACH, SHOREHAM. $8\frac{1}{2} \times 12\frac{1}{4}$ Victoria and Albert Museum

MARINE, SHOREHAM. $8\frac{3}{4} \times 13\frac{3}{8}$ GG 1926 | A. E. Anderson | Given 1927 Fitzwilliam Museum Cambridge

COAST AT SHOREHAM. $7 \times 11\frac{3}{4}$ Sir Edmund and Lady Davis | Given South African NG Cape Town

COAST SCENE (?SHOREHAM). $8\frac{7}{8} \times 13\frac{1}{2}$ Laing AG Newcastle-on-Tyne

BOATS DRAWN UP ON A BEACH. Sir Michael Sadler Coll | CAS 1942 | Given Ashmolean Museum Oxford

1927 CHELSEA REACH. $9 \times 11\frac{1}{4}$ Laing AG Newcastle-on-Tyne | Empire Exh Glasgow 1938 | *Old Watercolour Soc* 1942

1928 A PARK SCENE, SUFFOLK. $8\frac{3}{4} \times 12\frac{1}{2}$ Victoria and Albert Museum, 1928

FRAMLINGHAM CASTLE. $7 \times 11\frac{1}{2}$ Maleham Beq Permanent Loan Graves AG Sheffield

FRAMLINGHAM. $7\frac{1}{2} \times 11\frac{1}{2}$ H. M. Hepworth | Given 1934 Leeds AG | Leeds Exh 1944

WATER MEADOWS, FRAMLINGHAM. $9\frac{1}{4} \times 13$ Steer Chr 1942 | Bristol AG

1929 PADDLERS, HARWICH. $9\frac{1}{4} \times 13\frac{1}{2}$ NEAC 1929 | Chantrey Fund Purchase | RA 1930 | Tate Gallery | BC New York 1939 and South America 1943

HARWICH CHURCH. $8\frac{1}{4} \times 12\frac{1}{2}$ Huddersfield AG 1929

MALDON, ESSEX. $9\frac{1}{4} \times 11\frac{3}{4}$ Graves AG Sheffield

COAST SCENE WITH BOAT. $9\frac{1}{2} \times 13\frac{1}{2}$ Friends of the Gallery gave 1937 Birmingham AG

THE OLD SHIPYARD, HARWICH. $9\frac{3}{4} \times 13\frac{1}{2}$ Aldridge | Worthing AG 1944

1930 THAMES BARGES AT ANCHOR. $7\frac{1}{2} \times 14\frac{3}{4}$ R. J. Dyson | Beq 1943 Victoria and Albert Museum

THAMES BARGES, EVENING. $8\frac{3}{4} \times 12\frac{1}{4}$ Hereford AG

DOVER. $7\frac{1}{4} \times 11\frac{1}{2}$ Graves AG Sheffield

UNDER THE CLIFFS, DOVER. $9\frac{1}{4} \times 13\frac{1}{2}$ Steer Chr 1942 | NACF and Williamson AG Birkenhead

DOVER DOCKS. $8\frac{3}{4} \times 12$ Ballarat AG

SHRIMPERS. $7\frac{3}{4} \times 11\frac{1}{2}$ Crawford Municipal School of Art, Cork

BOATS ON THE BEACH, DOVER. $9\frac{1}{2} \times 12\frac{1}{2}$ Crawford Municipal School of Art, Cork

IN THE DOCKS, DOVER. $9\frac{1}{2} \times 13\frac{1}{2}$ Crawford Municipal School of Art, Cork

1931 SHIPPING AT WHITSTABLE. $8\frac{3}{4} \times 11$ Steer Chr 1942 Agnew | Walker AG Liverpool | Leeds Exh 1944

WHITSTABLE. 9×12 Graves AG Sheffield

RICHBOROUGH. $8\frac{3}{4} \times 12$ Maleham Bequest Permanent Loan Graves AG Sheffield

SHIP & CLOUD. $9\frac{1}{2} \times 12\frac{1}{4}$ H. Collison Coll Winchester College

WHITSTABLE. 10×14 BH | Martin Birnbaum | Grenville L. Winthrop NY | Beq Fogg Mus Harvard University Mass

STORMY SKY, WHITSTABLE. $9 \times 11\frac{1}{4}$ BH 1939 | British Council (Wakefield Coll) BC Sweden 1942

1932 OYSTER BOATS, WHITSTABLE. $8\frac{1}{2} \times 11$ CAJ | Oldham AG 1933

1933 HARWICH. 9×12 Graves AG Sheffield

MILL BEACH NEAR MALDON. 9×12 H. M. Hepworth | Beq 1943 Leeds AG | Leeds Exh 1944

A VIEW OF TOTLAND BAY, ISLE OF WIGHT. $9 \times 12\frac{1}{4}$ Steer Chr 1942 | Victoria and Albert Museum | BC Sweden 1942

LOW TIDE, MALDON. $8\frac{1}{2} \times 10\frac{3}{4}$ Steer Chr 1942 | NACF | Given British Museum

DATES UNKNOWN

LADY WEARING EVENING DRESS, SEATED ON A SETTEE. $7\frac{1}{2} \times 6\frac{1}{2}$ pastel Artist's Executors gave 1943 Victoria and Albert Museum

LANDSCAPE. G. Beatson Blair | Beq 1944 Manchester AG

RICHMOND. Municipal AG Durban South Africa

BRIDGNORTH, ST. MARY'S. NEAC Paris 1939 | Jeu de Paume Paris

FROM RICHMOND HILL. $8\frac{1}{4} \times 12\frac{1}{4}$ CAJ | Oldham AG 1933

INDEX

Titles in italics are of pictures or drawings by Steer

INDEX

R

W.S.